NTERNATIONAL
REGGAE

INTERNATIONAL
REGGAE

EDITED BY:
DONNA P. HOPE

PELICAN PUBLISHERS LIMITED
Kingston, Jamaica W.I.

First Published in Jamaica, 2013 by Pelican Publishers Limited

44 Lady Musgrave Road
Kingston 10, Jamaica, W.I
Tel: (876) 978-8377 Fax: (876) 978-0048
Email: pelicanpublisers@gmail.com
Website: www.pelicanpublishers.com.jm

© 2013, Institute of Caribbean Studies, University of the West Indies
Mona, Jamaica

ISBN 978-976-8240-12-5

Cover design by Pelican Publishers Limited

TABLE OF CONTENTS

PART 3 – MUSICAL CONVERSATIONS

PART 4 – REGGAE/RASTA INTERNATIONAL

ACKNOWLEDGEMENTS

The second staging of the International Reggae Conference in 2010, which generated the articles in this volume, owes a great deal to the contribution of the staff and student assistants of the Institute of Caribbean Studies/Reggae Studies Unit at the UWI, Mona Campus – in particular Nicole Edwards, Georgette McGlashen, and Latoya Tulloch. In her capacity as Director of the ICS/RSU in 2010, Professor Claudette Williams provided the necessary foundation, backed by financial support and professional guidance for the staging of the IRC2010. The UWI Open Campus office, then headed by Dr. Luz Longsworth, gave sterling contribution to the overall planning and execution of the IRC2010, with staff members Jennifer White-Clark, Delroy Banks, Delroy Waugh and Stacey Meggo working above and beyond the call of duty to ensure that every single aspect of the conference was efficiently and effectively executed. The overall IRC2010 Conference Committee who gave unstintingly of their time and effort throughout the entire process deserve high commendation, including Dr. Anna Perkins, Dr. Livingston White, Dr. Michael Barnett, Dr. Lloyd Waller, Charles Campbell, Patricia Valentine, Ava-Loi Forbes, Lenford Salmon, and Dennis Howard.

Many thanks to Professor Gordon Shirley, Principal and Pro-Vice Chancellor at the UWI, Mona, for his continued support for the International Conference, and the work of the ICS/Reggae Studies Unit.

Where this publication is concerned, Tanya Francis-Thomas' sterling support in the final editing and indexing of this work is commendable. I owe her a debt of gratitude. Latoya West-Blackwood and the team at Pelican Publishers worked assiduously to meet the demands of a rigorous publication schedule. And to all the reviewers of the chapters published herein, your contribution to this work is highly appreciated.

If I have inadvertently omitted anyone by name or designation, Nuff Respect to you for your contribution to the continued dissemination of knowledge on Jamaican culture and music.

INTRODUCTION

J amaican popular music has enjoyed a rich history since the first strains of drums resonated from the slave plantations during plantation slavery. The cementing of its music industry in the 1950s and the seminal contribution of songwriters, singers, players of instruments and their financial backers over several decades, has contributed to the development and spread of several Jamaican music genres, including mento, ska, rocksteady, reggae and dancehall, that have become internationally renowned, loved and replicated. The dissemination of thought on these genres and the exploration of socio-cultural, political, gendered and other interconnections, plus the exploration of regional and international movements across multiple borders, has been an integral part of the development of these genres.

The essays that make up this collection all originated from presentations made at the 2010 International Reggae Conference. As a component of the move to enable multiple conversations across genres, the International Reggae Conference provides a platform for academics, researchers, artistes, musicians, scholars, journalists, cultural practitioners, entrepreneurs and music lovers from around the world to share their experiences with and perspectives on Jamaican culture and popular music as well as on popular music internationally. These essays represent the research, reflection and interrogation of Jamaican popular music from varying intellectual perspectives, methodologies, spaces and geographical locations in what is a truly internationalized frame of thought and idea on music and cultures that began in the physically small location of an island in the Caribbean Sea - Jamaica.

This volume has four sections. In Part one, Cultural Interpretations, focus is placed on Jamaican popular music, reggae and dancehall, in relation to contemporary debates on violence, homophobia and youth identity negotiation in Europe, Jamaica and Canada. In Part two, Gendered Ruminations, debates on gender and sexuality in the dancehall are interrogated through Christian theology and linguistic methodology. Part three, Musical Conversations, presents important conversations with Jamaican popular music, particularly reggae, in varied formats, including an interview, journalistic discussion and an analysis of a seminal component of Jamaican culture - radio serials. In the final Part four, Reggae/Rasta International, the emphasis shifts to the internationalization of Jamaican music and culture with focus on manifestations of Reggae and Rastafari in diverse spaces, and the raising of an international reggae nation which all re-turn to the nexus of Jamaican music and culture for their birth and sustenance.

PART 1
CULTURAL
INTERPRETATIONS

1 FROM ONE LOVE TO ONE HATE?
EUROPE'S PERCEPTION OF JAMAICAN HOMOPHOBIA EXPRESSED IN SONG LYRICS

INTRODUCTION

This paper, a version of which was presented at the International Reggae Conference in 2010, originated from the authors' perception that the very topical issue of homophobia needed discussion, since it was clear that it would not disappear anytime soon, unless the Reggae community starts to finally deal with it in a proactive way

As editors of the German reggae/dancehall magazine *RIDDIM* we deal with Jamaican culture very often, and as such Jamaican culture has become a huge part of our life. But as Non-Jamaicans we are of course aware that we are not directly a part of this culture, which is so rich that it has spread all over the globe. What *we* would like, is to see the musical energy that is ignited in Jamaica, continue to burn in Germany as well as in other European countries. Based on the foregoing, this paper focuses on the shifting parameters of Reggae's reception in Europe - a shift which has occurred because of the general awareness that homophobic lyrics exist in Jamaican dancehall songs. It is important to note that some conservative Jamaicans, who are negatively biased against contemporary popular Jamaican music, might use the criticism that Jamaican music gets in Europe to support their stance. One should note, however that this paper, is clearly distinguished from this position, as it is underscored by the conviction that art mirrors rather than creates realities.

Since 2004, there has been a dramatic shift in the perception of reggae in Europe. As such, while it had been falsely reduced to the message of 'One Love' in the first instance, it is now – again falsely – reduced to the expression of 'hate' music, in the second. Since Germany's views can be seen as a reflection of that of other European countries, and with the authors also acting as editors of the German reggae magazine *RIDDIM,* this paper focuses specifically on the events in Germany which changed the mainstream perception of reggae from 'One Love' to 'hate' music. This paper also focuses on the media coverage of reggae and dancehall in the general press while showing how *RIDDIM,* as a special interest magazine, has dealt and is dealing with the situation. At the same time, the point must be made that none of these actions represent any judgement of Jamaican culture because of homophobia, even while it also doesn't suggest agreement with it. In addition, we want to stress that we are not homophobic at all, even though some publications in Germany have tried to portray us this way because we have often written about this issue in defence of reggae. Our publications took it for granted that people are people, no matter the race, class, gender or religion, that we apparently didn't emphasize it enough in the past. As such, the intent of this paper is also to help create a better understanding on both sides of the fence and attempt to provide an overview of the events that led to this shift in perception of Jamaican music from One Love to One Hate in Europe, particularly Germany.

The term homophobia is used throughout the paper, even with the understanding that it is quite problematic as the second part of the compound 'phobia' hints at irrational fears and a form of individual psychopathology. Indeed, even though the term has been widely used in the German media for the last couple of years, it still cannot be found in German dictionaries. The more neutral term which is used and refers to the rejection of a homosexual lifestyle is anti-homosexuality, however, because in English homophobia has become the common term to describe the range of negative attitudes and feelings towards homosexuality, as well as prejudice and discrimination against homosexuals, we will use it here as well, without getting into an examination or a discussion of the cause for this rejection.

GERMAN CULTURAL BACKGROUND

When writing about reggae, it is important to keep in mind that Jamaican culture is alien to a large percentage of the readers of *RIDDIM*. Therefore as Non-Jamaicans ourselves it is important to try to provide a cultural context and framework in which to embed the music we write about. For example, when discussing homophobia in Jamaican song lyrics it is important to also point out the specifics of reggae and dancehall language, and so we talk about religion, Rastafari, biblical interpretations, about Jamaican law, about different connotations of masculinity and the many other factors that come into play.

Now this discussion will focus on how German society and media deal with this type of dancehall lyrics and it is also crucial to provide some background information on why Germans are so sensitive when it comes to discrimination against minorities. This does not mean that there is no discrimination against minorities in Germany, but the expression of negative attitudes against any group of people publicly on stage is not tolerated – especially when it is done in violent, explicit language. A lot of this has to do with German history, mainly with the Holocaust, and the Nazis' mass murder of minority groups like gypsies, homosexuals, communists, socialists, disabled people and others. The fact that human beings were literally burned to death by the millions has resulted in a national trauma in Germany which the population's psyche has yet to overcome, even now, more than sixty years after the end of the Nazi regime. In 1968 during the course of the student revolts a serious discussion took place about how to avoid a repetition of anything like Auschwitz - the Polish concentration camp which is often used as pars pro toto for all the atrocities of the Holocaust, hence the slogan 'Nie wieder Auschwitz' ('Auschwitz never again') which refers to Theodor Adorno's 1970 essay *Education after Auschwitz* that stated:

'The premier demand upon all education is that Auschwitz not happen again. Its priority before any other requirement is such that I believe I need not and should not justify it. I cannot understand why it has been given so little concern until now. To justify it would be monstrous in the face of the monstrosity that took place.'[1]

Another popular slogan that evolved out of the perpetrator experience of the Holocaust is a quote from the Roman Cicero: 'Wehret den Anfängen' - 'To nip things in the bud'. This means that whenever someone expresses racist or sexist attitudes in public, he or she creates strong opposing reactions. For example when Neo-Nazi skinheads burnt down asylum-seekers' hostels in Germany in the early 1990s, hundreds of thousands of people all over Germany demonstrated against these openly racist and xenophobic attacks.

For this paper it is also important to note that the music the Neo-Nazi skinheads were listening to was so called Nazi rock, in which bands lyrically demanded the killing of all kinds of minorities. While the general consensus was that the song lyrics were not to be blamed for the gruesome attacks, nevertheless, the result was that most Nazi rock band releases were placed on an *Index of Youth Harming Media* and these songs are no longer available to people under the age of eighteen years.

Now, an example of institutionalised sexism and homophobia that existed was Article 175 of the German criminal code which made any sexual act between men a punishable offence until 1973. In the following years the law was only applied to homosexual acts with minors, and in the 1980s the Green Party tried to overturn the law, but it was not abolished until 1994 when - following the unification - the East and West German laws were adjusted. So, based on this timeline, it has only been a span of about fifteen (15) years between the legalization of homosexuality, to having openly gay politicians in high ranking positions, and same-sex marriages in Germany. This is not to say that homophobic sentiment does not exist in Germany. While this sentiment had decreased among German adults in the last century due to changing media representations of homosexuals, various awareness campaigns, a higher visibility of homosexuals in public life, as well as altered legal implications, there seems to be an increase in homophobic sentiment among the youth. According to a survey from 2002, 61 per cent of 12 to 17 year olds expressed a negative attitude towards homosexuals.[2] Many young people have detached the German adjective 'schwul' – 'gay' – from its original meaning and use it as a curse word for anything bad or boring. Additionally, as in many other places in the world you find homophobia in religious or clerical contexts, as well as in traditionally male-dominated areas – for example on German football fields. In general, there is less homophobia in the big cities compared to in small towns and villages. But many gays in Germany still do not come out of the closet for fear of career-related disadvantages and other negative reactions from those in their environment. Where German music is concerned, especially in so-called Deutsch Rap or German hip hop, there are strong verbal expressions of homophobia. However, before this is examined in any great detail it is necessary to explore the general public reception of reggae and Jamaican music, prior to the European general public's awareness of homophobic lyrics in the music.

PERCEPTION OF THE REGGAE ARTIST IN THE PAST

While hip hop has for quite some time been perceived as a musical genre that glorifies violence, that is at least in part sexist and misogynist, reggae for a long time lived off the reputation it had gained in the 1970s as being a distillation of Bob Marley's music and the mistakenly interpreted message of 'One Love'. While Marley's lyrics indeed spoke of black emancipation, religion, and a mystic world view, that had little to do with the lives of his European audience, his use of proverbs and biblical references as well as his universal approach left enough space for free interpretation. Music fans picked out familiar slogans according to their own needs like 'Revolution', 'Burnin' & Lootin'' or 'Get Up Stand Up', all the while ignoring the fact that Marley was referring to a black revolution. At this time his songs were a popular choice for chanting at demonstrations against military armament or nuclear power-plants. The white European audience, intent on escaping the confines of their rationalist society, was also good at incorporating the religious aspects of Rastafari as an esoteric retreat that promised to fulfil an 'alternative' hippie utopia. Marley's Rasta messages embodied a long-lost 'authenticity', credibility and a contemplation of 'true' values. The world promised by Marley was a mythical Africa and a symbol of black identity. But this world could not simply be translated into a 'white' European lifestyle. Therefore Marley's audience simply seemed to ignore the central aspects of his message. In general reggae was received as liberating music, rebellious on one hand, but also promising the utopia of a peaceful world, where people of all nations would live together in unity and harmony.

Journalistic coverage of Reggae was still scarce in the 1970s and 1980s. The mainstream press in Europe more or less ignored reggae or equated the music with mythical ganja-smoking Rastas. The harshness of ghetto life was often romanticized from an anti-capitalist view, according to the motto: 'poor but happy'. Many of these writers might have had the best intentions, but often failed to do justice to their 'object of observation' and this resulted in naive, if not racist judgements highlighting a 'Jamaica no problem, soon come attitude', that up until today creates a misleading image of Jamaica as an easy-going place, where everybody smokes ganja all day long, without acknowledging the fact that a lack of opportunity leads to this seemingly inactive lifestyle. It is also important to note here that upon Bob Marley's passing the German music press proclaimed the death of the whole genre of reggae music.

When a renewed interest in reggae took place at the beginning of the 1990s, Shaggy, Shabba Ranks, Chaka Demus & Pliers and Snow (mainly dancehall artists) entered the German national charts. Since Jamaican music – next to the reduction to 'One Love' – had also always been perceived as sunshine music and was therefore always a perfect soundtrack for the summer, the German media welcomed the arrival of dancehall in the summer of 1993. Suddenly, in what seemed like media frenzy, the entire German media, from daily newspapers to radio stations and even TV programmes, were introducing this supposedly new genre of Jamaican music. The coverage of dancehall helped the press to pep up their summer issues with a breath of fresh air and a touch of exoticism. But when the artists disappeared from the charts, the media soon lost interest in the genre. What remained were features or articles in leftist and more or less underground magazines that had just discovered that reggae and its offspring dancehall were not so much reflecting their own political views and dreams of a harmonious, peaceful lifestyle, but rather the harsh ghetto realities of which homophobia and misogyny were a part. In the general public's eye dancehall was still regarded as a novelty, which had had its heyday in one short hot summer.

The uproar caused by Buju Banton's song *Boom Bye Bye* in the early 1990s was mainly restricted to English-speaking countries with significant Caribbean communities, where dancehall found popularity not so evident in continental Europe, where the language barrier was a problem. In Germany and other European countries there was only a core audience that was still small in numbers (but growing steadily over the years) that was aware of homophobic song lyrics. This audience had learned to live with the fact that dancehall did not necessarily reflect their values and culture – a discrepancy that many white listeners of black music have problems with, because European Pop often functions as a means of shaping people's identities by voicing the values, fears and hopes of its listeners.

When reggae and dancehall started to gain more popularity again at the turn of this century – this time pushed by German artists like Gentleman, Seeed and Patrice, as well as Sean Paul – its growing number of fans was living under the illusion that the message of 'One Love' was still prevalent in Jamaican music. However, since the inception of

RIDDIM magazine in 2001 we have received many Letters to the Editor which have asked us to address the issue of homophobia in Dancehall lyrics. In 2002 we published an essay entitled 'Burning All Illusions,'[3] in which one *RIDDIM* writer, Ulli Güldner, explained, that homophobia is not so much a thing of the music, but rather a reflection of components of Jamaican society, and that artists should not be condemned for lyrics that many of their Jamaican listeners agree with. Güldner also dismissed the notion that homophobia in lyrics is restricted only to dancehall artists, and explained further that even artists such as Peter Tosh or Luciano agreed or agree with these views, even if they themselves did not express their aversions to gays as harshly as some of the dancehall artists. Ulli Güldner's article was *not* intended to denounce Jamaica and its culture, but rather to show that there are certain contradictions that you have to deal with as a European listener of reggae music. In the same issue, Cecil Gutzmore[4] gave a rundown of the history of homophobia in song lyrics and offered possible explanations of where the complex anti-gay sentiments in Jamaica came from, which he contextualised by portraying common homophobic manifestations in other parts of the world. Ulli Güldner's article did indeed burn quite a few illusions as the reactions from our readers clearly showed. Many had thought roots reggae to be untouched by homophobia as it was - again - all about 'One Love.' But what was most surprising were the accusations that the writer and editors of *RIDDIM* were also homophobic because of the efforts to offer a different perspective other than simply denouncing homophobia.

At this point, do keep in mind that *RIDDIM* is a special interest magazine and that, despite a circulation of 45,000 copies per issue, it is far from being considered mainstream. After its 2002 publication, the issue of homophobic dancehall lyrics took a much longer time to become an issue in the general, mainstream media.

CHANGING PARAMETERS

The focus on homophobia changed drastically in the summer of 2004, when Brian Williamson - Jamaican gay rights activist and founding member of J-FLAG - was found murdered in his New Kingston home. While the Jamaican police spoke of a murder with robbery, J-FLAG as well as its British equivalent Outrage! referred to the murder as a hate crime. Outrage!'s spokesperson Peter Tatchell, who in the early 1990s had coined the term 'murder music' to refer to Jamaican dancehall songs with homophobic content, appropriated Williamson's killing as a cause to revive his 'Stop Murder Music' campaign. This time Tatchell also sounded the alarm to continental European and American gay rights organizations, informing them about the content of certain dancehall songs and sending out word for word translations of the lyrics from Jamaican to standard English. He also provided 'black lists' of the respective artists including Beenie Man, Elephant Man, Vybz Kartel, Sizzla, Capleton, Bounty Killer, T.O.K. and Buju Banton. The aim of Outrage!'s campaign was to pressure local promoters to cancel the concerts of these artists and thereby deny the artists the possibility of making money from their performances in Europe. This campaign coincided with the commercial peak that reggae and dancehall had been enjoying, a peak which had both on the verge of establishing themselves as permanent features on the urban pop culture scene. Gentleman's album *Confidence* had gone straight to number one in the national charts, the Berlin-based group Seeed were enjoying the success of their dancehall album *Music Monks*, and Sean Paul's hit tunes were rotating in every dance club - in fact, at this time Jamaican artists were touring Europe like never before.

As a part of this timeline, in the late summer of 2004 Buju Banton became - once again - a welcome scapegoat providing the 'Stop Murder Music' campaign with the desired publicity it wanted. Shortly after having been accused of taking part in a homophobic attack against a group of homosexuals in Jamaica, Buju's presence on a European tour made him an easy target as his then twelve year old but still catchy tune *Boom Bye Bye*, was more popular than most hardcore dancehall tunes with homophobic lyrics.

The German gay rights group Association of Lesbians and Gays in Germany (LSVD) successfully mobilised the German press for its cause. Most publications merely repeated the LSVD's press releases – including all the mistakes the activists made out of sheer ignorance. They confused artists' names – for example, they called Beenie Man a band, T.O.K. a single artist and so on. But at this point in time it would have been too much to ask these publications to first do some research into Jamaican culture. Can you imagine the shock of suddenly finding out that Jamaican music is not only about 'One Love'? Having been confronted with word for word translations of dancehall lyrics that did not leave much to the imagination, the power of the written word did not fail to show its effects, not only among the activists and the media, but also among many reggae and dancehall fans who did not understand Jamaican language. Yet again symptoms were identified as the cause, and the music was blamed for the alleged persecution of gays in Jamaica. Some publications even went so far as to hold the homophobic lyrics responsible for the murder of J-FLAG's Brian Williamson. Indeed, the current chairman of the LSVD, Klaus Jetz, headlined an article for *Ila* magazine 'Deadly Baiting in Dancehall Reggae – The Murder of Brian Williamson and Jamaican Hate Songs.'[5]

Other German opinion leaders jumped on the bandwagon: local and national politicians from many different parties, regional and national newspapers, magazines as well as public prosecution departments and offices of criminal investigation all took the same line as the gay rights activists. Without checking the facts or looking at and researching the cultural context, they all repeated the gay rights activists' allegations with a feigned liberal approach. The consensus: Buju Banton is inciting murder against homosexuals – or more generally speaking 'Hate Music Equals Incitement of the People' the title of an article by Klaus Jetz published in February 2008 in a magazine called *Respekt.*[6] Incitement of the people is a punishable offence in Germany. Article 130 of the penal code says, someone is guilty of 'Volksverhetzung' (incitement of the people) if he or she:-

'In a manner that is capable of disturbing the public peace: (1) incites hatred against segments of the population or calls for violent or arbitrary measures against them, or (2) assaults the human dignity of others by insulting, maliciously maligning, or defaming segments of the population.'

This law, in this form is uniquely German, and has to do again with Germany's past, when the Nazis did just that - incite hatred and violence against minorities. This is the same law which also makes it a punishable offence to deny the Holocaust or to glorify or justify the Nazi regime.

Klaus Jetz wrote in his article:

'The situation in Jamaica showed us the scope of anti-homosexual violence that hysterical gay bashing by flipped out artists can take. From the stage people are incited to slay homosexuals. In Kingston and in other places on this Caribbean island this then leads to the regular wild chasing of (allegedly) gay men, with an often deadly outcome.'[7]

While violence against homosexuals in Jamaica cannot be denied and should not be downplayed, this description is exaggerated and again a symptom - the music - is taken for the cause. But articles like these have helped to manifest the image of Jamaica as a country where it is commonplace for wild lynch mobs to chase gays through the streets - to the soundtrack of dancehall music.

On the other hand, reggae and dancehall concerts and festivals in Germany are known for their peacefulness - especially compared to other genres like rock or hip hop. To our knowledge there has been no reported incident of any kind of violence, much less against any minorities, and the reggae scene as such has not been known to be at all homophobic. However, the gay rights activists and politicians referred to the incitement of people (Volksverhetzung) act to support their argument. Despite having much better knowledge of the issues, they claim that homophobic lyrics would incite German reggae fans to harm gays and lesbians.

When Buju Banton toured Germany in 2004 he was not willing to apologize in public for a song he wrote twelve years before, but he was willing to meet with representatives of the LSVD to start a dialogue on the issues. However, the organisation demanded that Buju Banton fulfil a 'worldwide unified' catalogue of five demands before they would agree to meet with him. Buju was asked to apologise personally in front of a camera, to apologise to gays and lesbians in particular for his 'incitement to violence' against homosexuals, to assure that he would never again in future call for violence against homosexuals during performances, on records or in speeches and that he would withdraw his records with 'hate lyrics' from circulation (if this was not possible due to contractual agreement then he should donate the money generated from the sale of these records to a Jamaican organisation, which would assist homosexual victims of violence.)[8]

While promoters, Donovan Germain who was Buju's manager at that time, and reggae-affiliated lawyers tried to appease the hardened fronts by sending out official statements or trying to provide explanations about the cultural background of Jamaica, Buju's offence seemed too harsh for the gay activists to back down from their stance. Consequently, the campaign against Buju Banton proved to be a successful one from the gay rights activists' point of view, as most of the shows on Buju Banton's tour were cancelled. Only a few promoters dared to hold the shows despite growing pressure – among them the U-Club in Wuppertal, that offered to donate the entrance fee from the show to J-FLAG in order to calm the gay rights activists, to express their own non-homophobic belief and to get their name out of the media, but J-FLAG refused to take any 'blood money' from Buju Banton.[9]

Even though *RIDDIM* had already planned another cover story at the time of these events, we as editors of a reggae magazine felt a sense of responsibility to give an account of the events without parroting the LSVD's press releases as most other publications were doing and so we decided to take a stand by putting Buju Banton on RIDDIM's cover. We had conducted various interviews with the artist before, but this one proved to be very difficult because Buju was obviously under a lot of pressure and was very sceptical despite the mediation of a mutual friend. He expressed his disappointment about the fact that nobody in the general media seemed to have noticed the changes he had gone through since the release of *Boom Bye Bye*. When confronted with the gay activists' accusation that he still performed the song despite his claim of the opposite, he answered with an angry laugh, that he couldn't believe that globalisation had gone so far that he couldn't even be left undisturbed in his homeland, in his bathroom. After this comment he refused to answer further questions.

Accompanying the interview excerpts *RIDDIM* offered a cultural contextualization by examining the legal, social, historical and linguistic situations in Jamaica that contributed to the fact that songs like *Boom Bye Bye* could come out of Jamaica. We also verbalized our own opinion, which is expressed in the following excerpt from the cover story of *RIDDIM* 06/2004:

> 'Yes! Parts of the Jamaican society are homophobic. Yes! Along with various other issues you will find homophobic content in dancehall lyrics. Yes! A lot of Jamaican artists reject homosexuality. This becomes a problem, when the music reaches an international mainstream of listeners, who think of themselves as being enlightened, liberal, tolerant and politically correct and who search in reggae and dancehall a pristine, authentic, rebellious, status quo rejecting outlaw or underground culture. It all goes back to the old problem of Black music and white listeners. Even though some of the mentioned aspects can to a certain extent be found in Jamaican music, the historic and social realities that are the backdrop to this music culture can't be ignored only to satisfy ones own expectations of what the music should be like. A ghetto is no amusement park! We cannot ask Jamaican culture to model itself according to our somewhat romantic illusions. This music is not first and foremost made for us, but for a Jamaican audience, mainly for so-called ghetto people. Therefore it is no surprise that we sooner or later have to face strong inconsistencies, which one can either endure by tolerat-

ing homophobic songs without adopting the point of view, or from which one can take what suits them considering the rich selection that the music has to offer. Any form of reinterpretation is legitimate as long as one doesn't fall back into the trap of master and servant, where one thinks one can force their world view on the originators of the music. We also need to keep in mind that it has been a long and painful process to overcome homophobia in Germany and that we still have a long way to go. Putting it clearly: We are not homophobic. And while we can even to a certain extent understand the LSVD's outrage, we only want to defend the music from the arrogance that this issue is dealt and judged with. This is cultural imperialism! To use the words of the cultural critic Stuart Hall, globalization should not equal cultural conformity, globalization has to always include the local, for only the uniqueness of the voices, the points of view, identities, cultural traditions and histories make expression possible – for example in song lyrics. The methods and strategies of the current campaign against Buju Banton raise the question: What are the actual aims of gay rights groups? Are they merely seeking media attention? Mission accomplished! Or do they want to rid the Jamaican society of its homophobia? Mission Impossible?'[10]

In the same issue with the cover story on Buju Banton, *RIDDIM* also included an interview with the cultural critic Paul Gilroy, who initially had helped to inform the English public of Buju's homophobia in the early 1990's together with film maker Isaac Julien, but who now condemned the gay rights activists' inconsiderate campaign. Also in the same issue, another essay titled 'The Third Way'[11] made it clear that certain lyrics are indeed unacceptable for an international market, and that artists who want to reach this market should be open to play by its rules.

While things seemed to calm down after Buju had left Germany in 2004, it soon became obvious that this was only the beginning. Gay rights activists staged campaigns against tours of Beenie Man and Capleton in the US; in England, Germany, Switzerland, and France one reggae concert after the other got cancelled. Elephant Man and Vybz Kartel were excluded from the British MOBO-Awards. In Germany, radio stations were pressured to take certain artists off of their playlists. The cancellation of shows is said to have resulted in a loss of 4 million Euros for Beenie Man, Sizzla and Capleton alone.

And so, in order to restore the reputation of dancehall outside of Jamaica and to safeguard their means of income European bookers in cooperation with Jamaican artists and gay rights activists from England developed the so-called 'Reggae Compassionate Act' (RCA) at the beginning of 2007, which is outlined below:

'We, the artists of the reggae community, hereby present this letter as a symbol of our dedication to the guiding principles of reggae's enduring foundation ONE LOVE. Throughout time, reggae has been recognized as a healing remedy and an agent of positive social change. We will continue this proud and righteous tradition. Reggae artists and their music have fought against injustices, inequalities, poverty and violence even while enduring some of those same circumstances themselves. Over the years, reggae music has been popularized and is enjoyed by an unprecedented audience worldwide. Artists of the Reggae Community respect and uphold the rights of all individuals to live without fear of hatred and violence due to their religion, sexual orientation, race, ethnicity or gender.

While we recognize that our artistic community is comprised of many different individuals who express themselves in different ways and hold a myriad of beliefs, we firmly believe that the way forward lies in tolerance. Everyone should be allowed to follow his own convictions and we must be respected for our freedom of speech as far as we respect the law, but it must be made clear that there is no space in the music community for hatred and prejudice, as well as no place for racism, violence, sexism or homophobia. We do not encourage nor minister to HATE but rather uphold a philosophy of LOVE, RESPECT and UNDERSTANDING towards all human beings as the corner-stone of reggae music.

This compassionate act is hereby calling on a return to the following principles as the guiding vision for the future of a healthy reggae music community: Positive Vibrations, Consciousness raising, Social and Civic Engagement, Democracy and Freedom, Peace and Non-Violence, Mother Nature, Equal Rights and Justice, One Love, Individual Rights, Humanity, Tolerance and Understanding.

We, as artists, are committed to a holistic and healthy existence in the world, and offer our greatest respect to the human and natural world. We pledge that our music will continue to make a positive contribution to the worldwide dialogue on peace, respect and justice for all. To this end, we agree not to make statements or perform songs that incite hatred or violence against anyone from any community. One Love.'[12]

While the authors of the 'Reggae Compassionate Act' surely had the best intentions in mind, some of the artists on the so-called 'black list', such as Bounty Killer and Vybz Kartel, refused to sign the act, because of the image that they had created for themselves and the fact that the signing of this act would have been equal to a sell-out to the gay rights activists. Other artists who allegedly signed the 'Reggae Compassionate Act', like Capleton, Sizzla, Beenie Man and Buju Banton later denied having done so. Buju even claimed that his signature had been falsified. So, only months after the introduction of the RCA, such claims undermined its effectiveness, especially because scanned copies of the act that had been signed by artists could be found on the internet. At this point, the artists were in a catch-22 situation, because not signing the RCA meant they could not tour Europe, but signing it meant losing the respect of their core audience in Jamaica. Some of them might have remembered Shabba Ranks whose career pretty much ended after his record company, Epic, released a statement of him apologising to the gay community.

One problem for the RCA was that it had again reduced reggae to the notion of 'One Love' allegedly 'for the future of a healthy reggae community', but it was very much stuck in the past and ignored the fact that dancehall music of the new millennium had little in common with reggae of the 1970s. Another problem was that it followed the line of argument of the gay rights activists being that certain songs were indeed inciting violence, and so by signing the act the artists would have admitted that they had done so in the first place.

While Outrage! and other British gay rights organizations still accepted the signatures and refrained from boycotting the tours, the German LSVD and member of parliament, Volker Beck from the Green Party, who had been fighting for gay rights for many years, no longer felt obliged to fulfil their part of the agreement and continued with their campaign against the respective artists. They accused the artists of being hypocritical because, on the one hand, they had signed the RCA and stopped performing homophobic lyrics in Europe, while, on the other hand, they denied having signed the act and continued to perform these songs in Jamaica. Through Youtube videos and online concert reviews it was and is possible to know exactly which artist said what at any show around the world – another clash of the global and the local. As such, the LSVD put together dossiers of each of the respective artists that included transcriptions and translations of the lyrics in question, highlighting the sensitive parts. They continued to feed this information to the mainstream media, which then started to react not only by reporting on cancelled shows from the gay rights activists' point of view, but also by reporting on homophobia in Jamaica at a more general level – all the while still arguing in the interest of the LSVD and Volker Beck.

One TV feature, which was aired on a national broadcasting network at prime time, showed 'daggering' patrons at a street dance while an MC repeats a line from the song being played that talked about 'killing gays'. The commentator, obviously alien to the expressiveness of dancehall culture, interpreted the dancing as a display of violence and connected the music to actual killings of gays in Jamaica.[13] While attempting to describe homophobia in Jamaica in a broader cultural context, such reports failed to do justice to the issue and at the same time scared clueless viewers with images of 'daggering', without any further explanation of dancehall and its rituals.

A lengthy article in a magazine called *Neon* headlined a story on homophobia in Jamaica in its February 2008 issue 'Murder Sound', thereby again claiming that the music was responsible for violence against homosexuals. The introduction of the article highlights its main line of thought thus:

> 'Dreadlocks, Bob Marley stickers and walls painted in the Ethiopian colours are part of the dominant culture of left wing Germany. At the same time homophobia in reggae music is likely to be ignored. Many hate songs *(note that this term is not used in quotation marks)* explicitly incite the murdering of gays and lesbians. With great success: Homosexuals in Jamaica are fair game.'[14]

On the one hand, such features are a result of the campaigns of the gay rights activists while on the other hand, these same activists use these features to support their claim that gays in Jamaica have to be protected from a homophobic society. In 2008 Volker Beck of the Green Party used quotes from these reports in conjunction with translations of lyrics, to get Sizzla's name on a database of the Schengen Information System (SIS) to deny him his visa for the European Union. Beck painted a picture of a Jamaica, where wild lynch mobs chased homosexuals through the streets on a regular basis and even demanded that the Foreign Office give out Travel Alerts for Jamaica, which are usually given out for regions like Afghanistan, Iraq, the Gaza Strip and Somalia.[15] The German government made it clear though, that such measures were disproportionate and pointed out that even J-FLAG had spoken out against any form of Jamaican boycott. Since Sizzla had already entered the Schengen area at that time, he could only be deported back to Jamaica when he tried to re-enter Europe via Spain, after having played a single show in Miami in between.

The German government later erased his SIS-entry and Sizzla's Schengen visa was reinstated for a tour of Europe in November 2009. This tour was again accompanied by massive gay protests, one-sided media reports, and cancellations of shows. A promoter from Berlin, together with the gay rights activists, even worked out a new version of the Reggae Compassionate Act that said that the artist had agreed not to perform homophobic lyrics globally, not even in Jamaica[16] which Sizzla is said to have signed - but even this was to no avail, as the promoter came under so much pressure that he finally gave in and cancelled the show at the last minute.

During the time of Sizzla's tour, Volker Beck, in an interview for the internationally broadcasted radio station Deutschland Radio used the term 'pogrom'[17] to describe the situation of gays in Jamaica, a term, that in Germany is almost exclusively used in connection with the persecution and killing of Jews under the Nazi regime. The climate was so agitated, that the U-Club in Wuppertal, one of the few venues that would not give in to the demands and pressure of the activists and local politicians, became the target of a butyric acid attack by an anti-fascist organisation that had earlier demanded the shutting down of the club because of its support for homophobic artists. Fortunately, no one was hurt and Sizzla's show could take place as planned the following day - accompanied by gay protests outside the venue.

It had meanwhile become common practice that the police and State Security were called in by the gays who claimed that incitement of the people would take place at concerts featuring the respective artists. Therefore, the State Security and police would send their representatives, along with a translator to monitor the shows, only to find out that neither had the artists performed homophobic lyrics nor had the audience been incited to violence against anyone. Yet, when even Mr Vegas whose name had never appeared on any so called 'black list', toured Germany at the end of 2009, he had to sign an agreement saying that he would not incite violence, and his performance was monitored by the police. This goes to show that the gay rights campaign was being extended to other Jamaican dancehall artists.

Since Volker Beck and the LSVD had not been able to fully succeed in outlawing the music by claiming its role in inciting people to violence, they developed another strategy to fight reggae artists and their music by making use of the Law for the Protection of the Children and the Youth to get records with homophobic content on a list of media that was harmful to youth - *Index of Youth Harming Media*. This meant that the records couldn't be sold or advertised in places that youths under eighteen years of age have access to, including the internet. According to Groove Attack, the German distributor of the most reggae albums in the country, this means de facto a complete disposal of these records as there is no outlet that youths do not have access to. It has been common practice that chain stores often get rid of the complete catalogue of an artist, or sometimes even of a record company, that has an album on the *Index of Youth Harming Media*. The aim of this strategy was again, to find a legal foundation for visa withdrawals and concert boycotts.

In *RIDDIM* 02/10, in a lengthy feature titled 'War On Reggae - Final Destination Illegality or Index?' Ulli Güldner presented detailed research on the matter.[18] At that time, 35 reggae albums were put on the Index, among them releases by Baby Cham, Bounty Killer, Buju Banton, Capleton, Elephant Man, Sizzla, T.O.K., Vybz Kartel, as well as compilations such as *Reggae Gold*, *Strictly The Best* and various one riddim samplers. It is striking that from the 978 records, which have been put on the Index in total so far (November 2009), almost all of them are composed in German language and about 80 per cent of them contain radical right wing propaganda and glorifications of the Nazi regime. What is even more striking is that not *one* single American hip hop artist can be found on this Index, 'despite nearly two and a half decades of gangster and gangbang rap.' Next to Nazi rock records there are about 50 Deutsch rap (German hip hop) albums on the Index. While the reggae and dancehall albums were put on the Index between 2008 and 2009 at the request of the Federal Ministry of Families, it was concerned parents, teachers and social workers, that had reported Deutsch rap and Nazi rock releases to the Federal Department for Media Harmful to Young Persons. It is no secret that the Ministry of Families was alarmed by the LSVD and Volker Beck from the Green Party.

In the aforementioned article Ulli Güldner quotes from a protocol about the decision whether to put Sizzla's song *Mash Dem Down* on the Index, a song that the Ministry of Families classified as glorifying violence which notes:-

'The twelve members of the Department for Media Harmful to Young Persons screened the song and came to the conclusion that only single words like 'Selassie', 'mash', and 'mek' could be understood. Further content was not accessible.'[19]

The song was therefore not put on the Index. It is also noteworthy that for decades there had only been one reggae record on the Index, Peter Tosh's *Legalize It*, and that was in 1980. This entry was removed from the Index 25 years later.

As mentioned earlier, there are quite a few Deutsch rap songs with homophobic content that have also been put on the Index. In the song *Keine Toleranz (No Tolerance)* the rappers G-Hot and Boss A, talk about cutting gays in half with an axe; in the song *Das Leben ist hart (Life is Hard)* one of the most popular German rap artists, Bushido, even talks about 'gassing gays' referring to the gassing of Jews during Holocaust. Yet, these German artists have not been persecuted like their Jamaican counterparts. On the contrary, Bushido has appeared in all major talk shows, has written a best-selling autobiography, and is about to star in a movie about his life. Even though Volker Beck and the LSVD have been campaigning against German rappers as well, these rappers are present in Germany, they speak the German language, and so they can explain themselves and even apologize for their lyrics without losing their core audience. And last, but not least, these German artists have a much stronger lobby group in the form of major record companies than the reggae industry, which basically does not have any lobby group(s) in Germany at all. Or, perhaps you could argue that *RIDDIM* magazine and a handful of promoters are the lobby groups on behalf of the reggae and dancehall artists.

In January 2010 the German booking agent for T.O.K. asked Jamaican academics for help regarding translations of T.O.K. songs such as *Chi Chi Man* that differed from those circulating in Germany. In his detailed interpretation and explanations of Jamaican metaphors Prof. Hubert Devonish of the UWI, Mona showed that T.O.K. was not inciting violence, but merely expressing their disapproval of a homosexual lifestyle. Thanks to Prof. Devonish's work T.O.K.'s 2010 tour of Germany took place as scheduled and the gay protests announced for their show in Munich were cancelled. Hopefully this was proof that there are ways to successfully demobilise certain gay rights campaigns with what Jamaicans term as *reasoning,* and that the local can still make itself be heard in a globalized world.

CONCLUSION

This conclusion focuses on a description of the state of reggae and dancehall in Germany today and with a suggestion on what can be done on the part of the reggae industry in Germany and in Jamaica to restore the music's image - an image restoration that is neither reduced to 'One Love' nor to 'One Hate,' but rather one that does justice to the myriad aspects covered in reggae and dancehall music.

When it comes to reggae and dancehall in Germany the situation right now is challenging. For someone who has a general interest in music, but no deeper knowledge of Jamaica and its culture, it seems almost impossible to pick up a reggae or dancehall CD without immediately associating it with 'hate' music, homophobia and horror scenarios of lynch mobs attacking and killing gays to a dancehall soundtrack. Worst of all, this image has begun to rub off on and tarnish the entire perception of Jamaica as the gay rights activists claim to speak on behalf of gays in Jamaica, without seeing that they also stir up even more anger against them by cancelling shows and denying the artists a means of income. Yet, Jamaican artists who perform homophobic lyrics are not 'fighting' gays as they might believe, but, instead, are furnishing the gay rights activists with more opportunities to get their agenda into the media.

Finally, the German gay rights activists seem to be less concerned about reggae or dancehall, but regard the music as a welcome vehicle to provide them with more visibility and create a greater public awareness for the gay community in Germany. Being fully aware that they would find common consensus with their demand for political correctness in Germany, these activists are successfully looking for cheap 'forwards' in the same way that the artists who perform homophobic lyrics are also looking for cheap 'forwards.'

It is arguable that enforcing the gay rights activists' agenda at the expense of Jamaica and the ability of reggae and dancehall artists to earn a living equals cultural neo-colonialism. The fact that Volker Beck, who claims prerogative of interpretation, but is not even willing to try to understand at least aspects of Jamaican culture, shows that his main concern is not to better the situation of gays in Jamaica but to advance the agenda of activists in Germany and so it would be naive to expect him to be willing to compromise.

At this stage, the main aim of any type of agreement that is developed for the artists to sign should not be the avoidance of gay protests, but rather the creation of a legal framework for the artists to move within in order to prevent visa withdrawals and concert cancellations. Ulli Güldner, in his aforementioned article on 'War On Reggae' in RIDDIM 02/10, suggests that such an agreement can only be valid for Germany, since the legal requirements as well as moral values vary from country to country. As such, the agreement should neither idealize reggae in a romanticized way nor should it contain paternalistic and presumptuous demands for apologies and financial donations to victims of homosexual violence in Germany or elsewhere. Again, this most likely may not stop the gay rights activists from protesting against Jamaican artists, but it could enable the artists to tour Germany without having to fear further consequences.

In the long run only Jamaica can better the situation by answering to the allegations made by the gay rights activists. While there are homophobic lyrics in other genres as well the difference with reggae and dancehall lyrics is that they emanate from a country where homosexuality among men is illegal, where there have been actual acts of homophobic violence as documented by human rights groups, and because of the richness of its culture, Jamaica (despite its small size) is much more visible than many other countries worldwide. At the end of the day we think there are much more urgent issues to be discussed in the lyrics, and it would make it so much easier for some of the artists and the genre on a whole if the lyrics could go without verbal bashing of minorities.

REFERENCES

BOOKS

Tiedemann, Rolf (Ed.), *Theodor Adorno: Can One Live After Auschwitz - A Philosophical Reader.* Stanford: Stanford University Press, 2003.

MAGAZINES

Güldner, Ulli, 'Burning All Illusions.' *RIDDIM* 04/2002.

Güldner, Ulli, 'War On Reggae - Final Destination Illegality or Index?' *RIDDIM* 02/2010.

Gutzmore, Cecil, 'Auf den Spuren jamaikanischer Homophobie.' RIDDIM 04/2002.

Jetz, Klaus, 'Tödliche Hetze im Dancehall-Reggae - Der Mord an Brian Williamson und die jamaikanischen Hatesongs.' Ila, September 2004, 278.

Jetz, Klaus, 'Hassmusik ist Volksverhetzung - Homofeindlicher Musik Einhalt gebieten.' *Respekt* 02/2008.

Karnik, Olaf, 'Homophobie hier - Der dritte Weg.' *RIDDIM* 05/2004.

Köhlings, Ellen & Lilly, Pete, 'Buju Banton - Wanted Man.' RIDDIM 05/2004.

Mocek, Ingo, 'Murder Sound.' *Neon*, February 2008.

PRESS RELEASES

iconkids & youth press release, May 6th, 2002.

J-FLAG press release, 'J-FLAG Rejects Buju Banton's Blood Money.' September 1, 2004.

LSVD press release, 'Keine Hass-Songs auf Berliner Bühnen!', August 27, 2004.

Printed Matter of the Federal German Parliament No. 16/9714. 'Kleine Anfrage der

Abgeordneten Volker Beck (Köln), Josef Philip Winkler u.a. und der Fraktion BÜNDNIS90/Die Grünen: 'Lage der Homosexuellen auf Jamaika." June 20, 2008.

INTERNET

www.petertatchell.net/popmusic/reggaecompassionatescan.htm, accessed October 01, 2010.\

TELEVISION

ARD Weltspiegel, 'Jamaika: Jagd auf Schwule.' May 6, 2007.

RADIO

Deutschlandradio, 'Volker Beck: Hasssänger sollen nicht einreisen dürfen.' November 25, 2009.

NOTES

1. Theodor Adorno, 'Education After Auschwitz,' in: Rolf Tiedemann (Ed.), *Theodor Adorno: Can One Live After Auschwitz – A Philosophical Reader* (Stanford, Stanford University Press, 2003), 19.

2. See: Pressemitteilung, iconkids & youth, 2002- ww.iconkids.com/deutsch/download/presse/2002/2002_2.pdf

3. Ulli Güldner, 'Burning All Illusions.' RIDDIM 04/02, December, 2002.

4. Cecil Gutzmore, 'Auf den Spuren jamaikanischer Homophobie,' RIDDIM 04/02, December, 2002.

5. Klaus Jetz, 'Tödliche Hetze im Dancehall-Reggae – Der Mord an Brian Williamson und die jamaikanischen Hatesongs.' Ila, September 2004, 278.

6. Klaus Jetz, 'Hassmusik ist Volksverhetzung – Homofeindlicher Musik Einhalt gebieten.' Respekt 02/2008.

7. Ibid.

8. LSVD press release 'Keine Hass-Songs auf Berliner Bühnen!', August 27, 2004.

9. J-FLAG press release 'J-FLAG Rejects Buju Banton's Blood Money.' September 1, 2004.

10. Ellen Köhlings & Pete Lilly, 'Buju Banton – Wanted Man.' RIDDIM 05/04, November/December 2004.

11. Olaf Karnik, 'Homophobie hier – Der dritte Weg.' RIDDIM 05/04, November/December 2004.

12. Reggae Compassionate Act. www.petertatchell.net/popmusic/reggaecompassionatescan.htm (accessed October 01, 2010).

13. ARD Weltspiegel 'Jamaika: Jagd auf Schwule.' May 6, 2007.

14. Ingo Mocek, 'Murder Sound.' Neon, February 2008.

15. Bundestagsdrucksache Nr. 16/9714 vom 20.06.2008. Kleine Anfrage der Abgeordneten Volker Beck (Köln), Josef Philip Winkler u.a. und der Fraktion BÜNDNIS90/Die Grünen: 'Lage der Homosexuellen auf Jamaika.'

16. The authors have never seen a copy of the 'new' version of the Reggae Compassionate Act.

17. Deutschlandradio-Feature 'Volker Beck: Hasssänger sollen nicht einreisen dürfen.' November 25 2009.

18. Ulli Güldner 'War On Reggae - Final Destination Illegality or Index?' RIDDIM, March/April 2010.

19. Ibid.

2 DANCEHALL, VIOLENCE AND JAMAICAN YOUTH

AN EMPIRICAL SYNOPSIS

INTRODUCTION: VIOLENCE, MEDIA AND JAMAICA

This paper presents a synopsis of the main findings of the Dancehall/Violence study of 2009 which assessed the relationship between dancehall culture and violence among youths in four parishes in Jamaica -Kingston and St. Andrew, Clarendon and St. Catherine - during the summer of 2009. Related components of this debate, including violence and the media, bear further discussion.

There have been multiple discussions about violence and its relation to crime in Jamaica. The Jamaican print and electronic media continues to feed its citizens with the images of violence and crime on a daily basis, almost as they occur in various parts of the country. Police blotters remain overcrowded with the myriad of violent and criminal incidents that occur on a regular basis. Indeed, there has developed a perception, that, in the current wave of sensational media that has become a global phenomenon, graphic reportage of extreme and violent acts are in high demand by media consumers. In Jamaica, several studies have been done and documents prepared that suggest ways to deal with or manage the country's pervasive challenges with crime and violence (see for example the Wolfe Report, 1993, the World Bank Report 1997, Harriott, 2008 and Headley 1986).

What is also relevant herein is that in Jamaica, force and violence have long been accepted components of the country's political history and culture. There are noted instances of the vertical, liberating use of violence in the numerous slave revolts against the British. For example, the most noted was the 1833 Christmas rebellion led by Sam Sharpe; the 1865 Morant Bay Rebellion led by Paul Bogle; and the 1938 disturbances in which the workers rioted against low wages and severe working and living conditions. In the post-independence era, violence in the Jamaican society has escalated significantly and can be disaggregated into six distinct types - violent crimes, political violence, drug violence, domestic violence, inter-personal violence and gang violence[1] and these are the forms of violence and crime that remain of immense concern in Jamaican society. In this instance, its relationship to Jamaican popular music culture is also a part of this arena of concern, particularly where its impact on youths are concerned.

MUSIC AND VIOLENCE

Jamaica has been blessed with an inexhaustible storehouse of cultural creativity for which it has gained tremendous international visibility - with significant country branding abroad. For example, where its music culture is concerned, Jamaican reggae and dancehall music have broken many barriers, including geographic, linguistic, ethnic and racial, among others. The themes of Rastafari that have been cemented in Reggae music have made it loved and appreciated by many persons worldwide - peace, love, unity, natural livity, African centrality, black pride etc. Yet, even while celebrations continue about the legacies of Reggae music these must also contend with the challenges that face its successor, Dancehall. Since its rise to prominence in the early 1980s, dancehall has faced harsh criticisms. It has been charged with multiple dastardly deeds that plague the society and more. I recall quite vividly an article in the *Gleaner* of January 21, 2000 where dancehall was identified as one reason why boys received poor grades in school.[2] Of course, it is also critical to note that dancehall culture's coming of age occurred at a time that was then seen as a spike in Jamaica's violent and criminal activities – 1980 - and which recorded, at that time, the greatest number of murders in one year – 800 (Hope 2006). Dancehall remains very popular among Jamaicans at home and abroad, as well as with its many fans and supporters across the world. Its impact or influence on Jamaican youths remains a point of discussion.

Jamaican debates on dancehall culture are also heavily coloured by perception. Here, dancehall culture is generally perceived and thus identified as a negative form of cultural and musical activity in many debates and discussions about its influence and impact in Jamaica. The constant dalliance of many popular dancehall artistes with extreme lyrics, particularly those which are graphically violent or highly sexual has ensured that the music and lyrics of dancehall are identified as contributory factors to violent and criminal activity in Jamaica, as well as to sexual promiscuity and perversity. This has remained so even with a lack of research to analyze any causal or correlational relationship between popular music consumption and behaviours and/or attitudes in Jamaica. This dearth of scientific information backed by adequate research continues to dog the efforts to make meaningful conclusions about the process, progress and impact of popular music and culture in modern-day Jamaica. Indeed, the greater proportion of studies conducted around music and behavior or socialization, have been carried out in developed countries (see for example Anderson and Bushman, 2002; Anderson, Carnagey & Eubanks 2003; Fried 2003 & 2006; Klein et al 1993; Rubin, West and Mitchell 2001; Martin et al 1993; Ballard & Coates 1995; St. Lawrence and Joyner, 1991; Wanamaker & Reznikoff 1989; Barongan and Hall 1995; and Wester, Crown, Quatman, & Heesacker 1997). Even with that focus, one must not lose sight of the fact that music is used for entertainment and communication. Arguments are also made that it is an important means of socialization, particularly in our media-driven societies. According to Klein et al (1993) music plays an important role in the lives of adolescents, particularly as they move through adolescence. Some correlational studies suggest a connection between the music and a wide range of troublesome behaviours, including violent and aggressive ones. For example, Rubin, West and Mitchell (2001) suggested that college students who prefer rap and heavy metal music, report more hostile attitudes than students who prefer other styles of music like country, alternative, or dance/soul. In another study, Martin et al (1993) reports a relationship between rock music preference and feeling low in mood.

On the other hand, some experimental studies of the effects of violent music lyrics on listeners have found no effects of lyric content on aggression-related variables including Ballard & Coates(1995), St. Lawrence and Joyner (1991), Wanamaker & Reznikoff (1989). Others have shown lyric-specific effects with a range of measures such as Anderson, Carnagey & Eubanks (2003), Barongan and Hall (1995), and Wester, Crown, Quatman, & Heesacker (1997). For example, Anderson and Carnagey's (2003) five experiments demonstrated that college students who heard a violent song felt more hostile than those who heard a similar but non-violent song, and these were replicated across song and song types. Importantly, trait hostility in the subjects was closely related to state hostility even while it did not moderate the song lyric effects.

Standing as the only study on popular music and behaviour of adolescents in Jamaica at the time of this work, Holder-Nevins and Bain's (2001) study on popular music and sexual behavior among female adolescents in Jamaica concluded that 'the data dispels popular beliefs that dancehall music promotes dangerous sexual behaviors'. In addition Holder-Nevins and Bain suggested that, based on its popularity, soul music (American R&B) could be integrated into interventions for responsible sexual health, and suggested that parents and teachers encourage adolescents to explore and understand feelings elicited by listening to music. My continued research on dancehall since 1996 (see for example Hope 2004; 2006a; 2006b; 2010 & 2011) has utilized mainly qualitative methods to explore dancehall music and culture from multiple standpoints. Based on my work it is clear that violence, as a critical component of the space from which dancehall music and culture draws its sustenance, remains interwoven with the narratives, lyrics, behaviour and performance of dancehall actors - Affectors and Affectees (Hope 2006), i.e. those who create and/or consume the products of dancehall. What remains unclear is whether dancehall music and culture stand as Art imitating life, i.e. drawing from on already violence and crime-ridden society; or works particularly to impose values of pure violence on the Jamaican society in isolation of other variables. Nonetheless, drawing from the foregoing synopsis of research on related and similar issues, it is arguable that many discussions around dancehall culture and its social impact in Jamaica have been fed, in the main, by ideas and perceptions of various individuals from different and often competing sectors of the society. As a general principle, these discussions are usually critically devoid of any scientific inquiry that specifically targets the issues at hand. As noted, earlier, the greater percentage of empirical work conducted on Jamaican dancehall have been mainly qualitative and have focussed particularly on the cultural production of music (Stolzoff, 2001) and the socio-cultural, political and gendered debates as they appear in dancehall culture (Cooper 1993 & 2004; Hope, 2006 & 2010).

Yet, despite continued protestation and denunciation of its social relevance by agenda setters, religious groupings and concerned Jamaicans, dancehall music and culture remains at the helm of popular cultural output in Jamaica and a favourite of Jamaica's youth. Dancehall's cultural influence runs the gamut from music, fashion, style, language, slang, and advertisements, through to traditional and non-traditional forms of theatre, poetry and into the journalistic and media debates that provide continued visibility for its output. An important component of this visibility is that dancehall music and culture continues to feature prominently in discussions around problematic levels of violent and criminal activities in Jamaica. Notwithstanding this, the continued focus on perception as the foundation for critical analysis of dancehall's social impact has failed to provide researchers, academics, pollsters and policy makers with data from which they can extract the information needed to craft meaningful strategies that can aid in the development of Jamaica. Thus, the main objective of this research was to initiate an exploration to assess the social impact of dancehall culture on Jamaica's young people by targeting youths who have been identified as violent and/or criminal as the main respondents. This research aimed to ascertain if, how and to what extent does dancehall music and culture actually influence violent behaviour in youths. In this regard, the key research objectives were (a) To determine if exposure to dancehall music influences violent behaviour among Jamaican youths 15-24 years old; and (b) To find out how and in what ways does dancehall influence behaviour among Jamaican youths 15-24 years old. Thus, this initial exploration had two key aims. While it is exploratory in nature, the first aim was to provide a more focussed and scientific point of entry for debates and discussions on this topic and the second was to add to the growing body of academic research around Jamaican popular music in general and dancehall culture in particular.

The size and flexibility of this project allowed the researchers an opportunity to explore the key aspects involved in the relationship between dancehall music culture and violence. Using a case:control approach, data was collected from youths who already displayed violent behaviours or tendencies towards such behavior, and some who had been charged for violent activities. The control group was closely matched to the non-control/case group for age, gender, location and other socio-demographics. Every effort was made to ensure that respondents in the control group had not been identified as violent or prone to violence. The actual fieldwork was set to end during the early summer, just before all the summer parties, stage shows and other dancehall events as generally, the lyrics and actions of dancehall artistes at these summer events often create opportunities for media and social controversy and debate, thereby acting as triggers for the high points for intense discussion and debate around dancehall culture in the media that often set the agenda for similar discussions in the society.

LOCATING THE RESPONDENTS

The sample for the study consisted of youths as defined by the United Nations which defines 'youth', as those persons between the ages of 15 and 24 years, without prejudice to other definitions. In the first instance violent-prone or at-risk teenagers, particularly in the age ranges 15-18, from secondary level schools, juvenile homes and other locations were identified. In addition, violent and/or criminal youths, 19 years to 24 years of age who may or may not have been charged and/ or incarcerated for their activities were also identified. This included youths in state facilities such as Children's Homes and Places of Safety and some individuals who had been released from jail or prison. The sample design drew on three hundred (300) youths 15-24 years of age from four parishes in Jamaica – Kingston, St. Andrew, St. Catherine and Clarendon[3] for the survey and two focus groups consisting of eight (8) youths each. The four parishes identified are significantly urbanized, with Kingston and St. Andrew at the highest point of this development. Levels of crime and violence have historically been highest in Kingston and St. Andrew; however, since the turn of the millennium the parishes of St. Catherine, and Clarendon also developed high levels of crime and violence. The preponderance of violent and criminal activities was borne out in the daily radio and television newscasts and newspaper reports that highlight the levels of criminal activity and the growing levels of gun violence and murders in these parishes.[4]

METHODS

The experimental method is generally the preferred method for studying impact and influence, as per several of the foregoing studies discussed, as it has been identified as the key means by which cause and effect can be established. This is so because it allows for the precise control of variables and involves the deliberate manipulation of one variable while keeping other variables constant. The fact that experiments are replicable also underlies their seminal role in studies of this nature as the experimental method consists of standardised procedures and measures which allow it to be easily repeated. However, the experimental method has often been criticized for particular flaws that are inherent to the study design including potential validity threats, ethical issues, artificiality which can often lead to distorted behaviour, high levels of behaviour control resulting in a narrow range of behaviour in the laboratory or experimental setting and demand characteristics, which often convey to the participant the purpose of the experiment resulting in participants trying to figure out the purpose of the experiment and maybe attempting to 'get it right'. Additionally, the experimental method (for e.g. as used in psychology) has a history of using biased or unrepresentative sampling. George Miller (1962) estimated that 90 per cent of U.S. experiments have used U.S. college students because they are easy to access and their participation generates little or no costs. Yet the results still tend to be generalised to the U.S. population as a whole, and often beyond the US to other societies globally.

As such, this study attempted to eliminate several experimental limitations including its artificiality by using a quasi-experimental design that sought to eliminate some potential validity threats and to move beyond a tightly controlled laboratory setting by utilizing a survey in the field, backed by a mixed method questionnaire, and supported by two focus groups. A case-control methodology was utilized with select respondents identified as confirmed violent cases and other respondents in the control group who were not. Case-control studies are most generally used in epidemiology to identify factors that differ in their frequency between case and control subjects, which could then be identified as possible risk factors for the disease and so these studies study compare individuals who have a disease or outcome of interest (cases) with others who do not have the disease or outcome (controls), and then retrospectively compares the frequency of exposure to particular risk factor in each group to determine the relationship between the risk factor and the disease or outcome (Schlesselman, 1982; Paneth N. et al, 2002a & 2002b). An important component of this quasi-experimental study was the use of pretesting, or analysis of prior achievement to establish group equivalence. This study design attempted to replicate some strategies utilized by Holder-Nevins and Bain (2001) since it bore particular similarities to their earlier work, particularly in terms of the phenomenon under study and the overall intent to capture impact on behaviour from the perspective of the respondents.

KEY FINDINGS: AN EMPIRICAL SYNOPSIS

An empirical synopsis of some of the key findings of the 2009 Dancehall/Violence Study, including some relevant graphs, tables and correlations which have been extrapolated from the broader study (Hope, 2010b) and are represented in the following. Where specific results are concerned, the study found that 98 per cent of all respondents in both control and non-control groups listened to dancehall music.

As a part of their music consumption patterns, respondents in both groups were asked to rank their music choices and the top 5 music choices of both groups are outlined below in Table 1.1 where both control and non-control (case) groups ranked Dancehall and R&B Souls as number 1 and 2 with 44 per cent, 45.2 per cent and 20 per cent, 19.6 per cent respectively. Respondents in the control group ranked Gospel as number 3 with 12 per cent while Reggae/Roots/Culture was ranked 3rd among non-control/case group respondents with 11.6 per cent.

RANK	CONTROL GROUP	%	NON-CONTROL GROUP	%
1	DANCEHALL	44.0	DANCEHALL	45.2
2	R&B SOULS	20.0	R&B SOULS	19.6
3	GOSPEL	12.0	REGGAE/ROOTS/ CULTURE	11.6
4	REGGAE/ROOTS/ CULTURE	8.0	GOSPEL	10.6
5	HIP-HOP/RAP	4.0	HIP-HOP/RAP	5.5

TABLE 1.1– RANK OF GENRE OF MUSIC BY RESPONDENTS (%)

Respondents in both groups were questioned as to whether or not they believed that dancehall promotes violence. This belief or perception that dancehall music promotes violence was higher in the control group at 55.1 per cent of respondents, than in the case group at 44.9 per cent as set out in Fig. 1.1.

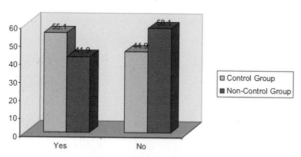

Does Dancehall Music promote violence?

FIGURE 1.1 – DO YOU BELIEVE THAT DANCEHALL MUSIC PROMOTES VIOLENCE?

Respondents also reported on their perception of Dancehall music's influence. The majority of responses in the control group reported that dancehall did not influence family members (58 per cent), friends (63.3 per cent) and self/respondent (64.6 per cent) as shown in Fig. 1.2.

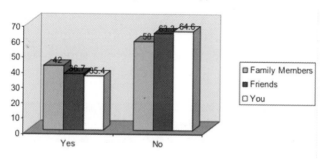

Categories of persons influenced by Dancehall Music (Control Group)

FIGURE 1.2 – CONTROL GROUP RESPONDENT'S PERCEPTION OF THE INFLUENCE OF DANCEHALL MUSIC ON FAMILY MEMBERS, FRIENDS OR RESPONDENT

In a related vein, higher numbers of respondents in the non-control or case group felt that dancehall had no influence on family members (70.3 per cent), friends (63.3 per cent and self/respondent (73.2 per cent) as outlined in Fig. 1.3.

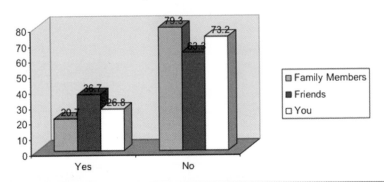

Categories of persons influenced by Dancehall Music (Non-Control Group)

FIGURE 1.3 – NON-CONTROL/CASE RESPONDENT PERCEPTION OF THE INFLUENCE OF DANCEHALL MUSIC ON FAMILY MEMBERS, FRIENDS OR RESPONDENT

Table 1.2 below outlines the perception of dancehall music and violence by respondents in both groups. Five statements were posited and respondents were asked to indicate their agreement or disagreement to each statement. The majority of the respondents in both groups (90 per cent-control group, 89.3 per cent-non control group) disagreed or strongly disagreed with the statement that 'Dancehall music is only listened to by bad and wicked people'. On the contrary, a total of 60.4 per cent of persons in the control group and 47.7 per cent of those in the non-control group agreed or strongly agreed that 'Dancehall music causes some people to become violent'.

STATEMENTS	RESPONDENTS	STRONGLY AGREE	AGREE	NEUTRAL	DISAGREE	STRONGLY DISAGREE
Violence is a good way to solve problems	CONTROL GROUP	4.1	2.0	4.1	36.7	53.1
	NON-CON-TROL GROUP	2.6	3.6	8.2	29.7	55.9

STATEMENTS	RESPONDENTS	STRONGLY AGREE	AGREE	NEUTRAL	DISAGREE	STRONGLY DISAGREE
Dancehall music is only listened to by bad and wicked people	CONTROL GROUP	2.0	2.0	6.0	30.0	60.0
	NON-CONTROL GROUP	1.5	1.5	7.6	26.4	62.9
Some people are just born to fight	CONTROL GROUP	4.1	16.3	8.2	32.7	38.8
	NON-CONTROL GROUP	14.4	18.5	11.8	31.8	23.6
Every argument leads to a fight	CONTROL GROUP	4.2	6.3	25.0	22.9	41.7
	NON-CONTROL GROUP	5.7	11.4	20.7	37.8	24.4
Dancehall music causes some people to become violent	CONTROL GROUP	10.4	50.0	12.5	14.6	12.5
	NON-CONTROL GROUP	22.3	25.4	18.1	17.1	17.1

TABLE 1.2 – RESPONDENTS' PERCEPTIONS OF DANCEHALL MUSIC AND VIOLENCE (%)

Ranking of Dancehall Artistes

The 2009 Dancehall/Violence study also identified the Most Popular and Most Favourite Artiste *at the time the study was conducted*. Table 1.3 below shows the **ranking of dancehall artistes** by respondents in both groups. The results revealed that respondents in the control group ranked the artiste as follows: Beenie Man (35.4 per cent), Vybz Kartel

(22.9 per cent) and Mavado (18.8 per cent) while respondents in the non-control group ranked Vybz Kartel (38.3 per cent), Mavado (27.7 per cent) and Beenie Man (20.7 per cent).

RANK	CONTROL GROUP	%	NON-CONTROL GROUP	%
1	BEENIE MAN	35.4	VYBZ KARTEL	38.3
2	VYBZ KARTEL	22.9	MAVADO	27.7
3	MAVADO	18.8	BEENIE MAN	20.7

TABLE 1.3 – TOP 3 DANCEHALL ARTISTES (2009)

Table 1.4 below highlights the ranking of the **most popular dance-hall artiste** at the time the study was conducted in 2009. The results revealed that for both the control and non-control groups, the respondents had the same ranking of the top three artistes with with Vybz Kartel (56 per cent and 45.2 per cent), Mavado (18 per cent and 38.6 per cent) and Beenie Man (18 per cent and 13.2 per cent).

RANK	CONTROL GROUP	%	NON-CONTROL GROUP	%
1	VYBZ KARTEL	56.0	VYBZ KARTEL	45.2
2	MAVADO	18.0	MAVADO	38.6
3	BEENIE MAN	18.0	BEENIE MAN	13.2

TABLE 1.4 – TOP 3 MOST POPULAR DANCEHALL ARTISTES NOW (2009)

With discussions prevalent about the influence of dancehall artists on youths, respondents were asked to rank, in order of most valuable (1) to least valuable (5), whose opinion mattered when they considered **whether or not they should do something violent or criminal.** Table 1.5 outlines the results for both groups. The control group indicated that parents/guardians (56.3 per cent) received the highest rank percentage for first place position. This was followed by friends (22.4 per cent) ranked at number two position, pastors (14.3 per cent) in third place. As for respondents from the non-control group, parents (54.3 per cent) and friends (25 per cent) were ranked number one and two respectively.

	CONTROL GROUP (%)	RANK	NON-CONTROL GROUP (%)	RANK
FRIENDS	22.4	2	25.0	2
TEACHERS	N/A*	5	5.2	5
DANCEHALL ARTISTES	6.4	4	11.9	3
PASTOR	14.3	3	9.7	4
PARENTS/ GUARDIANS	56.3	1	54.3	1

* Teachers did not receive any 1st place ranking for this group.

TABLE 1.5 – RANKING BY RESPONDENTS ON WHOSE OPINIONS THEY WOULD SEEK ON WHETHER OR NOT THEY SHOULD DO SOMETHING THAT IS VIOLENT OR CRIMINAL

Correspondingly, respondents were asked to rank, in order of most valuable (1) to least valuable (5), whose opinion mattered **on how you should pursue your education.** The results for control group and non-control respondents as outlined in Table 6 below indicated that parents/guardians received the highest ranking with 66 per cent and 64.2 per cent respectively. Teachers were in position number two with 24.5 per cent and 26.2 per cent respectively.

	CONTROL GROUP (%)	RANK	NON-CONTROL GROUP (%)	RANK
FRIENDS	4.0	4	6.9	3
TEACHERS	24.5	2	26.2	2
DANCEHALL ARTISTES	4.1	3	4.3	4
PASTOR	2.0	5	3.8	5
PARENTS/ GUARDIANS	66.0	1	64.2	1

TABLE 1.6 – RANKING BY RESPONDENTS ON WHOSE OPINION THEY WOULD SEEK ON HOW TO PURSUE THEIR EDUCATION

Some key statistical correlations were generated to find any correlation between respondents' violent tendencies or activities and their consumption of dancehall music and culture. Table 2.1 indicates that a statistical relationship exists between respondents who have been in a fight and attending dancehall events (0.020). The results also showed that approximately 79 per cent of the respondents who have been in a fight have attended a dancehall event in their lifetime. Using the Cohen and Halladay scale, however, the relationship was weak in terms of its strength (contingency coefficient [c.c] = 0.166) and 2.7 per cent of the variation in attending dancehall events can be explained by respondents ever being in a fight.

HAVE YOU EVER ATTENDED A DANCEHALL EVENT?	HAVE YOU EVER BEEN IN A FIGHT?	
	NO	YES
NO	38.3%	21.3%
YES	61.7%	78.7%

$X2$ = 5.438 ; Sig. value = 0.020; C.C = .166

TABLE 2.1

There was also a statistically significant correlation between respondents' levels of anger and whether or not they listened to dancehall music (0.021). The Spearman's Rho correlation value of 0.165 indicated that the more often persons got angry the more likely they were to have listened to dancehall music. However, the correlation was weak in terms of strength and the coefficient of determination indicated that only approximately four per cent of the variation in listening dancehall music among respondents can be explained by their levels of anger.

In addition, there was a statistically significant correlation between respondents' levels of anger and whether or not they have ever attended a dancehall event (0.001). The Spearman's Rho correlation value of 0.234 indicated that the more often persons got angry the more likely they were to have attended a dancehall event. Nonetheless, the correlation was weak in terms of strength and the coefficient of determination indicated that only 5.4 per cent of the variation in attendance of dancehall events among respondents can be explained by their levels of anger.

In addition, both the Focus Groups and the Survey data, provided valuable qualitative themes that are critical to this debate, and which are outlined in the following section.

GENERAL AND COMPLEMENTARY THEMES – SURVEY AND FOCUS GROUPS

Dancehall Music/Culture as Entertainment

Identification of Dancehall Music and Culture as a method of entertainment and fun was the main theme arising from the qualitative discussion in the survey and in the focus groups. The majority of respondents from both groups identified their personal use of the music and culture as a form of entertainment and a way of having a good time with friends. Terms such as 'crazy enjoyment', 'happy' 'hype', 'nice', 'vibes', 'vibesy', entertaining, 'relaxing', 'jiggy', 'energetic', 'enjoying', 'enjoyable', 'excitement', 'frass', 'hold a meds', 'feel good', 'good time with friends', 'party', 'party vibe', 'dancing mood', 'full of vibes', 'fun', 'lively', 'young people vibes', 'place hype', and 'mad tings', among others, were the main terms used to describe the feelings about dancehall music and feelings had at dancehall events.

Dancehall Music/Culture as Influential – Self and Others

The second theme arising from the survey and focus groups was one where the majority of the respondents from both groups felt that the music had some influence on young people in some way. The perceived influence on self and others is broken down into several categories as follows:

a. The motivation to learn new slang and dances stood out as one important category of influence on self and others that the respondents identified. The majority of the respondents from both groups stated that they had been personally influenced by the music to learn new slang and become proficient at new dances so they could be a part of the 'hype'.

b. The motivation to want to dress in a particular way 'like the artiste', 'like a superstar' was a second important and popular category of response that identified influence on self and others.

c. A career in dancehall culture was also an important point of influence on self and others across all respondents with terms like 'become an artiste', 'get a music career', 'buss big wid a new tune' used in this instance. This was particularly so among male respondents. Many identified points of convergence with what they 'liked' or wanted to become and what their friends, siblings and other peers found to be a component of their career choices. The 'superstar' and 'hype' nature of dancehall music and culture and the purportedly large fortunes earned by many individuals in the industry was a push factor – 'look how much ghetto yout buss', 'dem deh pon TV every day', 'Range Rover and X5'. Six of the respondents noted the positive influence of their future career plans including two respondents who claimed to be an aspiring artiste and producer respectively who stated that they used the music to make money as a part of their 'career', 'future', and 'future plans' while one noted that he was motivated 'to hustle harder to support myself'.

d. Respondents also highlighted the music's influence on their self-esteem where they were able 'love my body same way cause fluffy ah wear', 'listening to the music makes me want to achieve something better in life' while a female respondent noted that she was motivated to 'take care of myself and not be fooled by undeserving men'.

e. Negative influence on gullible young people, **but usually not themselves**—respondents also believed that other youths who were more gullible or improperly socialized could be influenced by the music in different and negative ways. During the focus group discussion there were two narratives about the experience in one instance of a cousin who was purportedly influenced by the music of a popular artiste to join a popular gang in his community, and a close friend who was lured by the music and culture to drop out of school and try to become an artiste. Others spoke of their friends or relatives' overwhelming desire to 'buss' as a dancehall dancer and make lots of money. In both the survey and the focus groups many individuals identified friends who had been influenced (negatively) to smoke marijuana (smoke weed, smoking). Another influence highlighted was the desire of many friends to dress and act like popular dancehall artistes even though they could not afford the true cost of these costumes. Several respondents also noted that intense partying and drinking of alcohol had negative repercussions on the pursuit of education. Terms such as 'frass', 'frass out', 'head gone', 'crazy hype' were used to describe the influence on these youths.

f.   Just under 4 per cent of all respondents suggested that dancehall influenced self and others towards sex or erotic activity. Respondents in both control and non-control categories stated that friends and family members were influenced to become more sexually aware, to become sexually active, have more than one sex partners, to have sex, 'have sex hard' or to have sex. They also noted that they had been influenced to have sex, to become sexy and several male respondents stated they had been influenced to become a 'gyalist' (multiple partners) and to go out and look girls.

Dancehall Music as Contributor to Violence – Artistes and Lyrics

The third overall theme arising from the qualitative discussions in the survey and the focus groups is the perception of the role of graphic and explicit lyrics on the one hand, and the perception of the influential role of artistes on the other hand, that were both identified as dancehall's main contributor to violence among youths. Respondents across both categories in the survey (just over 63 per cent) and focus groups (75 per cent) believed that dancehall influences violence. The main forms of influence identified by these respondents – via lyrics and artiste portrayal are discussed below:-

a.   For the Respondents who believed that dancehall contributed to violence, dancehall lyrics were identified as the primary contributor to violence. Respondents noted that 'Some lyrics are bad'. 'Some terms used encourage violence', 'Gun lyrics encourage badmanism'. 'Too much gun-talk', gun lyrics encourage people to use the gun', 'It's a ghetto thing, like in the streets', 'Badman tune', 'gun tunes motivate some to kill', 'illiterate people take gun lyrics out of context', 'It creates a negative impact on some people who are intellectually underdeveloped', 'It mirrors what is going on but glorifies violence to resolve issues', 'Lyrics influences especially inner-city youths by showing criminal means of achieving things', 'People are susceptible to messages in the media via dancehall music', 'Not everyone has self-control or great reasoning ability. Some are very gullible'. 'Some people take the words of the song literally'. Most respondents felt that young people should be safeguarded from too much exposure to gun and other lyrics in dancehall as they were too gullible and not ready for the adult world.

b. Of the respondents who believed that dancehall contributed to violence, dancehall Artistes were identified as dancehall's secondary contributor to violence. Beyond the production and dissemination of lyrics, their personas, and the response of fans to their music and exhortations, including clashes, was identified as problematic. For example, respondents noted the following:- 'This happens through lyrical feud. People get in fights over artistes', 'Young people idolize dancehall artistes and try to be like them as a result they influence their actions', 'When artistes clash and one loses the other will turn it into war', 'Most of the artistes are on coke and some man follow them', 'Clash between artistes cause people to be violent to one another', 'Artistes throw words at each other until it becomes violent', 'Artistes sing about violence and youths do what they say', 'Artistes promote violence and the youths listen', 'Artistes are very influential', 'Anything the artiste say they want to do it'.

REDUCING VIOLENCE AMONG YOUTHS – A WIDER SOCIAL ISSUE

Respondents felt that the issue of violence among youths was a wider social issue cutting across the family, peer group, education and religious groups. In their own words, suggestions for reducing violence among youths included'- 'Better parents', 'government must put in better education for the youths', help with lunch money. Church people should be more involved', 'Keep youths from bad company', 'Some don't know right from wrong', 'Look at what happened to me because I follow bad company', 'Some parents are not doing the right thing' The government must spend more money on children. 'Fathers are missing'. 'Too many violent movies and music', 'I never use to believe but it's true that some people just born bad'.

There were also several specific themes that arose from the qualitative data in the survey only, which are outlined below.

SPECIFIC THEMES - SURVEY

Music as anger control/conflict reduction mechanism

Approximately 14 per cent of all survey respondents across both control and non-control categories noted that they used music as a part of their anger control mechanisms. Among a variety of responses to the question 'What do you do when you are feeling angry/upset?' responses related to the use of music include:- 'control my temper and listen to music', 'fight or listen to music', 'listen to music and dance', 'listen to music and walk away', 'listen to some music to calm myself', 'sing a song', sit by myself and listen to music', 'write a song', and 'chill and listen to music'.

WEED/SMOKING/MARIJUANA USE AMONG YOUTHS

While it was not a primary focus of the study, youth smoking, especially of marijuana, was a recurrent theme in the responses to a variety of questions. During the survey, respondents identified smoking in general, and weed/ganja smoking in particular, as a youth activity in response to specific survey questions:-

Q. 11 - What do you do when you are feeling angry/upset? (Anger control/ conflict resolution mechanism) - Responses included 'Smoke', 'Sit by myself or smoke', 'Sit down and relax', 'talk to friends, do something stimulating or smoke weed', 'Sit, meditate and smoke', 'Smoke weed', 'Smoke weed and hold a meditation'.

Q. 28 - What do you do when you want to have fun? – Responses included 'Call my friends, smoke weed or party', 'drink and smoke', 'listen to music and smoke', 'smoke and chill with friends', 'smoke and listen to music', 'smoke chalice or have a conference'

Q. 34 - How has/have this/these family member(s) been influenced (by dancehall)? – Responses included 'Dress, violent behaviour and smoking', 'Drugs and ganja', 'Encourages and glorify weed smoking', 'Smoke weed and drink', 'Smoking of weed', 'Started smoking, drinking and dressing like dancehall artistes', 'To smoke weed', 'Influenced to smoke weed', 'Language, Dress, Smoking', 'Smoking ganja and became a rasta', 'They smoke a lot'.

Q. 36 - How has/have this/these friend(s) been influenced (by dancehall)? – 'Bad things like gun, smoking, extortion', 'Dress, smoke and drink'.

Q. 38 - How have you been influenced (by dancehall)? – 'Dress, smoke and drink', 'Smoking and dressing'.

Marijuana/Weed was also identified as the reason for suspension in four responses and the reason for criminal charges/penalties in eight other responses.

DISCUSSION AND CONCLUSION

The main findings of the Dancehall/Violence Study of 2009 were:-

1. Dancehall music is the favourite music choice of youths 15-24 years old.

2. The correlation between young people listening to dancehall music and being involved in violent behaviour is statistically insignificant.

3. Dancehall music generally invokes feelings described as 'hype, excitement, vibesy, nice, great, cool, energetic, excited, and fun' in youths 15-24 years old.

4. The findings of this study are not peculiar to the Kingston, St. Andrew, St. Catherine and Clarendon, as, based on the socio-demographics of the respondents they can be extrapolated across the island.

The study could not find any significant correlation between violent behaviour and anger levels based on exposure to dancehall music or events in both control and non-control groups and so the study concluded that the link between dancehall and violent behaviour among youths was statistically insignificant. In this regard, the preliminary findings of this study ties in with other studies of media and music which have been inconclusive in proving influence or impact of music or media on behavior. However, the dominance of responses regarding the perception of lyrics and artistes as influence, coupled with expressed personal desires and reported desires of friends and family members to learn new slang, dance and style from dancehall lyrics and artistes, suggests that dancehall music and culture are important for its youth fans as a source of self-identification. With the proliferation of cable television, popular music and dance programs on local and international TV channels, and explosion in new and alternative media (e.g. the Internet, Facebook, Twitter, etc.) the visibility and popularity of dancehall artistes, dancers and hype creators who present an aura of success and superstardom, is also important in affirming the career potential of dancehall for youths. This career focus is particularly important for young males who see the hype, materialism and visibility of dancehall culture as a quick and viable source of income and mobility.

The respondents identified the most prominent artistes at the time of this study as Vybz Kartel (#1), Mavado (#2) and Beenie Man (#3) who were voted as *Most Favourite* and *Most Popular Artiste Now* in the same order by youths in this study. Bounti Killa/Aidonia and Busy Signal were identified in fourth and fifth places respectively as *Most Favourite Artiste*, while Bounti Killa and Busy Signal were identified in fourth and fifth places respectively in the *Most Popular Artiste Now* category. Vybz Kartel was identified as number one in both categories. Notwithstanding the challenging and daring nature of many songs written and sung by Kartel, his position as the leading figure in Jamaican popular music at that time was indisputable. The youth respondents (15-24 years old) across all demographic levels in the survey and focus groups were particularly taken with what they viewed as his 'intellectual capacity' displayed in his prowess in media interviews, his endless capacity to pen lyrically dexterous treatises. This ties in with the Jamaican cultural predisposition to laud individuals who seem to have high levels of knowledge, or who are able to manipulate the English Language with dexterity. In addition, Kartel's fearless and rebellious attitude in the face of constant opposition from authority figures within dancehall culture and in the wider society, made him a favourite of youths, many of who are themselves challenging their personal and social authority figures and manipulating social and domestic taboos as a part of their move into adulthood. Each musical era throws up varying renditions of similar anti-systemic folk (anti) heroes who become identified with the rebellious inclinations of the youth of that era. For my work, I identify one strand of this cultural identity continuum that stretches from Peter Tosh through to Ninja Man, Bounti Killa and Vybz Kartel (now Tommy Lee) as popular cultural incarnations of that essence of 'badness' that pervades Jamaican popular music and culture. In their heyday, these men display the anti-social and anti-systemic bravado that made them heroes of their generations.

Where the issue of gender is concerned, the female artistes who were mentioned in the *Most Favourite* category include Lady Saw, Queen Ifrica and D'Angel. Lady Saw was the only female artiste mentioned in the top ten of the *Most Popular Artiste Now* category at that time. This ties in with another trend in the highly patriarchal realm of Jamaican dancehall culture, where male dancehall artistes who become dominant enjoy long-standing popularity over several years, but female artistes do not usually enjoy such longevity. As such, Lady Saw stands out as a special category of female dancehall artiste who has held the forefront of the dancehall imagination since the early 1990s and who has successfully continued to reinvent herself into the 21st century.

Additionally, the top five artistes identified as most favourite or most popular were those who were then attractive to youths and whose images gain the attention of the youths. At the time this study was conducted Vybz Kartel and Mavado were then at the highest point of dancehall's controversial divide, with the then ongoing Gaza/Gully debate which generated (or was generated by) intense media scrutiny. The high levels of publicity which the media scrutiny of the Gaza/Gully debate generated could be seen as a component of the media's agenda-setting activities, in line with work done for example by McCombs et al. (1972). It also means that they were most dominant in the minds of many Jamaicans, particularly youths, who consume media and entertainment products.

The survey respondents' identification of persons of influence to whom they turn for advice on key decisions, but particularly for advice on proposed violent/criminal behaviour was also instructive. Neither the control group nor the non-control group identified teachers in their top three choices of persons whose advice they would seek in this regard. Parents, friends, pastors (clergymen) and even dancehall artistes were selected by both groups as potential sources of advice ahead of teachers. The fact that teachers were second to parents/guardians for both groups with regard to seeking advice on educational choices suggests that teachers are mainly identified with formal education and not with guidance on how to deal with problematic behaviour choices among this youth group. Parents/guardians still remain a primary locus of perceived guidance and influence, followed closely by friends. With the growing problems of violence in schools and attempts to tackle this problem within the framework of the educational institutions, the issue of teacher role identification by some students, may prove a challenge and this demands some attention.

Of note also is the fact that individuals in both groups expressed similar views about their personal use and perceptions of dancehall music. A recurrent theme in the respondents' discussion on their perception of dancehall's influence in general, and their perception of dancehall's negative influence towards violence in particular, is the idea of an 'illiterate', 'intellectually underdeveloped', 'gullible' and 'young' person who must be protected. This parallels the general trend of longstanding and ongoing debates around dancehall culture for almost two decades, in Jamaica's formal print and electronic media. It also parallels similar debates (led by clergymen, Parent groups and politicians) that developed in the 1950s around the influence of the then popular mento (Jamaican calypso) and the purported influence its risqué and bawdy lyrics would have on the morality of children (Neely 2008). In this instance, the continuation of this debate highlights the continued role of sections of Jamaica in expressing its moral authority via a specific type of moral debate that is oriented around this infantilized citizen who is in need of 'care and protection' in an era when the Jamaican populace is far more media-savvy, cosmopolitan, and information-rich. This paternalistic debate also raises significant questions about the role of the formal media in influencing youth perceptions about dancehall, as a component of the media's agenda-setting practices, even while the same youth claim to have different and multiple uses for dancehall music and culture in their responses. Nonetheless, since perception forms a significant component of reality, popular dancehall artistes could be employed by relevant authority figures in the creation and production of production of songs and lyrics that suggest alternate modes of engagement and conflict resolution that moves away from the overwhelming focus on the gun and gun-related activity – which could be used in relevant public education efforts. The use of non-popular dancehall artistes in this endeavour will not have the same traction.

Additionally, based on popular knowledge, and the information gleaned herein, dancehall lyrics and artistes enjoy immense visibility and popularity among a significant component of youths aged 15-24. As such, it is suggested that popular artistes and dancehall-type lyrics are employed in public education campaigns that target youths in an effort to catch their attention about pressing social issues and influence their behaviour. Mobile companies, like Digicel, have successfully used dancehall artistes, or dancehall type settings (dancing, party or club scene, popular dancers and artistes) and lyrics to attract a significant component of their youth market.

The overwhelming perception of dancehall music and culture as areas for worthy career options and the desire to participate in this arena points to the increasing thrust for entertainment and creative/cultural industry careers among youth that form a part of the current era. Here, the development of training programmes and the provision of professional tool kits for these careers is an area that needs immediate attention.

One could argue that in order to find out if one variable say dancehall causes something else to happen say violence among youth, (i.e. establishing causality) three factors must be present: (1) correlation between the cause and effect; (2) time order - i.e. the cause must come before the effect); and (3) no alternative explanations. In this 'dancehall music causes violence' debate one can think of instances where the music and violence are not positively correlated and where the violence (effects) comes before the supposed dancehall music (cause). There may also be many alternative reasons for the violence in Jamaican society today. This suggests that there is a critical need for longitudinal studies of the phenomenon even while initial explorations such as this early foray, point the way forward.

In the final analysis, areas for future study are first, an exploration of the Jamaican cultural/creative industry's viable career and entrepreneurial paths towards provision of useful road maps and professional tool kits for youths and other interested parties. Second is the assessment of specially formulated and very catchy dancehall-type lyrics and songs as educational tools or teaching method that could possibly encourage youths to internalize and recall important educational material. Third, is the need for critical academic work to assess the role of the media in agenda-setting around dancehall culture, violence, crime and other social issues in Jamaican society.

REFERENCES

Anderson, Craig A. and Bushman, Brad J. 'The Effects of Media Violence on Society' in *Science*, Vol. 295, March 2002, pp. 2377-2379.

Anderson, Craig A., Carnaguey, Nicholas and Eubanks, Janie. 'Exposure to Violent Media: The Effects of Songs with Violent Lyrics on Thoughts and Feelings' in *Journal of Personality and Social Psychology*, Vol. 84, No. 5, 2003, pp. 960-971.

Ballard, M. E., & Coates, S. 'The immediate effects of homicidal, suicidal, and nonviolent heavy metal and rap songs on the moods of college students' in *Youth & Society*, Vol. 27 #2, pp. 148-168.

Barongan, Christy and Hall, Gordon C. Nagayama. 'The Influence Of Misogynous Rap Music On Sexual Aggression Against Women' in *Psychology of Women Quarterly*, Vol. 19 No. 2, June 1995, pp. 195-207.

Brown, Jane D., et al. 'Sexy Media Matter: Exposure to Sexual Content in Music, Movies, Television, and Magazines Predicts Black and White Adolescents' Sexual Behaviour' in *Pediatrics,* Volume 117, 2006, pp. 1018-1027.

Cooper, Carolyn. *Sound Clash: Jamaican Dancehall Culture from Lady Saw to Dancehall Queen.* Palgrave Macmillan, 2004.

Davies, Maire Messenger and Mosdell, Nick. *Practical Research Methods for Media and Cultural Studies: Making People Count.* Athens, Georgia: University of Georgia Press, 2006.

Fried, Carrie B. 'Who's Afraid of Rap: Differential Reactions to Music Lyrics' in *Journal of Social Psychology*, Vol. 29, Iss. 4, 2006, pp. 705-721.

_____. 'Stereotypes of Music Fans: Are Rap and Heavy Metal Fans a Danger to Themselves and Others?' in Journal of Media Psychology, Vol. 8, #3, Fall 2003.

Gayle, Herbert et al. *The Adolescents of Urban St. Catherine: A Study of Their Reproductive Health and Survivability.* St. Catherine, Jamaica: Children's First Agency, 2004.

Harriott, Anthony D. *Bending the Trend Line: The Challenge of Controlling Violence in Jamaica and the High Violence Societies of the Caribbean.* Professorial Inaugural Lecture, April, 24, 2008. Kingston: Arawak Publications, 2008.

Headley, Bernard. *The Jamaican Crime Scene: A Perspective.* Washington D.C.: Howard University Press, 1986.

Holder-Nevins, Desmalee and Bain, Brendan. 'Popular Music and Sexual Behavior Among Female Adolescents in Jamaica: A Case-Control Study', in *Journal of HIV/AIDS Prevention & Education for Adolescents & Children* Vol. 4, Iss. 2-3, 2001, pp. 149-160.

Hope, Donna P. 'From Browning to Cake Soap: Popular Debates on Skin Bleaching in the Jamaican Dancehall.' *The Journal of Pan African Studies,* Volume 4, No. 4, June 2011, pp. 164-193.

_____. *Man Vibes: Masculinities in the Jamaican Dancehall.* Kingston: Ian Randle Publishers, 2010a.

_____. *The Social Impact of Dancehall Culture: Violence as a Key Indicator._* Unpublished Final Report of the 2009 Dancehall/Violence Study, 2010b.

_____. *Inna di Dancehall: Popular Culture and the Politics of Identity in Jamaica.* UWI Press, 2006a.

_____. Dons and Shottas: Performing Violent Masculinity in Dancehall Culture. *Social and Economic Studies,* Special Issue on Jamaican Culture, 55:1 & 2, 2006b, pp. 115-131.

_____. Ninja Man, the Lyrical Don: Embodying Violent Masculinity in Jamaican Dancehall Culture. *Discourses in Dance,* Volume 2, Issue 2, 2004, pp. 27-43.

Ivankova, Nataliya V., Creswell, John W. & Stick, Sheldon L. 'Using Mixed-Methods Sequential Explanatory Design: From Theory to Practice' in *Field Methods*, Vol. 18, No. 1, February 2006, pp. 3-20.

Klein, Jonathan D., Brown, Jane D., Childers, Kim W., Oliver, J., Porter, C., Dykers, C. (1993). Adolescent Risky Behaviour and Mass Media Use. *Paediatrics* 92:24-30, American Academy of Paediatrics.

Levy, Horace. *They Cry 'respect'!: Urban Violence and Poverty in Jamaica.* University of the West Indies, 1996.

Lynxwiler, John and Gay, David. 'Moral Boundaries and Deviant Music: Public Attitudes towards Heavy Metal and Rap' in *Deviant Behaviour*, Vol. 21, Issue 1, January 2000, pp. 63-85.

Mahari, Jabari and Conner, Erin. 'Black Youth Violence has a Bad Rap' in *Journal of Social Issues*, Volume 59, Issue 1, 2003, pp. 121-140.

Martin, Graham, Clarke, M. and Pearce, C. 'Adolescent Suicide: Music Preference as an Indicator of Vulnerability', in *Journal of the American Academy of Child & Adolescent Psychiatry*, Vol. 32, Issue 3, pp. 530-535, May 1993.

McCombs, Maxwell, E. and Shaw, Donald L. The Agenda-Setting Function of Mass Media', in *Public Opinion Quarterly,* Volume 36, Issue 2, 1972, pp. 176-187.

Miranda, Dave and Claes, Michael. 'Rap Music Genres and Deviant Behaviors in French-Canadian Adolescents' in *Journal of Youth and Adolescence*, Vol. 33 No. 2, April 2004.

Neely, Daniel T. *Mento, Jamaica's Original Music': Development, Tourism and the Nationalist Frame.* Unpublished Ph.D. Dissertation, Department of Music, New York University, 2008.

Paneth N, Susser E, Susser M. 'Origins and early development of the case-control study: Part 1. Early evolution' in *Soz Praventivmed* Vol. 47, 2002a, pp 282–288.

Paneth N, Susser E, Susser M. 'Origins and early development of the case-control study: Part 2. The case-control study from Lane-Claypon to 1950' in *Soz Praventimed*, Vol. 47, 2002b, pp. 359–65.

Roberts, Donald F., Christenson, Peter G., and Gentile, Douglas A. 'The Effects of Violent Music on Children and Adolescents' in Douglas A. Gentile (ed.) *Media Violence and Children: A Complete Guide for Parents and Professionals.* Connecticut: Praeger Publishers, 2003, pp. 153-170.

Rubin, A. M., West, D. A., & Mitchell, W. S. 'Differences in aggression, attitudes towards women, and distrust as reflected in popular music preferences', in *Media Psychology, 3,* 2001, pp. 25-42.

Schlesselman, J.J. *Case-Control Studies. Design, Conduct, Analysis.* New York: Oxford University Press, 1982.

Singer, Mark I., et al. 'Contributors to Violent Behavior Among Elementary and Middle School Children', *Pediatrics,* Vol. 104 No. 4 October 1999, pp. 878-884.

St. Lawrence, Janet S. and Joyner, Doris J. 'The Effects of Sexually Violent Rock Music on Males' Acceptance of Violence Against Women', in *Psychology of Women Quarterly,* Vol. 15 No. 1, March 1991, pp. 49-63.

Stewart, Kingsley. 'So Wha, Mi Nuh Fi Live To?': Interpreting Violence in Jamaica Through the Dancehall Culture', *IDEAZ*, Vol. 1 No. 1: University of the West Indies, Mona, May 2002, pp. 17-28.

Stolzoff, Norman. *Wake the Town: Dancehall Culture in Jamaica.* Durham and London: Duke University Press, 2000.

Wanamaker, C.E. and Reznikoff, M. 'Effects of aggressive and nonaggressive rock songs on projective and structured tests' in *Journal of Psychology*, Vols. 1,2 &3, Nov. 1989, pp. 561-70.

Wester, Stephen R., Crown, C., Quatman, G., Heesacker, M. 'The Influence of Sexually Violent Rap Music on Attitudes of Men with Little Prior Exposure' in *Psychology of Women Quarterly*, Vol. 21 No. 4, December 1997, pp. 497-508.

NOTES

1. See World Bank's report on Jamaica, 1997 'Violence and Urban Poverty in Jamaica: Breaking the Cycle', pp. 39-42.

2. Morais, Richard. 'Popular Culture blamed for boys' poor grades' in *The Gleaner,* Friday January 21, 2000.

3. Jamaica has fourteen (14) parishes which are sub-national administrative divisions of the government.

4. During the development of this research and the selection of the appropriate sample, the Behavioural Unit at the Ministry of Education identified several schools across these parishes, whose students have been targeted by their remedial programmes in an effort to reduce the incidents of violence in schools.

3 CULTURES OF RESISTANCE:
HIP HOP MUSIC AND BLACK YOUTH CULTURE IN TORONTO

INTRODUCTION

This paper considers how Black Canadian youth employ Jamaican popular music, fused with hip hop, to articulate national and personal identities and register protest about the social conditions they face. More specifically, the paper uses an analysis of lyrics and interviews with musicians to problematize the popular notion that hip hop, dancehall and reggae do not represent sites of social resistance given their dilution to suit commercial markets. In contrast to this notion, both the mainstream and underground artists surveyed in this chapter continue to meld hip hop, dancehall and reggae in ways that challenge definitions of Canadianness, address social issues, and raise African diasporic consciousness.

To contextualize my argument let me explain that Caribbean migration to Toronto began in earnest during the early 1960's. Today, many Black youths, like their parents, suffer high unemployment and systematic racism. However, their situation is different. These youth are more conscious of belonging to Canada, because, unlike their parents, many of them are not immigrants and do not have a desired 'home' to return to in the Caribbean. While these Black youths celebrate and maintain their Caribbean background, they want to be seen as Canadian citizens. Their marginalization from Canadian society is one important reason why they embrace their Caribbean roots, and more specifically, for the purposes of this discussion, immerse themselves in Jamaican popular music aesthetics and Jamaican *Patwa*.[1] In its embrace they have claimed the right to practice independent forms of cultural expression, thus shaping a unique identity expressive of 'other' Canadianness.

In her article, 'From the margins to mainstream: the political power of hip-hop,' Katina Stapleton says: 'Protest music is characterized by objections to injustices and oppressions inflicted on certain individual groups.... typically, the intent of protest musicians is to oppose the exploitation and oppression exercised by dominant elites and members of dominant groups' (1998, p. 221). Using this definition, a case can easily be made that hip hop, reggae and dancehall fall squarely into the spectrum of protest music. Musicians from these genres regularly use their music to critique political and social systems which oppress and disenfranchise Black communities (wherever they may be), and to redefine themselves and their communities thereby creating alternative narratives. Musical artists of Caribbean heritage living in Canada, England and the U.S have brought something new to this musical heritage by combining hip hop, dancehall or reggae to speak about the challenges of belonging vs. non-belonging and the fluidity of 'in-between' and hybrid identities in their new diasporic homes. Stapleton's thesis can certainly be extended to apply to this unique pairing of hip hop, and Jamaican popular music, which has created novel sites of activism for formulating new identities and contesting traditional notions of who belongs in the nation.

In his rap lyric *Jamaican in New York,* for example, Jamaican American dancehall-hip hop artist, Shinehead, speaks about the transitions, aspirations and challenges of Jamaican immigrants living in New York,

> *I'm an alien, I'm a legal alien*
>
> *I'm a Jamaican in New York*
>
> *I'm an alien, I'm a legal alien*
>
> *I'm a Jamaican in New York* (1992).

The foregoing lines are a rewrite of Sting's 1987 song *Englishman in New York*. Sting's alienation in the metropolis however, is a satirical take on British mannerism versus that of the Americans, while Shinehead's alienation is based on the stereotypes surrounding Black Jamaican male criminality, which was heightened in the 1980s.

Although Shinehead positions himself as legally permitted to reside in New York, he still sees himself as an outsider whose main purpose in the United States is to seek opportunities. And despite what can be argued as his monolithic representation as a ragamuffin yardie, Shinehead also attempts to tease out the distinctive position of being Jamaican in a diasporic context. On the same track he goes on to rap,

> *Don't drink coffee, I drink roots my dear*
>
> *And I love my morning ride*
>
> *You can see it in my motions when I walk*
>
> *I'm a Jamaican in New York*
>
> *See me walking down Church Avenue*
>
> *With my hat leaned to one side*
>
> *You can see it when I walk.* (1992)

Shinehead's music and lyrics illustrate the ways in which artists of Caribbean descent living in the diaspora combine hip hop and dancehall to maintain ties to their cultural heritage while simultaneously creating alternative cultural narratives in their host countries.

Like Shinehead, many Black Canadian rappers of Caribbean descent have also blended reggae or dancehall and hip hop to offer counter-narratives for Black youth. The Dream Warriors and Jamaican-Canadian Michie Mee are two early, and seminal, examples of this tradition. Cultural critic, Professor Rinaldo Walcott notes that Canadian rap artists have been 'at the forefront of challenging various fictions of what Canada is, and their work attempts to produce new fictions of what Canada might be' (1997, p.80). He goes on to use the Dream Warrior's popular song *Ludi* to exemplify these new fictions, describing how they 'celebrate black diasporic connectedness and passion in their song *Ludi* by naming Black home spaces in Canada and the Caribbean' (1997, p. 50). The *Ludi* song also reinforces a Caribbean presence in the imagination of Canadians by employing an old reggae rhythm (and a minor ska sample) taken from the reggae track *My Conversation* originally recorded by singer Slim Smith and choosing to set the accompanying video on a Caribbean island. By inserting Black Caribbean peoples into the Canadian narrative, the Dream Warriors trouble the dominant perception of Canada as solely and predominantly British and French.

Unfortunately, although the Dream Warriors managed to achieve commercial success with *Ludi*, in general, reggae, dancehall and hip hop all continue to occupy a marginal space in the Canadian music landscape. Despite their popularity among youth, these genres are often confined to community radio stations and alternative newspapers. These genres are also often sidelined by the Canadian Juno awards.[2] Nevertheless, every now and then an artist manages to break through this relegation to the margins and find a broad audience for music that gives voice to the African Caribbean experience in Canada. Jamaican Canadian hip hop artist Michie Mee is an example of such an occurrence in the mid-1980s.

In her rap, *Canada Large*, Michie Mee gives a shout out to various Black Caribbean communities in Toronto,

> *As you know, good things grow in Ontario*
>
> *Like Mississauga, Thornhill, Brampton, and Scarborough*

> *And Bad men to find them is a cinch*
> *Jungle, Regent Park, Martingrove, Flemington and Jane & Finch*
> *(1991)*

Michie Mee is mindful of the socio-economic distinction between the various Jamaican communities in Toronto.

These lyrics work to disrupt Canada's notion of Canadianess and Whiteness by recognizing and validating various African Caribbean communities in Toronto while at the same time using commonly known Canadian references.[3] Mixing dancehall and hip hop, Michie Mee expresses pride in her Jamaican culture, indicated by the title of her album, *Jamaican Funk Canadian style*, and her lyrics,

> *I'm not mistaken, I am Jamaican,*
> *By the way that is my musical style* (1991)

While Michie Mee boldly affirms her place of birth here, in *Canada Large* through the same dancehall and hip hop blend, she draws from a verse of the famous Jamaican work song, *The Banana Man,* to not only highlight her 'Jamaicaness' but to also rightfully situate herself into Canada:

> *Come Mista Tally Man Tally Mi Banana*
> *Mi big up Canada although mi neva Barn ya* (1991)

Uniquely, the lines are sung with a folk like- ring game rhythm which adds a new and original flavour to hip hop genre.

By simultaneously claiming both a Jamaican and Canadian identity, Michie Mee resists Canada's traditional discourse around identity which often calls for a singular and White Canadian character. In doing so, Michie Mee also speaks to the tension of simultaneous belonging and not belonging experienced by many Black Canadians. Walcott comments on this theme when he notes that 'The people who live in the in-between, neither here nor elsewhere, redraw and rechart the places/spaces that they occupy...in doing this they take a political and ethical stance which refuses the boundaries of national discourse. To be Black and at home are to both belong and not belong' (1997, 50). The early musical work of both Michie Mee and the Dream Warriors provide powerful testimony to the in-between yet they also manage to expand on their 'in between' through their ability to confidently insert themselves into Canada's narrative as well as holding onto their Caribbean roots.

A more recent artist to add to the dialogue on Canadian identity is Kardinal Offishall. Like his predecessors, Kardinal amalgamates hip hop and Jamaican popular music to vocalize his place and space in the nation. In his piece *Lay Lay* for instance, Kardinal brags about his rapping skills but also employs dancehall slang to situate himself as both a 'yardman' and first generation immigrant who comes to 'represent and mash up di nation'. He raps:

> *From J.A. to di Hollywood sign*
> *Badman yardman pon di frontline*
> *Big man Kardinal first generation*
> *First man to mash it up and represent di nation*
> *B.K. J.A. Kardi combination*
> *Fire automatic and turn up di station*
> *Don't watch neither mix up inna boderation*
> *F all di frustration* (2003)

In this context the lyric 'yardman' represents Kardinal's Jamaican heritage while 'first generation' signifies his belonging to Canada. In contrast to Michie Mee and some of the members of the Dream Warriors who were born 'elsewhere,' Kardinal was born in Canada. His status as a Canadian born man who insists on holding onto his Jamaican roots complicates the notion of Canadianess to an even greater degree since he cannot be written off as a new arrival. Kardinal's lyrics maintain his ties to Caribbean heritage while also defining 'Canadianess' on his own terms. In this way Kardinal follows the advice of Jazzie B, from Black British funk and hip hop group Soul II Soul, who asserts in his song *Feel Free:*

> *Whatever you claim to be Yours,*
> *That's the nature of the game* (1989)

For Black British group Soul II Soul and others who either fall 'in between' or are from 'elsewhere,' the nature of the game points to the role and possibilities of individual agency in the process of self construction. Kardinal himself comments on this self naming in an interview with Del Cowie of *Exclaim*, 'For people that are first-generation Canadians or first-generation Englishmen or first-generation Americans, I represent somebody who was able to hold onto his culture yet still exist in a foreign [one]' (2005).

While Kardinal identifies himself as a Canadian, he is able to successfully occupy this in-between space without having to assimilate into the dominant culture or giving up his culture entirely.

Kardinal's dual identities are further articulated in the rap and dancehall lyrics of his popular *Bakardi Slang* song. However on this track, rather than solely affirming his Jamaican heritage Kardinal speaks to a unified Caribbean cultural identity in an attempt to inspire solidarity amongst the various African Caribbean communities in Toronto. His approach also claims and celebrates Black diasporic culture. He raps,

> *You all think we're all Jamaicans*
> *But nuff man a Trinis, Bajans, Grenadian,*
> *whole heap of Haitians, Guyanese*

> *The whole West Indies combined*
>
> *To make the T dot O, one of a kind* (2001).

Kardinal's lyrics highlight the shared experience of Canadians of Caribbean descent while also pointing to the complexities of creating and negotiating Black diasporic identities. Indeed Kardinal, the Dream Warriors, and Michie Mee all provide compelling examples of the way musicians have melded both African Caribbean and Canadian culture into their art as a way to protect their identities from 'the very real threat of erasure via misrepresentation by outsiders' (McLeod, p.148) and or to centralize their cultural expressions within Canadian narratives.

In addition to the alternative national narratives offered by Black Canadian rappers, it is worth noting that they also work to include and highlight African diasporic consciousness in their music. Somali born Canadian hip hop artist K'naan is a good example. Though he often underscores universal themes in his work, K'naan also uses hip hop and reggae aesthetics and a Jamaican inflected accent to raise an African diasporic consciousness. Accompanied by roots reggae style drumming, in *The African way* K'naan claims African diasporic connections by stressing the role of hip hop as a source of poor Black people's narratives globally and a potential tool for positive consciousness and change. In the same song K'naan also points to diasporic location and the continental Africa to invite people of African descent to embrace Africa 'the African way.'

> *Lyrically, I am flowing water*
>
> *Take it easy on me suckers*
>
> *Harass more niggas then a sleazy undercover*
>
> *But seriously, I remember when I was 7*
>
> *When rap came mysteriously and made me feel 11*
>
> *It understood me, and made my ghetto heaven*

> *I understood it as the new poor people's weapon*
>
> *But now it tap ass like a kid with one butt cheek*
>
> *Dusty foot philosopher came to change things, trust me*
>
> *From Ethiopia, Tanzania, Somalia*
>
> *Heathrow airport and customs in LaGuardia*
>
> *Uganda, Kenya, my people, up in Ghana*
>
> *Kingston, Jamaica, big up, because you know*
>
> *it's time for the African way* (2005)

K'naan, celebrates the 'African way', in a problematic manner where he employs the term niggas in the same verse to highlight the pervasive practice of racial profiling in Canadian cities, and to also signal a connection to other Black males being affected by police harassment. He unwittingly reproduces the derogatory designation and 'othering' of the Black male; a narrative he and other fellow rappers attempt to deconstruct through their music. On the other hand, other critics might argue that K'naan's use of the word niggas is a radical reappropriation of the term itself.

Similarly, in his rap *T.I.A* (a recording that samples The Wailers' ska hit '*Simmer Down*'), K'naan proudly celebrates African diasporic musical figures from around the world; in doing so he embraces the diversity of Black musical expressions from across the diaspora,

> *Around here we only bump Fela Kuti*
> *Tupac, or Bob Marley, Lucky Dube.*
> *So we don't really give a fuck about your groupies*
> *This Is Africa, Hooray* (2009).

The musical artists that K'naan names are all emblematic of Pan Africanist and Black nationalist struggles and for two of the musicians he identifies, Bob Marley and Lucky Dube, reggae music is used as a vehicle to articulate these struggles. Not surprisingly,   Jamaica has historically represented sites of revolution and activism, from slavery revolts to Pan Africanism. This revolutionary spirit has transcended into Jamaican popular music, and has inspired liberatory movements outside of the country in places such as Zimbabwe, South African and beyond.

This commitment to African consciousness is also witnessed in hip hop artists coming out of Quebec. Rapping primarily in French, some Quebec rappers have also incorporated reggae and dancehall aesthetics to assert Black consciousness and history. In the song, *La vie 'ti nèg* (*'A Black's Life'*) for instance, Impossible of Muzion, a rap artist of Haitian heritage, proclaims Black pride by pointing to the 1804 Haitian revolution that marked the end of French colonial rule,

> *En tant que les gens qui ont anéanti le pouvoir d'autrui en 1804*
>
> *Black & proud to be, j'vise les gens aptes*
>
> *As people who annihilated the power of others in 1804*
>
> *Black and proud to be,*
>
> *I'm aiming at people who are ready)* (1999).

In a similar fashion, Sans Pression, another Quebec rapper but this time of Congo descent, also makes links between African peoples when he raps to his friends of Haitian origin on the track *'Pathnai à vie'* (*'Friend for Life'*),

> *Tu me parlais d'Haïti, moi je te parlais de l'ancien Zaïre*
>
> *(You told me about Haiti, I told you about ancient Zaïre)* (1999).

Clearly then, as K'naan, Impossible and Sans Pression show, irrespective of what particular cultural heritage they bear, Black Canadian rappers often integrate dancehall and or reggae aesthetics as a means to express opposition to the dominant culture and to assert a Black diasporic identity and Caribbean cultural continuities.

ASSERTING NATIONAL IDENTITIES THROUGH VERNACULAR RESIS-TANCE

The use of Jamaican *Patwa* by many Canadian hip hop artists can be read as a challenge and protest to the stigmatizing notion that language as spoken by Black people is substandard. I would argue in this section therefore, as have Walcott (2003) and Stuart Hall (2000) elsewhere, that Black speech, and refiguring of English and 'White' spaces transmits the power to trouble, re-formulate and re-define Eurocentric patriarchal constructions of a national past and present. Notwithstanding the stigma that the Jamaican language and at times the music might carry in their homeland, music and language have been major imports for Jamaicans living abroad. Faced with marginalization and racism within their host country, the Jamaican community still maintains a strong attachment to the language of the Caribbean 'homeland'. It is through the music where Jamaican *Patwa* has been best represented and disseminated throughout urban diasporic spaces outside of Jamaica. This section will also examine how Jamaican *Patwa* has also represented site of protest in the ways African Canadian rappers mesh, hip hop, dancehall and reggae together. I pay special attention to how Jamaican *Patwa* is expressed in the hip hop lyrics of Black Canadian rappers and its further significance in forging a linguistic and cultural identity for Black Canadian youths in Toronto,[4] thus signaling protest and resistance against Canadianess and singular notion of African diasporic culture.

Similar to the way in which hip -hop music has penetrated Black youth speech in Toronto, the impact and popularity of dancehall music in the late eighties have also been key in transmitting Jamaican *Patwa* and dancehall slang into Black youth's speech. Amid an insatiable capitalist market where Black cultural production has become a commodity, dancehall and hip hop remain a thriving cultural expression among Black youth in Toronto. As both music represent resistance and are a site of contestation it is not surprising that Black youths in Toronto embrace these genres of music as a way to express their linguistic and cultural identities, separate from the typified English-speaking and Francophone Canadian image. With the popularity of both forms of music, youth of Caribbean descent and continental Africa living in Toronto have created a cultural hybrid space by combining the languages and speech of hip hop and dancehall in a manner very similar to the earlier linguistic styles of Jamaican-American rapper Shinehead discussed earlier. In his book *Dubwise: Reasoning from the Reggae Underground*, reggae critic and journalist, Klive Walker (2005) asserts that Toronto's hip-hop artists in particular, have always combined a distinctive reggae flavour in its rhythmic structure. Though I agree with Walker's argument, I would also add that the lyrics and speech of many of these rappers despite country of origin also include Jamaican *Patwa* and dancehall lingo to discuss the local realities of Black youth living in the city and to challenge the notions of Caribbean Creoles as being inferior and illegitimate language system.

Returning to Kardinal Offishall's rap *Bakardi Slang*, for example, the lyrics exemplifies the way in which Jamaican *Patwa* and Dancehall slang have been amalgamated into Toronto's Black youth's speech and act as forms of resistance to the standard code, English or French, as well as authenticating a unique Black Canadian hip hop culture. The rap *Bakardi Slang* is very similar to British reggae deejay Smiley Culture's single *Cockney Translation*. In his eighties single, Smiley Culture using wit and humor charts the variation between Black British youth speech and the Cockney dialect (spoken mainly by White England) with much of the translated word deriving from Jamaican *Patwa* and dancehall lyrics. And similar to Kardinal, Smiley Culture's *Cockney slang* underscores the legitimacy of Black British speech and culture in England. Smiley Culture also lyrically captures the dancehall culture. He chants:

> *11, 10, 9, 8, 7, 6, 5, 4, 3, 2, 1,*
>
> *It's I Smiley Cuulture with the mike in a me hand*
>
> *Me come to teach you right and not the wrong*
>
> *In a de Cockney Translation*

Cockney's not a Language it is only a slang

And was originated yah so inna England

The first place it was used was over East London

It was respect for the different style pronunciation

But it wasn't really used by any and any man

Me say strictly con-man also the villain

But through me full up of lyrics and education

Right here now you a go get a little translation

Cockney have name like Treey, Arthur and del-boy

We have name like Winston, Lloyd and Leroy

We bawl out YOW! While cockneys say OI!

What cockney call a Jack's we call a Blue Bwoy

Say cockney have mates while we have spar

Cockney live in a brum while we live in a yard

Say we nyam while cockney gwt capture

Cockney say guv'nor. We say Big Bout ya

In a de Cockney Translation!

In a de Cockney Translation!

Here, Smiley Culture lifts *Patwa* from the margins of the 'empire' and blends it with cockney to not only create and legitimize a new language for Black British youths but to also showcase his own ability to understand the language of White Britain.

In *Bakardi Slang*, however, Kardinal Offishall code switches between hip hop speech and Jamaican *Patwa* to highlight their differences. In doing so he demonstrates how Black youth speech in Toronto sources Jamaican *Patwa* and challenges the notions of African Canadian identity being an appropriation of African American culture. While the song reflects heterogeneous voices of the Anglo-Caribbean, Jamaican *Patwa* and dancehall lingo remain the dominant voice. Kardinal Offishall raps:

> [Kardinal Offishall]
>
> *We gonna put you on to something brand new, you Know what I mean*
>
> *My nigga's in the street throwin dot slang each and every single time we meet*
>
> *We don't say 'you know what I'm sayin'*
>
> *T dot says 'ya dun know'*
>
> *So when we singin about the girls we singin bout the 'gyal dem'*
>
> *Y'all talkin about 'say that one more time'*
>
> *We talkin about 'yo, come again'*
>
> *Y'all talkin about 'that nigga's a punk'*
>
> *We talkin about 'that yout's a fosse'*
>
> *For the kids that think I'm comin wit it*
>
> *Brother just watch me*
>
> *A shoe is called a 'crep'*
>
> *A big party is a 'fete'*
>
> *Ya'll takin about 'watch where you goin!'*
>
> *We talkin about 'mind whey you step!'*
>
> *Kardinal is gonna show you how the T dot rolls*
>
> *My style is off the thermostat plus I'm comin from the cold-yo*

Kardinal Offishall's expressions of how the T-dot (reference to Toronto) rolls demonstrate his attempt to articulate a distinctive hip hop style as well as a unique linguistic identity from African American youths, just as Smiley Culture tries to distinguish Black British speech from Cockney dialect while simultaneously asserting a Black British belonging.

Cameron Bailey, in his article *Hip-Hop Injects Toronto*, maintains that Black youths in Canada created a subculture based on integrating and adapting Black American culture to suit their particular circumstances because the dominant white culture offered them nothing that was familiar or attractive (19). While Bailey's argument might hold some truth in terms of Black Canadian youth embrace of hip hop as a musical genre and other elements of hip hop culture, Bailey overlooked the strong Jamaican dancehall presence that was also influencing the lyrics of the burgeoning rap acts of the late eighties and how this presence served as forms of resistance against singular and static notions of what constituted a Canadian or to dispel the singularity of Black Atlantic diasporic culture, but instead to express its diversity. This linguistic influence has continued right through to the nineties and more recently. Unfortunately, discourse around Black culture and history in Canada very often revolves around an African American context and it is also for this reason that rappers like Kardinal Offishall express not only a different style of hip hop music, but also a distinct Black Canadian cultural and linguistic experience. One can argue that Black Canadian rappers employ this to provide a Black Atlantic diasporic identity separate from the one imagined by many White Canadians. That perception that Black Canadian youth culture is just a replicate of their African American counterparts while also resisting the monolithic notion of Canada's official language as English and French.

In the introduction of the rap, Kardinal Offishall clearly signals to his listeners, '*We gonna put you on to something brand new, you Know what I mean'/ My nigga's in the street throwin dot slang each and every single time we meet*'. The 'we' used in the opening verse of the rap is in reference to Offishall's fellow Black-Canadian hip hop artists who have also adapted a similar style of rapping. The 'dot slang' is signaling the linguistic variation and the re-naming of space that Black youths in Toronto have taken the liberty to re-create. Jazzie B's advice therefore to freely name self has been extended here to not only claim self, but to also re-name and re-claim space.

To further reinforce how Black youth culture differs from his African American contemporaries, Kardinal alludes to Dancehall cultural aesthetics in Jamaica and the diaspora by explicitly utilizing a barrage of dancehall phrases and terms. He raps:

> *Y'all say 'a DJ battle'*
> *We say 'clash with two sounds'*
> *We rock the hottest We talkin about 'yo, lock it off!'*
> *Wheel that and tek it from de top*
> *And just flash up unno lighta and watch the dance rock*
> *Kardinal is gonna show you how the T dot rolls.*

In the same rap, Offishall code-switches to Jamaican *Patwa* which serves the purpose of dispelling the misconception that not all Blacks living in Toronto are Jamaicans, but instead asserts that the city is made up of a diverse Caribbean community. Kardinal Offishall raps 'You all think we're all Jamaicans/But nuff man a Trinis, Bajans, Grenadian, whole heap of Haitians, Guyanese/The whole West Indies combined/ To make the T dot O, one of a kind.' Ironically, Offishall uses Jamaican *Patwa* as the signifier of Black youth linguistic identity to dispel and challenge this popular myth.

Even though there is evidently identification of Caribbean culture in *Bakardi Slang*, Cowie observes how the use of the expression T-Dot 'expands the song beyond its African-American and West Indian influences and localizes it to the city of Toronto' (49). However, Cowie further notes how this moment of T-Dot entering the mainstream is not its beginning, but rather it represents a moment within grassroots hip-hop culture to re-name a space – Toronto. Kardinal continues to re-name and I add re-claim space in a more troubling way in other songs such as

Ol Time Killin. In his song *Ol Time Killin* for instance, Kardinal Offishall combines hip hop slang and Ebonics, Jamaican *Patwa* and samples of old reggae rhythms and verses taken from dancehall songs to localize Jamaican dancehall sound system culture into the T-dot. In *Ol Time Killin,* Deejay Korry Deez opens the rap exciting the T-Dot dancehall massive with a stream of dancehall lingo:

> *Everybody ah talk 'bout sound killing*
>
> *When dem dun know sey, we ah original sound killa*
>
> *Fassyhole you know we*
>
> *Anytime we start dance-dance a fi lock*
>
> *Girl follow back a we*
>
> *Yu know sey wi have di ting pon cock*
>
> *can't chat to we*
>
> *We start dance from 19-o-long*
>
> *Tink a only forty five we collect*
>
> *A dub plate we have*
>
> *Anytime we drop Kardinal, IRS and Wio*
>
> *A .....big tune dat*
>
>
> *Everybody is talking about sound killing*
>
> *When they know that we are original sound killers*
>
> *Punk, do you know us*
>
> *Anytime we start dance-dance shut down*
>
> *Girl follow back us*
>
> *Yu know we have everything in order*
>
> *can't chat to we*
>
> *We start dance from 19-o-long*

> *Do you think we collect only forty five*
>
> *A dub plate we have*
>
> *Anytime we drop Kardinal, IRS and Wio*
>
> *A .....big tune dat*

The chorus sung by Jully Black also uses dancehall slangs to speak to sound clashing culture as it was represented in Toronto in the past; not too different from sound clashes in Jamaica. The title 'Ol Time Killin' further gesturing to past sound clash sessions. Thus reinforces the notion of how reconfiguration of language can serve to challenge national histories. Black sings:

> *it's an old time, ol' time killing*
>
> *We a deal with, run and get your money clip*
>
> *For another day in another way*
>
> *De man dem, nuh take the ray ray*
>
> *We are a murderahs*
>
> *Killas...murder*

'Murderahs' and 'killas' refer to one sound system musically outperforming or musically defeating a competitor sound system. Jully Black's declaration, 'We are murderahs' 'Killas' therefore troubles the criminalization of the Black Jamaican male. In a society where Black males are written off as 'suspects', 'wanted men', and 'criminals', Black uses these (spoken in *Patwa*) stereotypical labels of Black males subversively to demonstrate the superiority of Canadian sound system selectors. In this way, Black, like her hip hop counterparts assert the transformative potential in Black linguistic and cultural expressions. Here the selectors and rappers associated with sound systems in the Toronto dancehall culture offer a cultural alternative for young Black men to perform their creativity and self worth.

In contrast to the Dream Warriors' video for the rap *Ludi* that is set in the Caribbean, Kardinal's video is situated in Canada and the backdrop is decorated with Rastafarian symbols (i.e. the lion of Judah symbol, red green and gold) as to re-imagine the dancehall sound clash and or session in the 'T-dot'. In the same song, Kardinal employs dance-hall slang to invoke the dancehall revelers to '*Lick a shot, wave your flag, gunfinga inna de air.*' Paradoxically, in the accompanying video, Kardinal sports a Jamaican flag around his neck (one of the MCs also wears a T-shirt with the words Jamaica printed on it), while the other revelers wave flags representing different Caribbean islands when instructed *to wave yu flag*. No Canadian flag is waved in the video. I argue therefore that Kardinal's video '*Ole Time Killin'*', like many others, have uniquely reflected the process of de-territorialization which in Anthony Giddens' term is defined as the 'disembedding' (lifting out) of people and symbolic forms from the places we expect them to be' (cited in Lull, 1995, p. 239). I extend Giddens' definition in my discussion here to include language as a vital part of the de-territorialization process of moving and re-inte-grating cultures. While this de-territorialization process seemingly ties with Canada's multicultural policy that allows one to move and retain cultures (exist in policy at least), the act of de-territorilization for these Black Canadian rappers serve to contest Canadian national narratives, in this case narratives given in another tongue other than the standard.

Equally as important to highlight is the Black diasporic connection that Kardinal alludes to (similar to K'naan's rap, T.I.A) when he boasts: '*Lick off a style, me-a-fi put dem all back/ Rap from T-dot to the Bronx and Bricks and come back*'. Indeed, Kardinal uses the term the T-dot to repre-sent Black Caribbean communities in Toronto and Bricks symbolizing Black Caribbean diasporic communities in Brixton, England; clearly the Bronx is referring to Black Caribbean communities located in New York. Thus, Kardinal's song *Ole Time Killin* can be read as the many ways Black Canadian rappers reconstruct and contest *Canadianess* through their blending of dancehall lingo and hip hop vernacular.

What remains ambiguous, however, is women's presence and role in the act of re-constructing Canadian identity. Hence, there is obvious machismo in this lyric and in his use of Jamaican *Patwa* where Kardinal Offishal proclaims a male dominant space in contesting notions of Canadianess. In the Introduction of the rap, deejay Koory Deez instructs female partygoers to '*Girl follow back ah we*' and in both videos *Bakardi Slang* and *Ole Time Killin* the girls are used as props within the male gaze, while the male participants in the video are positioned as central to the re-naming and re-claiming of a Canadian space. I take up these issues in greater detail in other work, in particular my chapter on 'The Black Diaspora North of the Border: Women, Music and Caribbean Culture in Canada'[5].

Pioneer rapper Michie Mee also inserted Jamaican *Patwa* and dance-hall lingo into her lyrics in order to distinguish her style of hip hop from Black American rappers. In *We're coming to America*, Michie Mee raps: '*Some say we try to imitate Americans/But like a true Canadian I know I can, I know I can/ be original and mash up de dance*'. Although Michie Mee proudly reaffirms her identity as a 'true Canadian,' she code switches to the Dancehall expressions '*mash up de dance*' to not only show off her lyrical dexterity but like Kardinal Offishall and other earlier and current Black hip hop MCs; she wants to express a distinctive linguistic identity for Black Canadian youths, as well as showcasing talented rap artists and or Black Canadian hip hop culture. Returning to Michie Mee's earlier song *Canada Large*, here she uniquely gives *Patwa* currency to decide on how Canada's Black cultural production has been recreated and received. Drawing on the popular dancehall expressions 'big up' 'and Large up'[6] Michie Mee extinguishes notions that Black cultural production emanates solely from the United States; thus changing the trajectory of the South and North cultural exchange. Like her male counterparts Michie Mee also drew on dancehall lingo and Jamaican *Patwa* to re-inscribe a Black Canadian presence in Canada's national narrative; I elaborate on this more in previous work.[7]

Some conscious hip hop acts such as Trinidadian-Canadian K-os draw on Jamaican *Patwa* and on occasion Rasta lingua that are found in conscious reggae as a way of politicizing and vocalizing experiences of racism and marginalization in Canadian society and globally. These hip hop lyrics often include themes, focusing on the despair and struggle of the Black Canadian 'yout'. Phrases such as 'chanting down Babylon' and fire metaphors used by Jamaican Rastafarian dancehall deejays are used to voice anger against racial profiling and to criticize the injustices they see in the media and educational system. In the chorus *Hallelujah* with an emphasis on Jah, K-os raps '*Hallelujah Babylon is falling, Babylon is falling*' to metaphorically call for the dismantling of white supremacy, so as to create equal opportunities for his Black brothers and sisters in Canada. In a similar vein, Kardinal's rap *Ole Time Killin* uses 'Babylon' metaphorically to allude to the transatlantic slave trade and the ongoing racial discrimination and class oppression that African diasporic people(s) faces. He raps '*Babylon fi get dust and let my people dem go*'.

Alternatively, the lyrics of Montreal-based hip hop act, San Precision are rapped primarily in French and Haitian kreyole. I find it interesting that in spite of their use of French and Haitian Kreyol, Jamaican *Patwa* and popular music lingo is sometimes inserted in some of their lyrical content, which demonstrates my position that Canadian youth, irrespective of cultural background and geographical location, tend to incorporate Jamaican *Patwa* and dancehall or reggae lingo as a way to express an African Canadian linguistic identity or to illustrate protest against social conditions, thereby empowering disenfranchised Black communities in Montreal. In the opening line of one of their rap songs *Le Soleil Se Couche; The Sun goes down*, for example San Precision asks their listeners, '*Ou sont les vrais rudeboys?*'/'*Where are the true rudeboys*'? When translated to English the word vrais means true, but in the context of this rap, vrais used here would connote original, as with the early ska/ rock steady and dance expression, 'original Rudeboy.' Like the problematic re-appropriation of the 'Murderah' and 'Killa' persona, 'Rude boy' is also used subversively here. The 'Rude boy' persona is taken from the early 1960s' ska and rock steady 'Rudeboy' cultural phenomena.[8] In this way, San Precision uses the 'Rude boy' archetype to revolutionize and to empower Black males resistance against racist and class stratified society.

In a few verses down, San Precision instruct their listeners, '*Rudeboy si t'est de chez nous lick one shot*'/'if you are from this neighbourhood lick one shot'. In later lines down they metaphorically (referring to street life) reiterate a Black Atlantic diasporic unity to clean up poor ghetto communities that are riddled with drugs and gun violence: '*C'est le street life, alright si t'es de chez nous, lick one shot*'/ '*It's the street life alright, if this is your neighbourhood lick one shot*'. In this rap, *Le Soleil Se Couche*, San Precision relates the poor social conditions of Black communities in Montreal and other diasporic communities, and in doing so, they, similar to Kardinal insert the dancehall expression 'lick one shot' to solicit unison among the community, and they summon the vrai (true) 'rude boys', not in a provocative sense, but to assert the rappers' own identity and to acknowledge other 'rude boys' who are from and have an understanding of the social ills that exist on the 'streets'. Using the gun metaphor, ('to lick a shot') to show sanction and comradeship against the same gun violence being challenged, again points to the linguistic creativity that emerges from these cultural art forms.

Diverting from the English-speaking rappers included in this paper, San Precision re-writes Black women into the process of reconfiguring the Canadian narratives. Here he challenges the vrai 'rude boys' to pay closer attention to female narratives in rap music, instead of simply focusing on the sexually provocative lyrics that are often glorified. San Precision encourages the 'rude boys to legitimatize female experiences and voices. And very much like the Black Toronto rappers, San Precision includes dancehall slang into their lyrical content to either speak of the social conditions of disaffected Black youth living in Montreal and Black diaspora or to demonstrate a unique linguistic identity and lyrical style.

In his book, *What the Deejay Said: a Critique from the Street*, British-Jamaican Anthropologist, William 'Lez' Henry cites the significant use of Jamaican *Patwa* in Dancehall music and the formation of a Black British identity in the seventies and early eighties. Henry maintains that the creativity of Black Caribbean British youth (e.g. Papa Levi, Smiley Culture) allowed for the blend of Jamaican *Patwa* and English language.

This fusing of language created a code that was only accessible at the time to British Black youths. This 'other' code provided alternative venues for Black youth in Britain. In this way, British Black youths had a sense of control, separate and apart from the racist establishment. As was the case with British Black youth, Jamaican popular music along with Jamaican *Patwa* has characterized Black youth's chosen arena in which to display a unique and new found confidence in African-Caribbean-Canadian linguistic identity as well as expressing belonging to Canada in a non-standard voice.

CONCLUSION

As the artists showcased in this paper demonstrate, Canadian rappers have extended the boundaries of protest music to move beyond solely singing against the oppression and exploitation of their marginalized communities. By combining hip hop, dancehall and reggae many Black Canadian musicians have asserted resistance to the dominant national ideology by creating alternative Canadian narratives and promoting an African diasporic consciousness. In one of his most cited works on Black identity formulation scholar Paul Gilroy writes:

> 'Black Britain defines itself crucially as part of a diaspora. Its unique culture draws inspiration from those developed by black populations elsewhere. In particular, the culture and politics of Black America and the Caribbean have become raw materials for creative processes which redefine what it means to be black, adapting it to distinctively British experiences and meaning. Black culture is actively made and remade.' (1991, p.152).

Gilroy's description of identity formation among Black British youth can also be accurately applied to Black Canadian hip hop artists as it relates to cultural exchanges between their African American counterparts. This has been demonstrated in the diverse ways that Black Canadian youth have borrowed from African American hip hop aesthetics to challenge and actively reshape the narratives of Canada. I argue however that

African Caribbean Canadian youths do more than just draw inspiration from the Caribbean. Instead I see the cultural dialogue between African Caribbean Canadian youths as cultural continuities with their Caribbean roots. It is evident through close textual analysis of these lyrics that much of them exemplify an expression of Black Atlantic diasporic identity and Caribbean cultural continuities, whereby these artists are seemingly conscious of the ways in which their belonging to Canada is an ongoing contestation, and yet they remain with no doubts that the space they occupy within the Canadian national narrative is in fact their rightful space.

In addition, British sociologist Simon Jones, in his PhD dissertation, acknowledges Black music as a cultural form and ideological vehicle which assists the Black oppressed in their winning of cultural spaces (cited in Henry p. 89). The second section of this paper attempted to map just how forms of Black music, dancehall and reggae, and to a lesser extent hip hop, have been instrumental in winning not only cultural spaces, but have also won a voice for Black youth living in urban areas outside of Jamaica. Black youths living in Toronto and other urban spaces have reproduced the voices of the dancehall deejays as a conduit for presenting alternative spaces from the white dominant culture. Therefore, regardless of geographical location, Jamaican popular music sounds and *Patwa* transmitted through Jamaican dancehall lyrics serve as an anchor for articulating an African-Canadian youth linguistic and cultural identity.

While critics assert that both hip hop and Jamaican popular music have of late become less political to suit mainstream listeners, this paper makes a strong case for the protest that can still be heard in the voices of African Canadians artists who continue to creatively combine these musical forms to articulate a social and political Black diasporic consciousness.

REFERENCES

Bailey, Cameron. 'Hip Hop Inflects Toronto' in *Fuse* Nov-Dec 1988: 17-26.

Cowie, D. 'Kardinal Offishall: Man on Fire'. *Exclaim.ca.* November, 2005. Retrieved from http://exclaim.ca/articles/multiarticlesub.aspx?c-sid1=75&csid2=778&fid1=4464.

Gilroy, P. *There ain't no Black in the Union Jack: The cultural politics of race and nation.* Chicago: University of Chicago Press, 1991.

Hall, Stuart. 'Old and New Identities, Old and New Ethnicities' In *Theories of Race and Racism.* Edited by Les Back and John Solomos. New York: Routledge, 2000.

Henry, William Lez (2006). *What the Deejay Said: A Critique from the Street.* London: Nu-Beyond Ltd, 2006.

Lull, J. *Media, Communication, Culture. A Global Approach.* Cambridge: Polity Press, 1995.

McLeod, K. 'Authenticity within hip-hop and other cultures threatened with Assimilation' in *Journal of Communication,* 49, 1999, pp134-150.

Stapleton, K. (1998). 'From the margins to mainstream: the political power of hip-hop' in *Media, Culture and Society,* 20, 1998, pp. 219-234.

Walcott, R. *Black Like Who? Writing Black Canada.* Toronto, Ontario: Insomniac Press, 1997.

_____. *Rude: Contemporary Black Canadian Cultural Criticism.* Toronto: Insomniac Press, 2000.

Walker, Klive. *Dubwise Reasoning from the Reggae Underground,* Toronto: Insomniac, 2005.

White, Garth 'Ska and Rock Steady' *Reggae International* ed. Stephen Davis and Peter Simon. New York: Rogner and Bernhard, 1982

DISCOGRAPHY

Dream Warriors. *And Now the Legacy Begins* [CD]. Fourth and Broadway Records, 1991.

_____. 'Ludi'. *Now the Legacy Begins* [CD]. UK: Fourth and Broadway Records, 1991.

Michie Mee. *Jamaican Funk: Canadian Style* [CD]. First Priority Music, 1991.

Muzion. *Mentalité moune morne* [CD]. BMG Quebec, 1999.

Kardinal Offishall. *Quest for Firestarter Vol 1* [CD]. MCA Records, 2001.

Kardinal Offishall. 'Bakardi Slang'. *Quest for Firestarter Vol 1* [CD]. MCA Records, 2001.

_____. 'Lay Lay'. *Fiesta: Riddem Driven* [CD]. VP Music Group, 2003.

K'naan. *The Dusty Foot Philosopher* [CD]. BMG Music, 2005.

_____. *Troubadour* [CD]. A&M/Octane, 2009.

_____. 'The African Way'. *The Dusty Foot Philosopher* [CD]. BMG Music, 2005.

_____. 'T.I.A.'. *Troubadour* [CD]. A&M/Octane, 2009.

Sans Pression. *514-50 dans mon réseau* [CD]. Disques Mont Real, 1999.

_____. *Réplique aux offusqués* [CD]. Disques Mont Real, 2003.

Michie Mee. 'Canada Large'. *Jamaican Funk: Canadian Style* [CD]. New York: First Priority Music, 1991.

Muzion. 'La vie 'ti nèg' (A Black's Life). *Mentalité moune morne* [CD]. BMG Quebec, 1999.

Sans Pression. 'Pathnai à vie' (Friend for Life). *514-50 dans mon réseau* [CD]. Disques Mont Real, 1999.

Shinehead. *Sidewalk University* [CD]. Elektra Records, 1992.

_____. 'Jamaican in New York'. *Sidewalk University* [CD]. New York: Elektra Records, 1992.

Soul II Soul. 'Feel Free'. On *Keep on Movin'* [CD]. London, UK: Virgin Records., 1989.

_____. *Keep On Movin'* [CD]. Virgin,1989.

Various Artists. *Fiesta: Riddem Driven* [CD]. VP Music Group, 2003.

NOTES

1. Patwa, also written Patois, are regional 'dialects' of English or French spoken across the Caribbean. I use this spelling to challenge the hierarchal connotation the French spelling Patois carries.

2. A Juno Award is the Canadian equivalent of a Grammy, both being the preeminent music awards in their respective nations.

3. The lyric 'Good things grow in Ontario' is taken from a well-known Canadian advertising campaign in the 1980s to encourage consumption of local fruits and vegetables.

4. I am cognizant of the fact that members of other ethnic groups have more recently taken up Jamaican Patwa and musical styles to also articulate their marginalization within the Canadian society. My concern in this paper, however, is to explore the genesis of how Jamaican Patwa and its popular musical forms have helped to construct Black youth identities in Canada, challenge Canadian singular narratives of 'Whiteness' and to create a distinct Black diasporas identity.

5. See 'The Black Diaspora North of the Border: Women, Music and Caribbean Culture in Toronto' in *Archipelagos of Sound: Transnational Caribbeanities: Women and Music*. Ed. Iefona Fulani. University of West Indies Press: Jamaica, 2012.

6. Dancehall expressions meaning giving or paying respect.

7. 'The Black Diaspora North of the Border: Women, Music and Caribbean Culture in Toronto' in *Archipelagos of Sound: Transnational Caribbeanities: Women and Music*. Ed. Iefona Fulani. University of West Indies Press: Jamaica, 2012.

8. 'Rude boy (bwoy) applied to anyone against the system. It described the anarchic and revolutionary youth of the poorer classes and the

young political goons (mercenaries of the two political parties), as well as the Rasta-inspired ‚cultural' rude boys (like the Wailers) who rejected white standards.' (White, 1982).

PART 2
GENDERED
RUMINATIONS

4 LOVE THE LONG DING DONG

TANYA TRANSGRESSES CHRISTIAN SENSIBILITIES?

> *It's all about the sex*
>
> *Mi jus love off di boom wok*
>
> *Love the way you have mi pum pum stuff*
>
> . . . .
>
> *Love the long ding dong....*
>
> **Tanya Stephens**

Many Jamaican Christians express discomfort with popular female dancehall artistes like Lady Saw, Spice, Ce'Cile and Tanya Stephens who are explicit about such personal matters as sexual desire, giving and receiving sexual pleasure and making choices about sexual partners based on material possessions and/or sexual prowess. These artistes deploy a woman-centred sexual politics in which they chose who, when, where and how they engage sexually (Russell 2010). So demands are made for "stab[bing] out mi meat" (Lady Saw) and invitations are issued to "kill mi wid di cocky" (Spice). Tanya Stephens, the self proclaimed "rough rider", in particular, jars the sensibilities of many Christians. When you listen to her... affairs abound; raw, rough sex is touted; cheating condoned; female rivalry and fisticuffs encouraged; sex explicitly described; expletives liberally sprinkled; women seduce men; babies are given to the wrong fathers; genitalia are worshipped... and, in the same breath, Christians are castigated as boring, thieving, hypocritical righteous freaks who fail to 'practice what [they] preach'.

In this chapter, a theologian takes a critical look at the dancehall lyrics of Tanya Stephens. Using the religious idea of transgressing (sinning), it explores the reasons that her open discussion/advocacy of sex and sexual 'wrongdoing' and radical excoriation of the Church engenders discomfort in some Christians, while averting to the transgressive value of her posturing on matters religious and sexual. Her advocacy of transgressive acts fall into five categories: 1) woman to man relationships, 2) woman to woman relationships, 3) sexual relations, 4) female self image, 5) Church mis-dealings. Most of her lyrics cluster around the important, heavily value-laden area of human sexuality. Social commentary/ critique is another powerful area of focus. In social commentary she addresses the Christian Church and Jamaican society directly. There is a clear inter-penetration/interweaving of the first four categories: male to female and female to female relationships are tied up with sexual activity and female/male sexual identity. While it may not be immediately obvious how the sexual dimensions of life are directly related to the social-developmental aspects, Ian Boyne (2009) argues that it is difficult to 'build an economy and promote peace and stability when large numbers of children are having children and when men engage in hit-and-run sexual behaviour'. In other words, sexual behaviour is relevant to the development of society because of its impact on the socialization and quality of life of people. There is a similar critique also at play in Tanya's work and so it is clear that the discomfort caused by her music rightly extends beyond sexual transgression and calls attention to a holistic vision of life. Perhaps we can play with her transgressive discourse in order to challenge the Church and its own sensibilities. The excessive sensitivities on the question of sex and sexuality among some Christians may disguise a discomfort with that dimension of life, which needs to be surfaced and addressed. The chapter examines lyrics from Tanya's albums: Rebelution (R, 2007), Gangsta Blues (GB, 2004), Ruff Rider (RR, 1998) and Too Hype (TH, 1997).

OF BOOM WUK AND LONG DING DONGS

The title of the chapter comes from the song 'Boom Wuk' (a great sexual encounter owing to the performance of the male partner) from her album Gangsta Blues. In this artful piece, the female protagonist professes her love (appreciation/desire) for good raw sex and a long penis (long ding dong), which connotes the possibility of untold sexual pleasure. She makes it clear that she is not attracted to her lover because of the way he walks, or the way he talks, or his beat-up car (and he 'definitely ain't no movie star'). 'It's all about the sex'. How he does the 'pum pum stuff' (deals with the woman's sexual needs; 'pum pum' being a common reference to female genitalia in Jamaican). In fact, his sexual performance is so spectacular that she is willing to transact sex with him without the usual expectations of being provided some material or emotional resource in return. This is so because there are deeply ingrained sexual patterns in Jamaican culture, including multiple partnering, early sexual initiation and transactional sex. High levels of poverty in Jamaica cause many persons, especially women, to engage in transactional sex in order to survive (Figueroa 2010). Indeed,

'Women may enter into transactional sexual relations with a man other than their main partner for economic reasons. Many Jamaican women, especially among the poor, expect to be supported financially by their male partner...Men who are not able to contribute financially to their babymother or girlfriend are at a serious disadvantage, and their relationship may be undermined' (Figueroa, 215)

The 2012 Knowledge, Attitudes and Behaviour Survey (KABS) has shown that sex is increasingly being used by young people "as a bartering tool rather than as a component of a healthy relationship" (Wilson 2013, p. 8). Transactional sex, which involves the exchange of sexual favours for material goods or money, was especially high among men and women between 15 and 24, who are both in live-in and non-live in relationships. Casual sex among this same group increased from 44 per cent in 2008 to 52 per cent in the 2012 survey. Of course, this is a worrying trend as it does not augur well for stable family life as well as posing a risk of pregnancies and HIV infections. As Sandra Knight, the chair of the National Family Planning Board, noted with concern, women jumping into bed with multiple men in exchange for material possessions play a part in the negative perception that men have of women.

Still, in eschewing these engrained sexual patterns, the protagonist turns the traditional male-female relationship on its head with the woman being the sexual aggressor and dominant partner. The man is denied his traditional role as provider, protector and hunter. Such willingness to go outside the accepted norm of male-dominated transactional sexual engagement—to cross boundaries that are clearly defined—is the mark of the transgressor, the brazen sinner.

THE QUESTION OF TRANSGRESSION

Etymologically transgression has been defined as the process of "crossing-over"; of moving from an ordered rational state to a disordered and irrational state. The act of transgression is the trans(a)gressing or passing over or beyond any law, either civil or moral. Indeed, it is a term that features prominently in criminology. In the Judeo-Christian tradition transgression has moralistic tones of judgement and is deeply tied to the biblical story of the original sin of Adam and Eve, who crossed a divine boundary through acquisition of forbidden knowledge (the eating of the fruit, often mistakenly referred to as an apple, from the tree of knowledge) and subsequent punishment (Genesis 3). To transgress in Christian terms is to sin against God, rebelling, disobeying the divine commands. It is a deliberate act/action that can be identified with certain specific activities that are labelled sinful. Christianity has had a peculiar preoccupation with sexuality and sexual morality and has instilled certain attitudes to sex that have often presented sexual sins as being the worst kind (Genovesi 1994, 114). (Many of these sins are "glorified" in Tanya's music, as our opening reflections pointed out). The perfect example of this is the term "living in sin," which clearly identifies sinfulness with engaging in unmarried sexual intercourse with a live-in partner. However, to assume that a person sins more often or more seriously in the area of sexual morality is questionable. Indeed, viewed theologically, to so associate sin with sexuality truncates the reality of sinfulness and certainly gives less attention to other harmful actions that are against justice.

At the same time, the Christian tradition has a notion of sin or transgression that focuses not on the individual but on the community. 'Social sin' is a key focus of Liberation Theology and Womanist Theology. The latter theology, like all Christian theology, is 'sourced by a community' (Williams 1993, p. 130). This means that Womanist Theology is informed by the experiences of the African-American community as well as the religious faith and social experiences of African-American women, which in many ways bears some similarity to Womanist theological readings from the Caribbean (of which, this chapter is an example). Womanist theologian Delores S. Williams maintains therefore that the womanist understanding of sin is social, placing the guilt on the side of society at large. In the context of the African-American community as well as the wider American society, Black women's humanity is devalued and their bodies are defiled by rape, overwork, domestic violence. This is the social sin of denying Black Women's humanity is in the image and likeness of God as is all humanity.

This focus on social sin raises the question of whether Black women are exempted as sinners? What does individual sin look like in Womanist perspective? "Individual sin has to do with participating in society's systems that devalue Black women's womanhood (humanity) through a process of invisibilization-that is, invisibilizing the womanist character of Black women's experience and emphasizing the stereotypical images of Black women that prevail and are perpetuated in the larger society" (Williams 1993, p. 146). Participating in the perpetuation of understandings of Black womanhood that dismisses them as frivolous and loose or other demeaning characteristics constitutes individual sin. There are significant resonances here with the Jamaican experience where women are dismissed as loose ('sketel').

THE PLEASURES OF TRANSGRESSION

Vytautus Rubavicius (2006), in an intriguing paper on the pleasure of transgression and the consumption of identities, gives us some further insights into the role of transgression that take us outside of the strictly theological realm. He points out that postmodernist philosophical discourse is replete with notions of flouting, breaking and overcoming various socio-cultural boundaries (p. 68). The influence of deconstructivism on philosophy teaches us several things about transgression: boundaries are conditional; there is a continual interaction between the familiar, normal, stable pre-boundary space and the ambiguous, abnormal open ended post-boundary space. At the same time, there is always a social and cultural struggle for the establishment and reinforcement of boundaries. This is the decisive factor in creating individual and group identifies connecting the body, consciousness and a territory. "The deconstructivist approach to transgression works by 'turning' unconditional things into conditional ones, 'turning' unconditional evidence, identities, taboos and norms into conditional social constructs, which are fixed in some established field of the configuration of power" (Rubavicus, p. 68). He links this deconstructive move of postmodernism with modernist artistic practices that consciously break with various taboos, especially those linked with "the expression of sexuality and the social control over that expression exerted by the clear-cut differentiation between the feminine and the masculine" (p. 69). This is perhaps to be seen at play in the struggle around the sexed female body and sexual interactions as is expressed in Tanya's music (and that of other female artistes).

The public/private boundaries are transgressed with her airing of her internal sexual urges and the happenings in the inner sanctum of her bedchamber. Suddenly the sharply defined and fixed boundaries between the personal and the public have become permeable and fused. Like various transgressive movements in fashion, innerwear has become outerwear, the personal has become public, and the sinful has become virtue. Indeed, boundaries are important for the creation of identities and Christians usually have very sharply defined boundaries of beliefs and behaviour that are closely interlinked, especially in the area of sexual morality, dress, food, etc. To join in transgressing these Christian sensibilities, especially in matters sexual as well as ecclesiastical, while heaping opprobrium on the nature of Christian faith and life seems to add insult to injury. Yet, it is evident that Christianity is having less and less of an effect on people's everyday lives especially in the area of sexual morality (Taylor 1992). This opens up questions as to the role of Christianity in Jamaican society and perhaps leads to the view that Jamaica as a 'Christian' country may indeed be a fiction (Lewis 2009).

TRANSGRESSING BORDERS THROUGH DANCEHALL

It seems like transgression/crossing borders is a hallmark of Dancehall. Tanya is one example – albeit a striking one – in a wider culture. Indeed transgression may be one of the hallmarks of popular cultural forms like Dancehall, which as Duncum (2009, referencing Storey 2003) describes it, is paradoxical in that it "reinforces dominant social values and so contributes to social cohesion while simultaneously offering pleasures associated with resistance to and even subversion of the social order..." (p. 233). Carolyn Cooper, herself a scholarly transgressor, discusses the notion of border clashes as both figurative and literal parts of the dancehall/Jamaican experience. DJs and sound systems clash over ascendancy on the stage and offstage there are individual clashes and violent encounters between members of their entourage/communities. The Gaza versus Gully saga is the most recent and perhaps ugliest manifestation of the border clash of the dancehall being acted out in the border clash of marginalised communities. The metaphorical clashes within the dancehall demonstrate the various ideological clashes and contestations of power that are part of everyday Jamaican life. Contention over the control of territory in the broadest sense speaks to the ideological conflicts between competing value systems in Jamaica (Cooper 2004, p. 35). Within the immediate context of the dancehall event, the idea of the border clash resonates with a range of conflicts within the Jamaican society: political (JLP versus PNP), religious (Rastafari versus Christianity), cultural (reggae versus dancehall, soca versus calypso), linguistic (Jamaican versus English), interests (browning versus Black woman, "middle-class" versus "poorer class").

Cooper further identifies the transgressive dancehall space as one dedicated to the "flamboyant performance of sexuality," which in the dominant discourse is framed as slackness (2004, p. 3). She, of course, turns this notion of slackness on its head and argues that "Slackness, though often conceived and critiqued as an exclusively sexual and politically conservative discourse, can be much more permissively theorized as a radical, underground confrontation with the patriarchal gender ideology and the duplicitous morality of the fundamentalist Jamaican society" (p. 3). Slackness therefore is not simply sexual permissiveness, although it is certainly that; it is a sometimes unwitting contestation of conventional, Christian-influenced definitions of morality and outrightly challenges the appropriation of the authority to define morality by one group. There is nothing underground or surreptitious about this contestation, as the "in-your-face" feistiness of Dancehall divas like Tanya demonstrates.

TANYA THE TRANSGRESSOR

Many people know Tanya Stephens as the artiste whose albums have parental advisory notices on them about explicit content. To others she is the self proclaimed gangsta gal who talks tough to men and is dismissive of her female rivals ("nuh haffi like mi, but yuh haffi respect mi skills"). She is one of those female artistes who Donna Hope says can be described as raunchy as she rides the sexual thrust of the dancehall in her own suggestive way (Hope 2006, p. 50). At the same time, she rebuffs attacks on the female body and feminine sexuality with lyrics that in turn derogate male arrogance in their sexual performance and right to conqueror the female body (Hope, p. 51). As Hope details further:

> "Tanya Stephen's release of the dismissive "Yuh Nuh Ready fi Dis Yet" in 1996 pushed at the gendered boundaries of dancehall discourse when she lyrically berated the self-praising man for his lack of sexual prowess and his inability to truly satisfy women...For men..., women like Tanya Stephens upset the traditional patriarchal structure of masculine dialogue into which the [male as] dancehall courtier or conqueror [of the female body] plays" (2006 p.51).

The dismissive fashion in which she treats the male performer in this song has earned her many an enemy in that camp. She has even been threatened with sexual violence for having so disrespected men and being so uppity and rude (Hope, 2006, p. 51). Clearly, as an artiste in the popular genre, her repertoire is as paradoxical as her medium. She both appears to support the status quo with transactional sex as a key feature of sexual interactions while, at the same time, clearly deriving pleasure from transgressing the norm by reframing the dominant partner in the transaction (from the male to the female party). Similarly, she challenges and thereby transgresses the male role as dominant and satisfying for women.

In her most clearly autobiographical piece "Who is Tanya" she states that her power does not reside in "stripping fi control dem man yah" yet she proclaims confidently that "di man dem fi get a good ride, ah dat Tanya believe" ("Don't Play", (R)). She declares that "although the mic is [her] favourite utensil, [she's] still #1 with a #2 pencil". She needs approval from no one and desires to be compared to no other. She proudly declares that "worl domination ah di plan". Her repertoire is liberally dotted with deeply "conscious" pieces in which she critiques social relations in Jamaican and the world ("Warn Dem" (R), "What a Day", "The Other Cheek" (GB)). She does not back away from social concerns like alcoholism, which she treats in a humorous but deadly fashion ("Cherry Brandy" (R)), racism and homophobia ("Do You Still Care", "Come A Long Way" (R)).

The artiste is revealed in her art and Tanya is unveiled in every piece of her music, but especially the more autobiographical pieces ("Who is Tanya" (R), "Don't Play" (R)," Intro" (GB), "I am Woman" (GB), "This is Love" (GB)). There is a very sensitive, romantic side to this "funky, feminine human" from Richmond, St. Mary. She croons about being woman and desiring respect from men in her life; her duet with Wyclef Jean, "This is Love", bears and bares her woman's soul and the vulnerability of every woman to the man she truly loves. "These Streets" (R) echoes her desire for affection and attention from her beloved. She is human, after all. Yet for all the failures experienced in relationship she does not give up.

In our attempt to capture the essence of Tanya Stephens it is worthwhile bearing in mind the thoughts expressed by Canadian songbird Jann Arden in her piece entitled "Never Mind" (Greatest Hurts: the Best of Jann Arden). In it Jann encapsulates the sense that the artist is never fully captured in her lyrics or in the impressions created of her in the public sphere—the artiste is veiled as much as revealed in the interaction. Much of what "Never Mind" says highlights some elements that are necessary to be explored as we ask who is Tanya? Also, who does Tanya's music say that she is? (Echoes of the very existential question that Jesus asks his disciples in John's Gospel: "Who do people say that I am?) Jann Arden tells us:

> Never mind what you think you know about me
> Never mind what you might have seen on the TV
> You can't believe every single word you're gonna read
> What I am is too far in for you to see

Arden's is a postmodernist trope, which brings to the fore the provisional nature of a person, especially the artiste, who really is in too deep for us to see simply by looking or watching the media. In the case of an artiste like Tanya, her reminder is very apropos:

> *Never mind who said that I was a bit far gone*
>
> *Never mind when they tell you sex is all I want*
>
> *You can't believe that I'm every word that I write down*
>
> *What I am is too far in and can't be found*
>
> *Never mind what they're gonna say is probably wrong*
>
> *Never mind ain't about the singer it's the song*
>
> *You can't believe how a person looks is who they are*
>
> *What I am is too far in and can't be found*

In "What a Day" (GB) Tanya expressed her desire to be judged by more than the style of her hair, what she wears (the perennial problem faced by women) and the music that she listens. Her in-your-face-no-holds-barred feistiness makes both men and women uncomfortable, particularly when she is explicit about female sexual desire and sexual needs and performance. Yet her on stage attire and performance is rather subdued and not in the least bit raunchy or explicit. In performing she pointedly stitches several of her pieces together to tell a story in a fashion that engages the participation of the audience.

The question of Rebelution

In postmodernist discourse, which challenges all absolutes including the overarching religious story/narrative (what Chimamanda Achidieze calls "the danger of a single story"), Art is expected to have a transgressive dimension. Hence there is the expectation that the art form of popular music can and does have this edge. The transgressive act is not an end in itself, however; rather it is a midwife that aims to bring a new life into the world—in Tanya's case: a new identity, a new society, a new world ("one which eradicates hunger by eliminating greed"... allows sharing of partners... removes religious counterfeits). This new realm to which we are to be transported is a realm of freedom, better perhaps— revolutionary freedom. It is no mistake that her second-to-last album is called Rebelution (a conflation of rebel and revolution; speaking to the role of the rebel in transgressing in order to bring about revolution). Somewhere in there is the key notion of the power of one, a one like Tanya. "All we need to change this shit is you..."

John Ransom maintains that revolutions in the West have had two primary goals: first, they are designed to reverse the unnatural condi- tion where a political regime pursues interests that are at variance with the purposes for which the regime was established; second, the liber- ation of the human spirit; human emancipation in its deepest sense. The first kind of revolution reasserts the rights and freedoms of the community and its members against an unjust usurpation of author- ity. It is the concern with freedom that links the two goals. "Revolution is not just that expedient employed in the last resort against a regime become tyrannical; it is, rather more ambitiously, the very midwife of a transcendence out of this world into the next" (Ransom, N.Pag.).

Tanya's agenda is Rebelution! She wants to create a change by inspir- ing one rebel at a time. There is a lot about how the world runs and about how people live their lives in it that she wants to change. And she knows that music—her music—is an important tool in changing the world. This rebel consciousness makes her, for me, one of the most lyrically exciting artistes in the Dancehall today. She has a talent for words and quite an impressive vocabulary. Her use of imagery, humour and satire is effective. "Spilt milk" describes a relationship that "would have gone sour anyway"; in a alcoholic funk she laments ruefully that "when it comes to passing the bar I'm not the best student"; in pleading with her gangsta man to spend more time with her and not the streets she describes herself by saying *"yuh girl is a perfect 10 but yuh benz dem is only a 5 and a 6"*.

Transgressing Christian Sensibilities

Tanya is a multi-vocal transgressor. She is indeed advocating much sexual transgression - adultery, 'jacketing', revenge, cheating... all that is sinful and wrong in the eyes of Christians.

She demonstrates versatility in her transgressions; she speaks in diverse oftentimes contradictory female voices. She knows the psychology of being a woman first hand. One minute she is the matey setting out like a goalie or a Red Cross volunteer to "save" or "rescue" the husband from a bad marriage that is "killing" him ("To the Rescue"(R)); the next minute she is regretting ending a relationship because she was "so caught up in what [she] wanted [her ex] to be, convinced that perfection meant spot free"("The Truth" (R)) or the jilted lover who prays to God for revenge, "Father, mi know yuh si him commit the atrocity, and vengeance is yours all me need is a little reciprocity, Nutten too major, just equal pain. Yuh know wah me a feel already father make him feel the same" ("Damn You" (R)). In describing her mistreatment at the hands of her lover as an atrocity, Tanya reclaims the value of her person and refuses to allow herself to be devalued by the wrongdoings of a patriarchal male who sees the female as simply an object of desire and consumption. There is certainly a shade of sinfulness in his act as she appeals for divine vengeance on her own behalf. Yet the vengeance that she demands is proportional—an eye for an eye, heartbreak for heartbreak. This approach echoes Williams's Womanist notions of sin, which regards individual sin as participating in acts that devalue the worth of the Black woman.

There is no question that male-female relationships in Jamaica are fraught with pain, hurt, anger, disrespect. Many of her lyrics capture this in painful, oftentimes, angry detail. There is a biblical flavour to her description of male-female relations. The helpmeet role is clear in "Gangsta Gal", a duet with Spragga Benz (GB). She facilitates her gangsta man's criminal activity through smiling and hiding the "piece" from the police, oiling his weapon and, when necessary, coming to bail him from prison. This gal's facilitative role seems to conform to the conservative view of a woman who is to cook and clean for her man ("Still a go lose" (R)); at the same time, a power struggle between men and women is in evidence. The perfect expression of this is "Goggle" from a previous album, Ruff Rider (1998). In this piece, she exhorts women to exert their power by refusing to goggle, i.e., engage in oral sex, when men demand it. Men are again the object of scorn for their slipshod sexual performance ("dem a slip saggle...dem a wiggle waggle"). (There may also be the concern about the inability to maintain a firm erection, which then requires "a gal fi bend an help him out"). The fact of her refusal to fellate the man is a means of maintaining her power vis-a-vis the man who constantly strives to dominate. Part of that domination involves spreading word about his conquest. The man is therefore implicated in gossiping with his friend, an activity which is often identified with women. Generally female and male approaches to sexual roles differ. Girls receive inadequate and conflicting messages regarding healthy sexuality while young men are given a double standard that endorses sexual prowess and promiscuity.

Evidently there is no longer any need for the woman to stroke the man's ego by lying about his sexual prowess and her sexual fulfilment at his hands. Many Jamaican women remain sexually dissatisfied after intercourse (Perkins 2012) and an airing of such dissatisfaction may put a women at risk, as the responses to Tanya's "unoo nuh readi fi dis", demonstrated. Without a doubt, Tanya refuses to buy into the Jamaican dancehall (and wider Jamaican) culture where male identity is concerned with subduing and conquering female sexuality. Rather, she cleverly turns that on its head and calls it into question—an act of transgression. She brings the pum pum stuff out into the public space so misrepresentation-by-subterfuge has to flee. Too often male prowess and performance is misrepresented and the truth remains hidden. Tanya and others say, "No more"!

Contradictory Voices

Tanya often places two contradictory perspectives one after the other on her CDs perhaps to provoke contention but certainly to give an airing to both sides. Both record authentic voices and experiences with which women can easily identify, e.g., "Boom Wuk" (great male sexual performance) is followed by "Damn" (poor male sexual performance) which is followed by "Good Ride" (woman giving man a great sexual experience). "It's A Pity" (man wanted but not touched) is followed by "Tek Him Back" (man wanted, taken and returned). The very popular "These Streets" is followed by the hard-charging "Home Alone"; in the latter song, the woman no longer declares an enduring loyalty to a male partner who is ignoring her sexual needs and the relational bonds. She forthrightly gives him many chances and pleads with him, but when he refuses to relent she draws on her exes and gives him all kinds of bun! "Bun for di Easter, bun fi di Christmas. Get so much him might as well put it pon him wish list" ('bun' is the Jamaican term for cheating on one's partner). In "Home Alone," which is dedicated to all "the playaz dem", she seems to dismiss the woman in "These Streets" as a prude, who keeps holding on. Indeed, the woman in "These Streets" professes loyalty to the point of him being away in prison. Her alter ego in "Home Alone" dismisses that by asking, "Tell mi would you save di kitty fi a man weh a chill out pon di street? All hours a day an refuse fi pressah di beef"? ('Kitty' and beef, of course, are euphemisms for the vagina) Undoubtedly, she rejects the loyalty demanded of women in a context where men refuse to meet their emotional needs or choose to be unfaithful. ("Two can play"). Later she does proclaim in a contradictory fashion that the only way he could keep her was if he was in GP (The General Penitentiary). There is in fact a warning being issued in "These Streets" ("di love weh tek so much effort fi buil you about fi blow dat. Just like a played out jersey you about fi get trow back"). The warning gets played out when the gangsta lover is imprisoned with only her loyalty to count upon.

The Jacket

She exploits the fairytale genre in "Little White Lie" to present a woman's perspective on a troubling situation in Jamaica where women are known to pick and choose whom they name as the sire of their offspring. A very disturbing situation ensues:

Once upon a time there was a happy family

There was a baby girl, a daddy,

And there was a mommy

Mommy had a secret

She told a little white lie

And when she tucked the baby in

At night, she sang her this lullaby.

Her opening is spoken softly in tones heavy with regret and perhaps self-loathing. The naming of this act of transgression as simply "a little white lie" is belied by the fear that being found out holds as well the potential for even greater damage for the child she loves so much that she is "willing to tell a million lies". (Nowhere in the piece is the term 'jacket' (i.e., the colloquial term for the child that is "given" to the wrong man) used. The acknowledged hurt that is caused to children who either do not know their real sires or have been deliberately given to the wrong father is humorously captured by a reference to ending up on the Ricki Lake show, but a humor that hides deep pain ('kin teet kibba hart bun'). Pain for everyone involved—the woman, the cuckold, the deprived father, their families and most of all, the child.

Verse 1

You've got your daddy's smile

You've got his eyes

I feel my heart breaking

Every time you cry

I'm gonna burn in hell but

It's no sacrifice

Your stability is worth a million lies

I see your daddy in everything you do

> And if you could talk, I'll bet you'll talk like him too
>
> but he can't be your daddy, I hope you understand
>
> the man who thinks he's your father
>
> is a much better man
>
> So I lied and baby I tried, but it kills me inside...

Lies preserve the fairytale, but one wonders for how long. Again, Tanya's transgressive discourse opens up to the public gaze the anguish of a woman "forced" to do the wrong thing for what she considers to be the right reasons. In ethical discourse there is the recognition that it is not a simple matter to determine the moral status of an action. Questionable acts may be performed for various reasons depending on the circumstances. The concern with premoral or ontic evil may be relevant in making a judgment upon this situation; the extenuating circumstances may be such that they constitute a sufficient or proportionate reason for performing the action or allowing it to be performed (Genovesi, p. 173). This is not a rush to validating "an ends-justifies-the-means" approach, but certainly the need to bring the tools of ethical analysis to all questionable activity. Superficial listening to the contrary, the men in Tanya's stories are not all deadbeats; the women are not all heartless, selfish 'sketels'.

Female–Female Relationships

Tanya narrates the usual trope of the wife versus matey. In Gangsta Blues, she includes what appears to be a real message from an answering machine in which she is cursed and threatened by a woman, who accuses her of stealing her husband ("The Message"). This message, which is liberally sprinkled with Jamaican expletives, is sandwiched between "Put it on You" (financially independent predatory female goes after a stranger) and "Still A go Lose" (accepts designation of matey/housewrecker and proclaims her superiority over the wife). The wifey in "Put It On You" is told if she doesn't like how Tanya puts a bruise on the man, "she fi tek it off back". The sense is that the woman is simply out for a good time and the wife need not waste her time fretting. In "Still A go Lose", a really defiant Tanya challenges the wife to go head to head with her to see who can get the husband ("Mi is a gal nevah flee nevah back dung yet, the tighter she hold him ah di closah mi get"). She had no doubt that she will win as the wife refuses to face her own shame. She sides with the man whom she says is unhappy: "Di man life lack suppen an him a hunt it..." (The male as predator and hunter of the female is perhaps the subtext of this statement). The wife is blamed for not taking care of the man (not squeezing blackheads, lacklustre flex, boring sex, etc), being out at night looking to fight her challengers, worrying about who will claim the husband's pension. She, the matey, is providing an important service of rescuing and caring for an abused man. Similar yet more trenchant sentiments are expressed in the song which follows, "To the Rescue". (Her charity does not stop at men; her attempts at rescue and aid also extend to hapless beverages: "Well, if two Heineken a freeze, mi haffi rescue dem" ("Cherry Brandy"). In between "Saturday Morning" and "Sunday Morning" comes a likkle "Cherry Brandy" (R).)

Clearly, the mutuality which ought to be at play in the intimacy of the marriage bond has been broken down. In any such breakdown one party is rarely to blame, however. In spite of acknowledging that the man has lied to them both Tanya continues to derogate the wife and pursue the relationship with the husband. You can almost hear another one of her "little" mistakes for which someone has to pay dearly coming. In the end, ironically, she will be the one to lose. Nonetheless, I wonder though if Tanya's pugnacious defence of the adulterous man may not be read as a blaming of the victim for her victimisation and justification for men in their continued culturally-sanctioned infidelities ("Wifey made me do it").

Perhaps my favourite of her satirical ballads is "Tek Him Back" in which a woman attempts to return to a wife the man she has "stolen". What ensues between them is a hilarious exchange where the wife refuses to believe that Tanya had changed and Tanya is insisting that she take back the man who is malfunctioning seriously. The metaphors of purchasing and stealing shade into each other and the question of the legitimate terms for returning an item needs to be answered. The male voice is silent and silenced as two powerful female opponents square off. The piece of masculine merchandise refuses to "look work" and so never has any money; he lured Tanya in with the pretence of wealth and in her haste to pose off with him she finds herself tricked. "Him have a cute face but im naw perform". Here performance may be both financial and sexual, although the former is the key complaint while having implication for the second. The male is refusing to carry out his cultural role as provider and that makes him less desirable property in the eyes of a woman who has the power to make choices. Tanya admits ruefully that "a man always looks better in a next gal arms, but it neva fail soon as de nex gyal gone de newness rub off and de man lose de charm an den him close dem reach the lawn. An yuh wish to hell im woulda pack up an gwan..." This is a warning against "covetousness" or envy, one of the seven deadly sins. She is a woman caught red handed and is barefaced in her adultery as adultery is laid bare. What has become of the cockiness displayed in "Still a Go Lose" and "To The Rescue"? If the wife refuses the return (against company policy, perhaps), the purchaser will simply dump the goods in the store/on the lawn. Picture the transgressing Jamaican woman arguing with the store owner:

> *And you can find im clothes dem pon de lawn*
>
> *If when you come you nuh see me me gone*
>
> *'cause me no love how yuh man ah peform*
>
> *So, tek him back, wifey, tek him back ....*

There is advice here for where shopping is to be done. Certainly not in someone else's backyard.

> *Well ah de 1st rule ah shopping*
>
> *let de buyer beware*
>
> *be careful how yuh tek a gyal man mi dear*
>
> *yuh might grab someting weh she jus about fi dash*

cuz one gyal treasure is anudda gyal trash

The matey does not always win, even if it is for the wrong reason.

Look how me used to brag and show off

down inna de end you have de last laugh

even if it even means dat mi haffi pop off

There is a clear warning here for women who set out to break up each other's relationships. The grass is always greener on the other side. Handsome is what handsome does, ladies!

Yet, again that is not the whole story. "It's a Pity" (GB) shows a bit more respect for the bonds of marriage and relationship, even as adultery is pursued. The legitimacy of multiple relationships is called into question in the face of a loving wife and family ("the respect weh mi have fi yuh woman fi yuh kids; mi woulda nevah want fi dis yuh queen, mi woulda nevah dis mi king".). She acknowledges having to play it by the "stupid rules of men" hence the inability of herself and the wife sharing him between them "in a civilized manner". The "stupid rules of men" may aver to the ideals of faithful monogamy which are enshrined in Christianity and are certainly honoured more in the breach in our society. The difference between this situation and the previous appears to be the presence of a relationship of her own, alongside his marriage and family. Does the married man become fair game when the transgressor is unattached? Perhaps finding true love is sufficient reason to cheat?

Female rivalry also exists within the dancehall community itself and Tanya constantly throws words at her detractors and female challengers. In "We a lead," for example, she claims the ability to outdo her rivals who are unable to "back it up pon di cock" or "wine pon di cock" like her (like a we). In any area that they seek to challenge her—hypeness, hotness, badness, money—she leads. This does play into the competition for resources that is seen to be the norm between women. Is the transgression here simply the airing of the rivalry? Or does surfacing such rivalry simply re-inscribe negative ways of relating among women?

Sexual Relations

The question of cunnilingus is treated up front and centre by Tanya. She is forthright in one voice calling for it and in another saying it is not even necessary once the man is able to perform. Unlike other artistes Tanya does not see the need to hide behind double entrendre when speaking of this sexual practice. The taboo subject of men performing oral sex is treated with from time to time by female artistes, some of whom call for it, e.g., Ce'cile in "Do it to me baby" (2003). Unlike the question of cunnilingus, Tanya is not as explicit around fellatio. In fact, as discussed previously, she cautions women "nuh goggle" (fellate) as this places a women in a position of subservience vis-a-vis her male partner. This is the same fear which is perhaps at the root of the male rejection of cunnilingus. In that same song ("Goggle"), however, she appears to reject cunnilingus and dismisses it as a habit picked up by the man abroad, something shameful yet addictive ("now mi have him like puppet pon a piece a cord"). In an earlier album (*Ruff Rider*) she speaks of her dissatisfaction with her lover's performance, which forces her to draw fi har fingah (engage in self-pleasuring). "Bwoy gone sleep lef mi hot like ginger". Similarly, the selfish and unfulfilling performance of the perfect man is lamented in "Damn" (R) – "you set a new record six seconds flat". The "perfect" man suffers from premature ejaculation and a decided unconcern about his partner's fulfilment. What this perhaps demonstrates is Donna Hope's argument that Jamaican men both fear and revere the punaany.

Hope identifies the use of sex and sexuality in the dancehall to reinforce and identify masculinity and its reflection in the paranoia against male homosexuality (79). Interesting, where Dancehall and Christianity seem to be on the same side is when it comes to homosexuality. Much of the Christian Church is stridently anti-homosexuality. Pinnock (2007) argues that:

> "Male homosexuality as a practice, therefore, is allowed only to the extent that it does not contravene accepted social norms and mores in the society which are adamantly defined as being

rooted in Christianity. In fact, it could well be argued that these attitudes and postures of 'hate'/fear in Jamaican popular culture are part of the fictive constructions of the nation state (of Jamaica) as Christian. Thus, in keeping with the biblical injunction to condemn (male) homosexuality, Jamaican popular culture at large, represents a state of extreme manifestation of Christendom's traditionally intolerant position of same gender sexual relations" (p. 4).

Pinnock's argument finds echo in Lewis (2009), as mentioned previously. The fictive nature of Jamaica's Christian essence is illuminated by the transgressions in Dancehall even as paradoxically some practices in Dancehall seem to confirm the fictivity. In GB and R, Tanya seems to depart from both these groups, making her own path as is demonstrated in "Do you still care?" In that ballad, she places the question of racial, sexual and economic discrimination and oppression within the context of the African American experience while linking it to the Israeli-Palestinian-Iraqi question. At the root of the problems she identifies is the refusal to accept difference and the desire to impose one's own opinions on others ("If you not doing it my way then you doing it wrong...If you don't look like me me ago pop mi piece."). She questions the man whose life is saved by a queer man, "How do you feel that you friends know you are hanging out with a queer?" She portrays the homosexual man as a regular caring human being which flies in the face of Christian and cultural notions of perversion and sinfulness. Hers is a bold move within the dancehall dis/place (Hope 2006).

Female Self Image

No doubt Tanya continues to upstage her male counterparts by taking control of the mic, her favourite utensil. She effortlessly represents herself and other women and puts paid to the claims of the male DJs to do this on their behalf. As Cooper points out, paradoxically, in so doing Tanya speaks in the same sexually explicit language of her male rivals (2004). This, of course, leads to the charge that she, like other female DJs, is complicit in-her own objectification. Again Cooper rejects this and sees self-assertion at play as these women talk back to the male, "challenging many of the chauvinist limitations that are imposed on her gender" (Cooper 2004, p. 21). This may be the case but the danger of re-inscribing male notions of the sexually available female as an object of male control and desire cannot be so easily dismissed.

Her self-image is not tied up with her sexuality in the way of other female DJs. Given the value of male heterosexuality and woman's role in facilitating this, the queens of the Dancehall like Tanya and Lady Saw "utilize their sexuality ruthlessly" (Hope 2006, p. 62). Women don't come across in her music as oppressed and marginalized. We meet women who are sexually aware and able to demand the pleasure and satisfaction which they are due. Some people would argue that her women actually behave like men of old (demand and gets sexual pleasure, sees/uses the male simply as an object of pleasure, etc). Women in Tanya's music are transgressors par excellence.

Returning to the notion of transgression and female identity, it is of note that Tauchert (2008) is not as taken with the notion of transgression as an absolute value. She acknowledges that in some cultural contexts transgression is a liberating act, a means of escaping a dead past (p. 2). I acknowledge Tauchert's concerns and argue that the Jamaican society is a space that requires transgression of the kind identified with the work of Tanya Stephens. The dead past that can be described in the Jamaican context was vividly captured by Cooper (1993), who presents a literary critique of a popular eighteenth century Jamaican popular song, "Me know no law, me know no sin". The female voice in the song, while born a slave, has reclaimed her body and her freedom to dispose of it as she chooses despite the often horrific consequences. Hers is an act of transgression in which she goes beyond the enslaving boundaries that delimit her person and place (Cooper 1993). "Transgression thus becomes the acknowledgement of a rehumanised identity" (Cooper 1993, p. 29). Fast forwarding to Dancehall today, it is possible to identify a subversive dimension in the relationship of Dancehall artiste Tanya to the dominant social/moral order. Her oeuvre has recaptured the female identity from masculine gaze and made it a site of self-definition and identity for women (and other marginalised groups).

Church Mis-dealings

Theologically Tanya also has what can be described as a strongly "prophetic" voice. This is not prophetic as it is understood as limited to predicting the futures. She is like a biblical prophet who "speaks truth to power". The powerful who need to hear the divine words to which she gives voice, includes the Prime Minister ("Mr you know mi naw try fi dis yah, but everyting not soh criss sah. We jus a look a likkle help Prime Minister"), some noveau riche ("pricks with money but no social graces"), members of the dancehall fraternity, baby mothers and baby daddys and members of parliament ("The Other Cheek" (R)). At the same time, the Church is also at the receiving end of her scolding and prophetic denunciations.

Tanya expresses her frustration at always leaving church and feeling like she has just been robbed ["What a Day" (R)]. She feels robbed because she spends two hours listening to ramblings and God is not mentioned. (It is not only women steal but Church also steals.) She identifies the richest man in church as the one who does not have a job (the pastor?). (Interestingly, the very material focus that Tanya excoriates as present in Church also is alive and well in Dancehall. The correlate of wealth/prosperity Gospel in Church is "bling" in the Dancehall.) Church people are "a bunch of righteous freaks extorting worse than the mob". Undoubtedly, she is expressing her distaste with certain ways of being Church that focus on prosperity and wealth without addressing the real social concerns of "life and death being sold as a pair". This distasteful "characteristic" of Church is not one that is present across Christendom, however. Indeed, even within the wider Church community there are ongoing discussions about the falsity of such theology.

In a certain Freudian vein she identifies a toxicity at work within organised religion that has her desperate for a new religion ("Sunday Morning" (R)). Christianity feels stifling and imprisoning to her.

Religion is a psychosis that is propagated by Christians who claim to be concerned about salvation. She rejects the God of Moses as the God who preaches peace while having Christians fighting war in His Holy Name. This is the God who sits idly by while evil is carried out in His name and Satan is given the blame. She excoriates Sunday Christians who for the rest of the week look down at her from a pedestal on which they super- ficially perch. She claims that the same set of people who believes that God lives in the sky are the same set of people who has a problem when she gets high (marijuana (weed) seems to be the drug of choice). The God of Love that she wants worship is the one that says to her, "You are still my child whether you sniff or you smoke" ("You keep Looking Up"). She questions, "Well if Jesus had a problem with drinking would he turn water into wine?" Furthermore, she rejects a mediator between herself and her God. The pastor and bishop are therefore to find themselves unemployed in her new religion. Her vision is such that it challenges the belief that everyone does and ought to worship this God of Moses, the Judeo-Christian God. Clearly, her vision of religion is fairly ecumenical and inter-faith, an approach that some Christian groups would reject out of hand. Her new religion is decided here-and-now as she envisions religion working at eradicating need, hunger, greed, war, and one that does not condemn her to the flames of hell if occasionally she smokes a "little b## c$$$ weed".

Stephens like many Jamaicans labour under the impression that the King James Bible was written/compiled by King James rather than being an influential translation authorised by him for his own polit- ical purposes. Her recourse is to the King James Bible as the source of inspiration even as she takes issue with the absence of a woman's voice from its pages. "Not even one likkle verse from a woman? Behold, the Chronicles of Tanya!" She openly contests the power of the Bible to speak on behalf of women while silencing women in the process. She sets herself the transgressive task of adding the woman's voice (her own) to a largely patriarchal discourse and in so doing challenges the one-sided vision of ecclesiastical/scriptural authority that has served to delimit female possibilities, as she demonstrates in many of her other lyrics. The Chronicles of Tanya seem to be encapsulated in "You Keep Looking Up".

So not only does Stephens speak in the voice of women who transgress. She also speaks in the voice of God to humanity. In "You Keep Looking Up"(R) she chastises Christians for their rejection of life on earth. She points out that in looking up they miss the divine presence in all dimensions of human life (flowers, plants, river flowing through the land, your greatest enemy). Her charge is that we are so heavenly focused we are of little earthly good. She is also deeply attuned to the kind of Christian spirituality that causes human beings to be so convicted of their sinfulness that they are literally bowed down by the weight of that knowledge. Yet she exhorts us not to believe that we are flawed and irreparable (unable to be repaired). Stephens seems to have rejected the notion of a fatal flaw or stain that each human being is born with (original sin) or that this stain cannot be removed. Interestingly, she is very Christian in that belief if she is rejecting the irreparable dimension as Christians believe that the flaw has been removed by Christ. If however she is rejecting both the sense of being flawed and that that flaw is irreparable then she has gone her own way and again transgressed Christian sensibilities about sin, particularly original sin. At the same time, hers is a decidedly apocalyptic vision as she desires for "everything to bun dung clean and start fresh again" (Echoes of 2 Peter 3.12?). She dreams of a better day but only one that can result from the destruction of the destructiveness that is at play now. There is some real irony in using destruction to destroy destructiveness.

LEAD US INTO TRANGRESSION

Donna Hope (2006) describes the dancehall dis/place as one where the overlapping symbols of power and domination are undergoing an ongoing struggle. In so doing, Hope averts to the dancehall as a transgressive space in which women claim sexual freedom and the ability to define themselves without the strictures of Christianity's sanctioned patriarchy. Tanya Stephens is one dancehall artiste who has mastered the art of transgression in the dancehall dis/place. Through her music she leads us into transgression, boundary crossing and contestation.

John Ransom points out that most human beings have a tendency to analyse ourselves, a desire to subject ourselves to critical scrutiny and even cultivate ourselves in a particular way. He argues that the primary vehicle for this activity is usually taken to be the Church; the Church has provided a key set of codes that has allowed us to identify psychic events and to interpret them. Jamaica is still a context within which the Church sets the agenda for the interpretation of human life and living in a significant fashion. To that end, artistes like Tanya Stephens are caught in the bind of having to use the very structures of Church to critique the Church. So she not only criticizes the Church but uses it as a point of legitimisation in her own discourse and self identity, as is demonstrated by her challenge to the King James Bible yet her dependency on it for framing the vision of her critique.

At the same time, reading her lyrics with a certain eye recognizes that her transgression has an ambiguous face. While she is calling women to self-knowledge, liberation, and challenging male-female stereotypes that keep both men and women in bondage she is deeply enmeshed in some cultural perspectives that bedevil her transgression, for example, her characters blame women for the behaviour of men including rape (based on dress), men are supported in their multiple relationships as a means of legitimising their masculinity, and women strive to emulate men in their destructive practice of devaluing womanhood. This does not totally nullify the transgressive value of her work, however. Her ballads call us to look again at the nature and meaning of sex and sexuality in human life. Her ballads call us to the provisional and ambivalent nature of Church. In spite of the highly conservative fashion in which much of Christian discourse around sexuality has been deployed, there is a space for a new discourse on Christian sensibilities in that area. Christian discourse around the body and sex calls us to a deepened understanding of the body and sex that can be deeply meaningful in light of the struggles for wholeness and affirmation that Tanya's lyrics demonstrate. She demonstrates that sexuality is one of the areas in which human beings connect with and grow towards their fullest potential, their truest selves. Boundary crossing with its ambiguity calls us to explore Christian ideas about sin that are often individual and often-identified with sexual transgressions. If appreciating such matters is the way of the transgressor, then maybe loving long ding dongs is not so bad after all.

REFERENCES

Boyne, Ian. "Dancehall debate a diversion?" *Sunday Gleaner*, February 22, 2009.

Cooper, Carolyn. *Noises in the Blood: Orality, Gender and the Vulgar Body of Jamaican Popular Culture*. Duke University Press, 1995 (originally published Macmillan 1993).

Cooper, Carolyn. *Sound Clash: Jamaican Dancehall Culture at Large*. Palgrave MacMillan. 2004.

Chang, Kevin O'Brien. "Licensing the Jamaican penis," *The Sunday Gleaner*, Sunday April 16, 2006. http://jamaica-gleaner.com/gleaner/20060416/focus/focus3.html

Duncum, Paul. "Toward a Playful Pedagogy: Popular Culture and the pleasures of Transgression," in *Studies in Art Education: A Journal of Issues and Research*. Vol. 50.3, 2009, pp. 232-244.

Figueroa, J. Peter. "Understanding Sexual Behaviour in Jamaica" in *The African-Caribbean Worldview and the Making of Caribbean Society*. Horace Levy, (ed.). Kingston: University of the West Indies Press, 2009, pp. 210-222.

Genovesi, Vincent J. *In Pursuit of Love: Catholic Morality and Human Sexuality*. Michael Glazier Books/The Liturgical Press, 1996.

Hope, Donna. *Inna Di Dancehall: Popular Culture and the Politics of Identity in Jamaica*. Kingston: The University of the West Indies Press, 2006.

Lewis, R. Anthony. " 'This is a Christian country!' The Limits of Popular Religious Discourse on Jamaican Identity". Paper Presented at the Caribbean Studies Association Conference, Kingston, Jamaica, June 2, 2009.

Perkins, Anna Kasafi. "'Oh, Daddy, That's My G-Spot": Women and Sexual Pleasure in Jamaican Dancehall Music' in *Handbook on Sexuality: Perspectives, Issues and Role in Society*. Nicholas E. Peterson and Whitney Campbell (Eds.). Nova Publishers 2012.

Pickstock, Catherine. "Postmodernism," in *Blackwell Companion to Political Theology*. Peter Scott and William T. Cavanaugh (Eds.). Blackwell Publishing Ltd, 2004, pp. 471-485.

Pinnock, Agostinho. "At the Ideological Cross Roads: Interrogating (Jamaican) Masculinities in Contemporary Urban Culture through Historical Discourse. Paper presented at the SALISES Conference, University of the West Indies, St. Augustine, Trinidad, 2007.

Ransom, John. "Transgression, Limit, and Oppositional Modes." http://sincronia.cucsh.udg.mx/ransom.htm

Rubavicius ,Vytautas. "The Pleasure of Transgression: Consuming Identities" in *Athena* 3, 2006, pp.68-80.

Russell, Heather. "Man-Stealing, Man-Swapping and Man-Sharing: Wifey and Matey's in Tanya Stephen's Lyrics", in *Caribbean Erotic: Poetry, Prose and Essays*. Palmer, Opal Adisa, and Donna Aza Weir-Soley (Eds.). Peepal Press, 2010, pp. 276-291.

Tauchert, Ashley. Against Transgression. Wiley-Blackwell, 2008.

Taylor, Burchell. Free for All? Grace Kennedy Lecture, 1992

Williams, Delores. "A Womanist Perspective on Sin," A Troubling in My Soul: Womanist Perspectives on Evil and Suffering, ed. Emilie M. Townes. Maryknoll: Orbis Books, 1993, 130-149.

Wilson, Nadine. "No to sex for dollar$", The Sunday Observer, January 6, 2013, p. 8.

SHE SE DIS HIM SE DAT

EXAMINING GENDER[1] – BASED VOWEL USE IN JAMAICAN DANCEHALL

INTRODUCTION

What men and women say are usually viewed differently by society. Women's language is seen as weak and powerless, and lacks assertion while the way men speak is seen as powerful and authoritative (Lakoff 1975; Coates 1998). As it relates to talk, men tend to dominate public spaces (Herring 1993). In this work, dancehall is considered a public space, through the music and the staging of dances. In this genre of music men are considered to be powerful and dominant, not just in numbers but in their language and popularity. Developing on preliminary work (Dawkins 2009) this paper presents information from ongoing research which focuses on vowel use by male and female artists in Jamaican dancehall, and considers how gender and identity in collaboration with style may account for the vowel selections demonstrated by artists. It also takes into account how specific target audience influences language use in popular recorded songs.

Relevant literature by linguists suggests that, when an option is available, men show a preference for back and low vowels, while women show a preference for high front vowels. In Jamaican dancehall lyrics, however, vowel choice appears to be influenced more by the target audience than the singer. Back and low vowels are used by both male and female artists when targeting men and high front and high-mid front vowels are used by both male and female artists when targeting women. Indications are that women target mainly male audiences and that this appears to be linked to male dominance in the music industry in Jamaica as well as the norm for this particular community of practice. The current study engages biological and social explanations for observed differences in male and female linguistic behavior. These include description of the size of the vocal tract (Gordon and Heath 1998); sociolinguistic issues such as acts of identity (Romaine, 1994, and Le Page and Tabouret-Keller 1985); social networks (Milroy and Milroy 1992); dominance (Coates 1998); and, most central to this paper, Bell's (1984) study, 'Language style as audience design,' which proposes that speakers will use particular language styles to identify with a specific audience. In addition, accommodation theory, and community of practice which outlines that 'a particular community focuses on groups of people in virtue of their regular engagement in common practices', such as language (Eckert 2006:22) are engaged.

DANCEHALL BACKGROUND

Dancehall can be defined by its many cultural styles; it is a style of dress, a style of dance, a style of talk and as such a style of rhythmic songs that brings forth this type of music and musical beats. Dancehall, according to Hope (2006), is also a place for the staging of dances. Dancehall music is one of the most popular musical genres in Jamaica today and its songs are 'climbing charts' and 'making waves' in other parts of the world such as Europe, Asia and the Americas. The most common language of dancehall music is Jamaican Creole, usually its more mesolectal form. Devonish (1998) defines dancehall as an art form involving the delivery of spoken language to a predetermined rhythmic pattern established by an accompanying recorded bass and rhythm sound tract. Hope describes the intense social situation which assisted in the breeding of a culture of dancehall; 'the intense social pressures at work in early 1980s Jamaica demanded a catharis, the opening of a safety valve to release the pent-up frustrations of many dispossessed Jamaicans. From within the heart of Jamaica, popular culture responded to the vacuum that had developed in the society. It projected a cultural music product that was indelibly marked by the political, economic and social tensions at work in the society. This was the evolution of dancehall music and culture' (Hope 2006, 9). This type of music is sung by artists known as deejays (DJs) and began in the early 1980s. It is well known for its fast, up tempo beats and energetic delivery by artists. This genre is at the heart of controversy in the Jamaican society; as the music is frequently viewed as 'raw,' 'raunchy,' and 'violent' by some members in the society Dawkins (2009). According to Cooper (2004:6), what the dancehall artists say 'is often dismissed as pure nonsense by elitist critics of the genre, or worse, is deemed seditious'. Hope posits that there is a constant struggle between what is seen as 'superior' European culture and African culture in negotiating the Jamaican identity. Dancehall music and culture, as the most contemporary manifestation of what is deemed Jamaican 'low culture', creates and recreates symbolic manifestations of the tensions that operate in the society Hope (2006).

Hope (2006) also declares that dancehall culture's identity re-presentations is a symbolic magic wand that many individuals from the poverty-stricken, inner cities of Kingston and St. Andrew use to transform and refine the subordinate roles and identities ascribed to them by traditional Jamaican society. The average Jamaican, particularly from the working class, finds refuge and hope through the expression of this type of music which has also gained international fame, giving recognition to artists via Grammy awards and American Music Awards. Dancehall figures prominently in annual concerts such as Sting and Reggae Sumfest, which attract audiences from all over the globe. Hope states that:

'Indeed since Bob Marley's international success as Jamaica's premier reggae artiste, dancehall has proven the most commercially successful form of Jamaican music to date. Reggae dance-hall artiste like Shabba Ranks (Winner of the Grammy for Best Reggae Album in 1991 and 1992), Patra, Cobra, Super Cat, Chaka Demus & Pliers, Beenie Man (Winner of the Grammy for Best Reggae Album in 2000), Bounty Killa, Shaggy (Winner of the Grammy for Best Reggae Album in 1995), Sean Paul (Winner of the Best Reggae Album in 2003). Wayne Wonder, and Elephant Man, among others have successfully broken into the Japanese, Europe and North American markets and have continued to ensure, the global spread of Reggae dancehall music and its associated images'. (Hope 2006:22).

There are few literary works examining the lyrics of dancehall music. The most popular authors of dancehall in Jamaica are Donna Hope and Carolyn Cooper. Research carried out on dancehall by Cooper, a strong supporter and avid writer on dancehall music, concentrates on the cultural aspect of the music. She notes that the genre comes from what is perceived to be an oral culture, it is the 'noise in our blood' and indicates that 'if you choose to ignore the noise, then you ignore part of the meaning' (Cooper, 1993). Cooper argues that, language is the medium via which the DJs articulate their preoccupations and commu-nicate directly with their receptive audiences. On the other hand, perfor-mance is dialogue with an audience that speaks back in no uncertain terms (Cooper, 2004). Therefore, the artists' lyrics are designed for their audience.

LINGUISTIC FRAMING

Linguist, Hubert Devonish (1998 & 2006) has conducted extensive work on the internal structure of dancehall lyrics, focusing on the linguis-tic aspects of dancehall lyrics. He examines vowel alongside stress patterns in the rhyming system and argues that the scientific study of the language forms which make up music lyrics is more obviously the field of the linguist than that of the literary musical critic. This is partic-ularly true when studying the phonetics and phonology of the lyrics, rather than the imagery and metaphor as such cases of creativity provide linguists with insights to help develop their understandings of the form and structure of the phonological system of Jamaican Creole.[2] Devonish (2006) examines the lyrics of DJ Vegas' song, 'Heads High', stating, that this piece performed by a man addressed to women, is a praise song to women. Devonish's main focus is on the rhyming words at the end of its lines and he notes that twelve lines in the verse have rhymes with syllables ending in /iip/, /iik/, /iit/ and another twelve in /iim/, /iin/ and /in/. I, however, point out that the chorus of the song contains 52 syllables with high front vowels and 30 syllables with low and back vowels. Additionally, Devonish (1998) states, 'the deejay/dancehall piece also possesses an internal structure which complements the structure laid down by the rhythmic backing. There is rhyme, the number of syllables per line, the number of lines per verse, etc' (p. 45). Devonish (2006) also provides an example of the stressed syllables in these lines of a song's chorus sung by Buju Banton.[3]

The data indicates that Buju uses a lot of back and low vowels in the chorus of this song, and stress is placed on the vowels of all the word final syllables at the end of each line. In earlier work (Dawkins 2009) I argue that vowel final syllables are more important in a song's chorus, and these syllables will contain specific vowels (high front and low back)[4] depending on the audience being targeted. This is supported by the view in the literature, and in the music studios, that final syllables play the greatest role in the songs' choruses. Devonish (1998 & 2006) states that, although every syllable per line in dancehall lyrics is very important, the most important syllables are those located at the end of each line in the chorus. These syllables are always heavily emphasized and carry high stress on the vowels.[5]

In dancehall music the final syllables of each line are always repeated on a second tract (audio recording track) to match the same syllable on the first tract. This is called 'doubling the ends' or 'doubling-up'. Earlier research confirms that music engineers frequently tell the artists that the last part of the word (the final syllable) must always be heard clearly during recordings. This is done with every professionally recorded dancehall song. Consequently, in almost every dancehall song, it is easier to remember the chorus, especially the final words, or syllables at the end of each line because of their rhyming scheme. Based on these observations therefore, it is not the amount of vowels in the overall chorus that are significant (although important), but actually the vowels located in the final syllables of each line, because they are more important for the purpose of rhyme and emphasis.

Research reveals that women tend to produce front vowels more front than men, and they also have the tendency to front back vowels and make them appear more front during speech production. Linguistic work conducted by Chambers and Hardwick (1986) find that women in Toronto have the tendency to front and raise the diphthong[6] /aw/ (aʊ) (in words like *how* and *now*) to produce [ew] (eʊ), while men led in the backing and rounding of the diphthong [ow] (oʊ) (in words like *show* and *glow*). Also, case studies such as Milroy and Milroy's (1985) observations of the Belfast speech community indicate that women led linguistic change in the raising and fronting of [æ] (as in *bad*) to [ɛ] (as in *bed*), while the backing and occasional rounding of /a/ is led by men.

Eckert's (1989) research looks at sociolinguistic variation among students at Belten High School in Detroit. Her study focuses on groups of students which she calls Jocks and Burnouts. These students are speakers of African American Vernacular English (AAVE). Her work focuses on three variables, vowels [æ] as in *bad*, [uh] as in *cut*, [ay] as in *fight*. The variable [æ] ranges from a conservative pronunciation [a] to a raised variant [e], so that *bad* sounds like **bade**. The variable [uh] ranges from its conservative pronunciation [ʌ] to a backed pronuncia-tion [ɔ], making **cut** sound more like **caught**, and the diphthong [ay] (aɪ) monophthongizes[7] to [aː], so that **right** is pronounced **rot**. Her findings reveal that boys led in the rounding and backing of the front diphthong [ay] (aɪ), with a pronunciation closer to [aː], a low vowel. Eckert's investi-gation also reveals that girls led in raising and fronting of vowels. The vowel [æ] is realized mostly by the girls with an actual production of [e], the high-mid front vowel. This is also common among the female artists in Jamaican dancehall music, Dawkins (2009). Eckert's study indicates that female informants produced more of the high front and high-mid front vowels and males produced more of the low and back vowels. Eckert (1989) posits that phonological variation, or nuances of pronunciation, can signal important information about speakers' social identities including class and gender and points out that the study of variation has traditionally focused on socioeconomic class, establishing that gender is also a significant and powerful force of linguistic variation. Her work helps clarifies why it is now common to speak of men's language and women's language in many circles, as gender is often seen as independent of other aspects of identity.

A THEORY OF IDENTITY

In examining the social aspects of gender and language, a theory of identity proves to be a crucial necessity, as identity is directly related to theories of gender. It should be noted that there are physical as well as social identities. Physical identity is directly derived from a physical description of a person's bodily characteristics; while 'social identity is that part of an individual's self-concept which derives from his knowledge of his membership of a social group(s) together with the value and emotional significance attached to that membership' (Joseph 2004:5). Baldwin and Hetch (1995) define two types of identities, personal identity and enacted identity, 'who I am and who I am for others' (qt. in Joseph 2004:5). Besnier (1991 & 1995), and Street (1993) states that 'self' is who I feel myself to be, emotionally and 'affectively', while 'person' is the identity projected to others in socially defined roles. As it relates to linguistics, Joseph (2004) states:

> 'A full account of linguistic representation would have to include how the identity of the speakers is manifested by them and read by others. It would have to recognize that the speakers themselves are a part of the meaning, represented within the representation. A full account of linguistic communication would have to start with, not a message, but again the speakers

themselves, and their reading of each other that determines, interactively, their interpretation of what is said' (22).

While it is quite easy to construct social identities and to modify these as well, this is not so easily done with already established physical identities, unless one chooses to undergo extreme physical surgery. In examining theories of identity, a distinction must be made between personal identity and social identity, 'but at the same time, our personal identities are in many respects collages of different social category characteristics, complete or fragmentary' (Joseph 2004:112). By using a theory of identity, this research can relate to dancehall artists establishing an enacted identity, that is, 'who I am for others' which leans more towards the social and not the physical.

Additional research posits that the phonological choices that men and women demonstrate may be linked not only to social factors, but also to the biological make-up of the sexes. Gordon and Heath (1998) argue that women are attracted to particular vocalic qualities, prototypically the high front unrounded vowel [i], while men are attracted to other vocalic qualities, prototypically back vowels rounded or not, namely [ɒ, ɔ, o, u]. They claim that these male/female preferences could be biologically determined, because of physiological differences in the vocal tracts of men and women. The physical evidence they describe shows that the larynx of adult males is typically 50 per cent larger than that of females, which implies longer vocal cords in men. Since the size of the vocal cord is related to the rate of vibration, men tend to have lower formants than women (Borden and Harris 1984). Formant values can be roughly translated into the traditional articulatory terms of description, using the first formant (F1) as the primary correlate of height and the second formant (F2) as the primary correlate of frontness (Gordon and Heath, 1998). The research holds that women show a greater tendency towards fronting. When both men and women produce front vowels, women's production is more front than that of men. Also, researchers have observed a tendency to raise or front back vowels among women, while men's production appears to be more back and rounded.

GENDER AND IDENTITY: A SOCIAL CONSTRUCT

Gordon and Heath (1998) argue that men and women may modify their articulatory lowering or raising of their formant frequencies to produce voices that aim towards archetypes of the opposite gender. This, they say, is motivated by social dynamics, such as those associated with the construction and performance of identity. According to Le Page and Tabouret-Keller (1985), acts of identity entail identities which people make within themselves as well as those that are shared with others. 'The individual creates his systems of verbal behavior so as to resemble those common to the group with which he wishes from time to time to be identified' (p.115). Romaine (1994) posits that acts of identity refer to speakers choosing the group with which they wish to identify. However, according to Le Page and Tabouret-Keller the process of choosing is neither necessarily conscious nor is it always uni-dimensional. Relevant research conducted by (Pierrehumbert et al., 2004) reveals that gay, lesbian, and bisexual ('GLB') speech patterns reflect learned manip- ulation of the phonetic space of the opposite sex. Thus, GLB speakers learned to model speakers of the opposite sex in specific respects. The formant values for the lesbians and bisexual women were more back than men for /ɒ/. These researchers note that the use of backness in back vowels to convey specific meanings associated with particular social identities is not unprecedented. Pierrehumbert et al., 2004 states that Habick (1991) finds that the freedom which English allows in the production of /u/ is exploited by adolescents to convey social identity. In his research, Habick found that the use of the back vowel /u/ was associated with a group known for its 'tough' stance. It may be that the lesbian and bisexual women in the (Pierrehumbert et al., 2004) study were using back vowels in a sense to portray social identification with certain aspects of maleness and/or men. Eckert (1989) also associates the use of the back vowel /ɒ/ among a group identified as 'burnouts' with perhaps a similar desire to portray a 'tough' stance. Farquharsen (2005: 107) states that 'gay-bashing is one of the ways in which (young) Jamaican men construct a heterosexual identity-which is the same cultural practice embodied in the public performance done on stage by dancehall artists'. Dawkins (2009) found that heterosexual male dancehall artistes will use what can be considered the 'female' vowels to bash homosexuals and issues pertaining to homosexuality in the Jamaican society.

While phonological differences between the voices of men and women in dancehall music might be seen by some as a result of sexual or anatomical differences, it is not my intention to attribute such findings purely to biological claims as social factors are significant. Specifically, an individual's identification with a particular group of speakers, such as a target audience, may have more influence on the artists' language style than biological differences between males and females. This lends support to Bell's (1984) claim that speakers' language styles are influenced by their audience, present or absent, and this assertion that in cases such as that of mass media communication, more pressure is on the speaker to identify with a particular target audience. Bell (1984) argues that 'style is essentially speakers' response to their audience' (p.145). He argues that speakers will style shift to sound like other speakers. The more attention that an audience pays to the speaker, the more likely the speaker will be influenced to style shift. Thus, speakers design their style for their audience. Bell (1984) points out that Hindle (1979) recorded the speech of a woman in a variety of situations and found that where a vowel change was being led by women, the speaker used more advance variants when talking to women. Where men were leading the change, the woman in Hindle's study used more advance variants with men who used more advance variants. The idea that musical artists style shift to sound like others is not unheard of either, Trudgill (1983) found that British punk music singers changed their pronunciation of particular phonemes to sound more American, because their style was seen as more prestigious by British audiences/fans. However, Schilling-Estes (2001) disagrees with Bell's (1984, 2001) claims, that speakers do not merely style shift, or primarily in reaction to the elements of the speech situation but rather are quite active and highly creative in their use of stylistic resources. Thus, not only are speakers not bound to elements of the external situations as they shape their speech, but they use their speech to help shape and reshape the external situation (whether the immediate interactional context or wider societal forces), as well as their interpersonal relationships and crucially their personal identities. She further goes on to say that Labov (1990) believes that style shifts are triggered primarily by the amount of attention people pay to their speech as they converse, how self-conscious people are as they speak. But, Bell argues that variation on the style dimension within the speech of a single speaker derives from and echoes the variation which exists between speakers on the 'social' dimension (Bell 1984, 151). Therefore, individual style is drawn from and shaped by wider societal norms.

Another theory that could account for stylistic behaviours in speech is the Accommodation Theory, first proposed by Howard Giles (1987). 'The accommodation model is a social psychological theory in which a speaker's perception of the interlocutor[8] and his conversational needs are related to his speech style' (Boves 1992:6). The way in which people adapt their speech style to the interlocutors, the topic, and the situation in which a conversation takes place, is a key topic in sociolinguistics (Boves 1992:1). Boves also goes on to refer to some facts about ecology as it relates to accommodating to things around us in our daily lives as it relates to our environment. He notes Higgins (1981) who states:

> 'living orgasms are constantly in touch with each other, and with their environment. The ability to perceive and respond to signals is generally considered essential for all organisms in order to survive in a strange and changing environment. With regards to the exchange of signals between human beings, free conversations can be taken as the canonical setting. In this setting, people communicate for a certain purpose, and the conversation takes place in a socially defined context in which they assume interdependent roles. They 'follow conventional rules, strategems and tactics for making decisions and obtaining various goals' (Higgins 1981:346).

Boves posits that the substantial point behind the accommodation theory is that during interaction individuals are motivated to accommodate their speech styles for different goals, such as, 'evoking a listener's social approval, attaining communicative efficiency, or maintaining positive social identities' (Boves 1992:6). This can be considered as an attributive factor in dancehall among dancehall artists who may accommodate their speech to suit that of an intended audience being targeted.

Convergence and Divergence are two key areas of Accommodation Theory. Boves states that in co-operative conversations speakers will converge to the speech of their interlocutor and in competitive conversations speakers will diverge from the speech of their interlocutor (Boves 1992). Convergence is 'a linguistic strategy where individuals adapt to each other's speech by means of a wide range of linguistic features. Divergence refers to the way in which speakers accentuate vocal differences between themselves and others' (Giles et al. 1987:14). Boves agrees by stating that 'convergence was interpreted as a strategy of identification with the interlocutor, whereas divergence was seen as a strategy of identification with some external reference group' (Boves 1992:11). He also mentions Genesee and Bouhis (1982) who concluded that in some context, it is better to adhere to socially accepted norms than to converge to an interlocutor.

METHOD

For the overall research a total of 452 songs were examined but only, 64 songs were utilized for this paper.[9] From the total of 452 songs selected on the charts 414 were recorded by males and 38 by females. This is represented in the following chart:

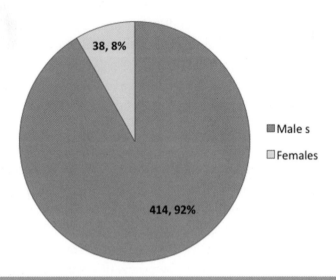

CHART 1. TOTAL NUMBER OF MEN AND WOMEN ON CHARTS BETWEEN 1990-2006[10]

Of the total of 64 dancehall songs (with an addition of two collaborations) selected for this paper, 32 were performed by men and 32 by women. All the selected participants have been in the dancehall industry for over 10 years. The lyrics and titles for each of the songs which were examined for the present research were also supplied by varying websites and VP records, and the choruses of the songs were transcribed using the International Phonetic Alphabet (IPA)[11] and then given an English gloss. Next, the final syllables in each line of the choruses containing the vowels were counted and recorded to determine the frequency of their occurrence. Each was classified as back, low, high front or high-mid front and the results presented in tables that pair these variables with a specific target audience.[12]

Praat (Dutch word for talk), is a software used for analyzing phonectic sounds which was also used to measure the vowel formants, F1 and F2 for both Lady Saw and Gyptian for their 'Hold You' song, where they both used the same vowels on the same rhythm to sing about an identical topic.

FINDINGS

Table 1 presents the data for the male artists and table 2 has the data for the female artists.

NAMES OF ARTISTS AND SONG TITLE	NUMBER OF SYLLABLES with high front and high-mid front vowels [i], [e], [ɪe], [aɪ], [ɛ]	NUMBER OF SYLLABLES with low and back vowels [ʊ], [u], [o], [ʌ], [ʊo], [oʊ], [a], [ɒ]	NO. OF VOWELS contained in final syllables at the end of each line	TARGET AUDIENCE Male, Female, General	TOPIC DISCUSSED
BEENIE MAN					
. **Old Dog** [ʊol dag]	44	32	10 [i]	Females	Being a womanizer
?. **Memories** [mɛmriz]	46	58	2[u], 10[a]	Males	Memories
?. **Who am I** [hu am aɪ]	25	28	3[a], 3[o]	Males	Brags about his posses-sions
?. **Noff Gyal** [nof gjal] (Lots of girls)	16	56	6[o], 2[a]	Males	Encourag-ing men to have lots of girls
?. **Ketty Drum** [kɛtɪ dʒɹom]	54	38	8 [oʊ]	General	Music
?. **Suzukie** [sʊzukɪ]	42	40	4[ɪ], 4[ɪe]	Females	Sex
?. **King of the Dancehall**	28	32	6[a], 2[i]	Females	Sex
?. **Wickedest Slam** [wɪkɪdɛs slam] (best sex)	46	42	8[a]	Males	Telling men about specific women who give good sex

NAMES OF ARTISTS AND SONG TITLE	NUMBER OF SYLLABLES with high front and high-mid front vowels [i], [e], [ɪe], [aɪ], [ɛ]	NUMBER OF SYLLABLES with low and back vowels [ʊ], [u], [o], [ʌ], [ʊo], [oʊ], [a], [ɒ]	NO. OF VOWELS contained in final syllables at the end of each line	TARGET AUDIENCE Male, Female, General	TOPIC DISCUSSED
SIZZLA					
1. Give it to them [giv it tu dɛm]	65	58	8[ɛ]	Females	Sex
2. Dry Cry [dʒɹaɪ kɹaɪ]	39	47	12[e]	Females	Heart aches
3. Babylon [babɪlan]	32	50	8[a]	Males / Rastaman	Government
4. No White God [no waɪt gad]	22	26	6 [a]	Males/ Rastafarians	Religion
5. Praise Jah [pɹɪəz dʒa]	12	18	4[æ], 2[ɛ], 2[ɪ]	Males/ Rastafarians	Religion
6. Rise to the Occasion [ɹaɪz tʊ ðɪ əkeʒən]	21	46	4[æ], 2[ʌ], 2[a], 2[aɪ]	General	Motivation of Self
7. Words of Divine	32	13	4[aɪ], 4[e]	Females	Love
8. Take myself away	35	30	8[i]	Females	Love
BUJU BANTON					
1. Browning [Bɹaʊnɪn]	24	24	6 [i]	Females	Women of lighter complexion
2. Murderer [mɔɹdaɹa]	28	58	4[o], 4[a]	Males	Senseless killings
3. Deportee [dɪpoʊɹti]	32	50	8 [a:]	Males	Deportation
4. Bumbai Bai [bʊmbaɪ baɪ] (sound of shooting)	18	25	4 [e]	Homosexual men	Homosexuality

NAMES OF ARTISTS AND SONG TITLE	NUMBER OF SYLLABLES with high front and high-mid front vowels [i], [e], [ɪe], [aɪ], [ɛ]	NUMBER OF SYLLABLES with low and back vowels [ʊ], [u], [o], [ʌ], [ʊo], [oʊ], [a], [ɒ]	NO. OF VOWELS contained in final syllables at the end of each line	TARGET AUDIENCE Male, Female, General	TOPIC DISCUSSED
mi tu bad (I'm too bad)	17	51	4[i], 4[æ]	Males	Female obsession with Buju
ʃɪaɪ afa jʊ ry after you)	29	73	8[ʊ]	Females	Trying to get females attention
Love Sponge	30	40	2[ɪ],2[aɪ], 2[o]	Females	Love
Flex	12	23	4[ɛ]	Females	Fabulous women
BOUNTY KILLA					
Man Heart [man hɑɪt] (Men's heart)	35	56	8[ɛ]	Females	Relation-ships
Magnum [magnʌm]	20	38	8[o]	Males	Gun war
Can't Be lieve [kjan bɪliv]	61	36	3[e], 2[aɪ], 3[ʊo]	Homosex-ual men	Homosexu-ality
wʌtlɪs bwaɪ (Worthless Man)	28	48	8 [a]	Males	Men who sexually underper-form
man a bad man am a bad man)	50	33	8[ɪ]	Males	Men with effeminate behavior
Dangerously	36	28	8[i]	Female	Women who cheat
Mystery	46	58	8[æ]	Males	Conflict
Fed up	21	19	3[ʌ] 1[a]	General	Social

1. SYLLABLE COUNT IN THE CHORUSES OF SONGS BY MALE DANCEHALL ARTISTS

NAMES OF ARTISTS AND SONG TITLE	NUMBER OF SYLLABLES with high front and high-mid front vowels [i], [e], [ɪe], [aɪ], [ɛ]	NUMBER OF SYLLABLES with low and back vowels [ʊ], [u], [o], [ʌ], [ʊo], [oʊ], [a], [ɒ]	NO. OF VOWELS contained in final syllables at the end of each line	TARGET AUDIENCE Male, Female, General	TOPIC DISCUSSE.
LADY SAW					
1. Man a di least a mi problem (Men are the least of my problems)	39	32	8[ɛ]	Females	Relation-ships Among men and women
2. Fling It Up [flɪŋ ɪt ʌp] (Throw it up)	30	18	4[aɪ], 2[e]	Females	Sex
3. If Im Lef [ɪf ɪm lɛf] (If he leaves)	26	20	3[i], 1[a:]	Females	Sex / relation-ship
4. Belly Rubber dub [bɛlɪ ɹʌba dʌb]	20	38	4[ʌ]	Males	Sex
5. Hardcore [haɹdkoʊɹ]	59	29	8[ɪ], 3[ɪe], [a]	Females	Sex
6. Sycamore Tree [sɪkamoʊɹ tʃɹi]	49	40	8[i]	Females	Oral Sex
7. Good Wuk [gʌd wʌk (Good work [sex])	38	38	4[ɪ]	Males	Sex
8. Ehm ehm	44	48	4[ɛ]	General	Sex
D' ANGEL					
1. Blaze [blez]	42	48	8[ɪe]	Females	Fashion Style
2. Downtown Girl	30	33	6[aɪ]	Females	Her lifestyl
3. wan man mɪ gat (I have one man)	14	30	6[a]	General	Drama i relation-ships

NAMES OF ARTISTS AND SONG TITLE	NUMBER OF SYLLABLES with high front and high-mid front vowels [i], [e], [ɪe], [aɪ], [ɛ]	NUMBER OF SYLLABLES with low and back vowels [ʊ], [u], [o], [ʌ], [ʊo], [oʊ], [a], [ɒ]	NO. OF VOWELS contained in final syllables at the end of each line	TARGET AUDIENCE Male, Female, General	TOPIC DISCUSSED
. Woman Power [ʊman powa]	24	66	10 [aː]	Male politicians / Men in society	Politics
. My Life [maɪ laɪf]	24	18	4[æ]	Females	Bragging
. First Lady [fɔɹs ledɪ]	55	23	8[i]	Females	Bragging
. Dream [dʒɹim]	24	19	5[aɪ], 1[u]	Males	Love
. Baby Father [bebɪ faðəɹ]	39	28	6[aɪ], 2[ʌ]	Females	Being a mother and a wife
ANYA STEPHENS					
. It's A Pity [ɪts a pɪtɪ]	32	28	4[ɪ], 4[aɪ]	Females	Infidelity
. Bun [bʌn] (an xpression for heating)	46	68	5[a], 2[ʌ], 3[i]	Males	Why women Cheat
. Ninja Bike [nɪndʒa baɪk]	35	38	6[a], 4[ie]	Males	Sex
. These Streets [ðiz stʃɹits]	23	32	4[a], 2[u]	Males	Gangster love
. Goggle [gɒgl]	26	49	6[æ], 2[oʊ]	Males	Sex (Male bashing)
. Handle The Ride [handl ðə ɹaɪd]	13	19	4[aɪ]	Males	Sex (Male bashing)
. bum wok [bʊm wʌk] (great sex)	37	53	8[ʌ], 2[I],	Males	Sex
. Breathe [bɹiθ]	27	34	4[i], [I]	Males	Broken heart

NAMES OF ARTISTS AND SONG TITLE	NUMBER OF SYLLABLES with high front and high-mid front vowels [i], [e], [ɪe], [aɪ], [ɛ]	NUMBER OF SYLLABLES with low and back vowels [ʊ], [u], [o], [ʌ], [ʊo], [oʊ], [a], [ɒ]	NO. OF VOWELS contained in final syllables at the end of each line	TARGET AUDIENCE Male, Female, General	TOPIC DISCUSSE...
CECILE					
1. Do It To Me [du ɪt tʊ mɪ]	34	24	6[ɪ]	Females	Sex
2. Can you work [kjan yʊ wʌk] ('work' here carries a sexual connotation)	10	29	4[ʌ]	Males	Sex
3. Looser [luza]	27	63	8[a]	Males	Worthless men
4. Woman Tings [ʊman tɪŋz] (Women's Things)	38	38	8 [ɛ]	Effemi-nate men	Men who dress like women
5. Hot like we (us)	19	14	3[i], 1[æ]	Females	Flossing
6. Take Care of Your Man [tek kɪəɹ əf jəɹman]	40	26	8[aɪ]	Female	Relation-ship
7. Got a Man [gɒt a man]	24	46	4[o], 4[au]	Males	Sex
8. Nah Stress Ova Man [nɑ stʃɹɛs ova man] (Not stressing over a man)	41	39	8[ɛ́]	Females	No Fussing over men

TABLE 2: SYLLABLE COUNT IN CHORUSES OF SONGS BY FEMALE DANCEHALL ARTISTS

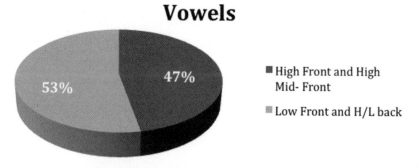

Vowels

53% 47%

■ High Front and High Mid- Front

▨ Low Front and H/L back

CHART 2: SONGS BY MALE ARTISTE

Of the 32 songs analyzed from the four male performers, only 34 per cent (11/32) had more high-front and high-mid front vowels than back and low vowels. Seven of these eleven songs target females; in other words, the artiste sings directly to females. Three songs target males, with two specifically talking about men who display homosexual behaviour, while the final song targets a general audience. Sixty six percent (21/32) of the remaining songs contain more back and low vowels than high front and high-mid front vowels. Of these twenty-one songs, fourteen specifically target men; one of which deals with the issue of homosexuality and all final syllables in word final position in this song contain a high front vowel. Five target females and two songs target a general audience. According to Bell (1984) non-audience factors like topic (in this case 'homosexuality') derive their effect by association with addressee types.

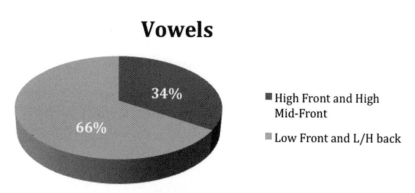

Vowels

34% 66%

■ High Front and High Mid-Front

▨ Low Front and L/H back

CHART 3: SONGS BY FEMALE ARTISTS

In the case of the data on the female artists, 47 per cent (14/32) of the songs have more high front and high-mid front vowels than back and low vowels, this is 13 per cent more than that of the same statistic for the data from men. Of these fourteen songs, thirteen target women and the other one target males. Of the remainder, sixteen songs by the female artists contain more low and back vowels and two contain an equal distribution of both of these vowel types. Of the sixteen songs with mainly low and back vowels, a pattern emerges: twelve target men, two women, and two a general audience.

The findings also reveal that both male and female artists perform songs targeting female audiences and listeners. Although they contain more low and back vowels overall; these do show more high-front and high-mid front vowels in the final syllables of each line. As mentioned earlier, the final syllables are very important as they are the last syllables heard by target audience or listener, and these are the syllables that are emphasized more by the artists as shown in Tables 1 and 2. The following examples are from Bounty Killa's *Man Heart,* Sizzla's *Dry Cry,* and D'Angel's *Blaze* and *Down-town Girl.* An example of the first two lines in Sizzla's song is shown below in Example 1:

EXAMPLE 1: *dʒɹaɪ kɹaɪ ivn teɹz*   *Dry cry, even tears*
                       ivn maɪ haɪt kɹaɪz   *even my heart cries*

The other six lines also contain the same set of vowels [e], [aɪ] in the final syllable.[13] The artist provided information about his intended audience in an interview stating that it was targeted at women.

In examining the data by individual artists, Table 1 shows that out of every eight songs selected for each male artist, an average of 5 songs contain more back and low vowels while the other three songs contain more high-front and high-mid front vowels. Table 2 reveals that out of the four female artists in the study, three (Lady Saw, D'Angel and Cecile) have more songs targeting women, five out of eight, four out of eight and four out of eight respectively. Lady Saw uses more high- front and high-mid front vowels in the chorus of all the songs targeting women, and more back and low vowels in the one song she has targeting men. The other two women in the study have seven out of eight songs that target males, and one song targeting females. All the songs targeting males contain more low and back vowels; and those targeting women have more high front and high-mid front vowels. Tanya Stephens tends to target men more than she does women, unlike the other three females in the study.

The foregoing findings suggest that both men and women in the study use more low and back vowels, and more specifically when targeting men, and more high and high-mid front vowels when targeting females. Beenie Man's lyrics *Memories* and Lady Saw's *Men are the least of my problems* illustrate this, as shown in examples 2 and 3, respectively:

DJ BEENIE MAN

XAMPLE 2: | Mɛmɹiz dʋon lɪv laɪk pipl **du** | Memories don't leave like people
| Dɛ alwiez mɛmba **yu** | do They always remember you
| Wɛda tɪŋz ar gʋd ar **bad** | Whether things are good or bad
| ɪts jos dɪ memɹiiz dat wɪ av | Its just the memories that we have

The target here was actually an individual, Bounty Killer, Beenie Man's arch-rival in the dancehall for over 15 years. This song was recorded during the mid-1990s as a component of an ongoing clash/feud between the two artists. Here, Beenie Man uses syllables containing 46 high front and high-mid front vowels and 58 low and back vowels. All final syllables end with a low and back vowel. Example 3 below includes lyrics in which Lady Saw targets women:

DJ LADY SAW

EXAMPLE 3: | man a dɪ lis a mɪ pɹablɛmʋ | Men are the least of my problems
| sʌ mɪ lɛf ɪdjat fɪ salv dɛm | I leave it to idiots to solve them

Here she uses more syllables with high-mid front vowel [e] in all the lines of the chorus. Lady Saw informs (females) that men are the least of her problems and holds that only 'idiotic' women try and solve the problems associated with men.[14]

Another pattern discerned in analysis concerns sexuality as was observed that when male and female performers alike talk about homosexual males, they tend to use more of the high front and high-mid front vowels, than back and low vowels, most notably in the last syllable of each line. For example, this is found in Bounty Killa's and Buju Banton's *Can't Believe My Eyes* and *Bum Bai Bai* respectively, as well as in Ce'cile's *Woman Things* (see Tables 1 and 2). An excerpt from Bounty Killa's song is presented in Example 4 below:

EXAMPLE 4:	mɪ kjan bɪlɪv sʌm niem mɪ æ ier sɛ a mɛn	I can't believe some names I'm hearing are 'men' (gay)
	sɛ mɪ kjan bɪlɪv sɛ taɪt pants kʌm in ægɛn	I can't believe that tight pants are back in again
	mɪ kjan bɪlɪv sɛ gʌnman an batɪman an frɛn	I can't believe that gunmen and gaymen are friends
	mi kjan bɪliv mɪ jaɪ, mɪ kjan bɪliv mɪ jaɪ	I can't believe my eyes, I can't believe my eyes

As suggested by these lyrics, in dancehall culture, gay men are referred to negatively as 'men' or 'guy' and it is considered taboo to refer to a heterosexual man in dancehall or in the wider society as a 'guy' or 'men'. Dancehall artists like Bounty Killa and Buju Banton frequently express their shock about the growth of homosexual behavior in Jamaica, which is considered to be a homophobic society. The data indicate that the high – front and the high-mid front vowels are used by both male and female artists when addressing homosexuals. It could be argued that this is so because they are perceived by both male and female dancehall artists as being effeminate.

Analysis also suggests that, in collaborations involving men and women sharing a chorus, all the lines by women have more high-front and high-mid front vowels than low and back vowels; and all the lines by men have more low and back vowels than high-front and high-mid front vowels. This phenomenon can be seen in the song *Healing,* recorded by Beenie Man and Lady Saw a segment of which is outlined below in Example 5:

LADY SAW'S LINES

EXAMPLE 5:	mɪ man nʌf gjal a aːks mɪ wat jʌ dilɪ n	Beenie man, lots of girls are asking me what's the deal
	mɪ tɛl dɛm a av dɪ ilɪn	I tell them that you have the healing
	aɪ kant fagɛt oʊ ju mek mɪ stʃɹɛtʃ tʊ dɪ silɪn	I can't forget the way you make me stretch to the ceiling

BEENIE MAN'S LINES

	Lady Saw dʊon jʌ wʌɹɪ jʌsɛlf ka mɪ na tʃa:	Lady Saw, don't you worry yourself cause I won't chaw
	jʌ nʊo man a bad man man a oʊtlaː	You know I'm a bad man and an outlaw
	ju ar dɪ gɹʌl hu brat dɪ dʒɔɪ ɪn maɪ wɜɹl	You are the girl who brought the joy in my world

In this song Lady Saw tells Beenie Man that other ladies have been asking her about him and she relays her responses to their queries. Here, we see both genders using specific vowels influenced by the gender of the target audience. Not only do these vowels dominate the syllables in the overall lines for each, but they also dominate the final syllables of each line. Beenie Man utilizes a similar strategy in a 2010 song with his wife D'Angel, which was recorded two years after their bitter separation. This song suggested that their separation had ended and they were still very much in love with each other as outlined in Example 6:

D' ANGEL'S LINES OF THE CHORUS

EXAMPLE 6:	maɪ juːt jʊ æ mɪ fɛɹs mæn	My youth (slang for man) you are my first man
	gæd mɜk jʌ mɪ hʌsbæn	God made you my husband
	mɪ æ mɜk mɪ sʌdʒʒʃæn æn mɪ nʌ mætæ wɪʧ fuːl waːn ɹɪspæn	I am making my suggestion and I don't care which fool wants to respond

BEENIE MAN'S LINES OF THE CHORUS

	jʊ æ mɪ fɛɹs lɪedɪ	You are my first lady
	bɪkaːz jʊ æv mɪ bɪebɪ	Because you have my baby
	nʌ ɪf bʌt aɹ mɪebɪ	No if buts or maybes
	nɜvæ wæn bɪfʊo jʌ aɹ bɪfʊo mil	Never anyone before you or before me

The foregoing song reveals that D'Angel uses more back and low vowels in the lyrics she used to target Beenie Man, and these (vowels) are also evident in the final syllable in each line's final word. Beenie Man also does a similar thing, in that he uses the high front vowels in his lyrics to D'Angel.

The following outlines lyrics and Praat values for a song originally performed by Gyptian, with a cover version done by Lady Saw:

GYPTIAN

CHORUS 1	gjal mɪ glad sɛ mɪ ʊol jʌ	Girl I just want to hold you
	pʌt mɪ aɹmz ɹait aɹoun jʌ	Put my arms all around you
	gjal jʌ gɪv mɪ dɪ taɪtɛs ʊol mɪ ɛva gɛt ɪn a maɪ laɪf	Girl you give me the tightest hold (literally means 'hole' referring to vagina) I have ever gotten in my life
	gjal mɪ dʒʌs waːn fɪ skwiz jʌ	Girl I want to squeeze you
	pʊt mɪ tɪŋ aːl aɹoun jʌ	Put my thing right around you
	gjal jʌ gɪv mi dɪ taɪtɛs ʊol mɪ ɛva gɛt ɪn a maɪ laɪf	Girl you give me the tightest hold I have ever gotten in my life

Analysis of the foregoing shows that Chorus 1 contains 27 back vowels and 31 high front vowels with final syllables containing 4 back vowels and 2 high front vowels.

LADY SAW'S COVER OF GYPTIAN'S SONG

HORUS 1	bwaɪ mɪ glad sɛ mɪ ʋol jʌ	Boy I'm glad that I hold you
	juz dɪ pʊsɪ kanʧʋol jʌ	Use my pussy to control you
	bwaɪ jʌ gɪv mi dɪ bɪgɛs wʋd mɪ ɛva gɛt ɪn a maɪ laɪf	Boy you give me the biggest wood (penis) I have ever gotten in my life
	bwaɪ mɪ nɛva bɪliv jʌ	Boy I never believed you
	wɛn jʌ tɛl mɪ sɛ mɪ wʋda nid jʌ	When you told me that I would have needed you
	bwaɪ jʌ gɪv mi dɪ bɪgɛs wʋd mɪ ɛva gɛt ɪn a maɪ laɪf	Boy you give me the biggest wood I have ever gotten in my life

Analysis of the foregoing shows that the Chorus 1 contains 22 back vowels and 40 high front vowels and the final syllables of Chorus1 contains 4 back Vowels and 2 High front vowels.

Overall, analysis of the foregoing shows that lady Saw uses more high front vowels in the song's chorus than Gyptian does and less back vowels, while he does the opposite - using more back vowels and less high front vowels.

PRAAT VALUES FOR GYPTIAN'S HIGH BACK VOWELS IN THE CHORUS

CHORUS LINES	VOWEL TYPE	F1 VALUES	F 2 VALUES	MEAN
LINE 1	/ʊ/	666.528 Hertz [15]	1478.456 Hertz	1072.492 Hertz
LINE 2	/ʊ/	784.194 Hertz	1759.485 Hertz	1271.8395 Hertz

CHORUS LINES	VOWEL TYPE	F1 VALUES	F 2 VALUES	MEAN
LINE 4	/ʊ/	833.100 Hertz	1678.221 Hertz	1255. 6605 Hertz
LINE 5	/ʊ/	771.764 Hertz	1783.366 Hertz	1277.565 Hertz
TOTAL		3055.586 Hertz	6699.528 Hertz	4877.557 Hertz

PRAAT VALUES FOR GYPTIAN'S HIGH FRONT VOWELS IN THE CHORUS

CHORUS LINES	VOWEL TYPE	F1 VALUES	F2 VALUES	MEAN
LINE 3	/aɪ/	856.872	1798.621 Hertz	1327. 7465 Hertz
LINE 6	/aɪ/	506.505	1628.27 Hertz	1067.3875 Hertz
TOTAL		1363.377 Hertz	3426.891 Hertz	2395.134 Hertz

PRAAT VALUES FOR LADY SAW'S HIGH BACK VOWELS IN THE CHORUS

CHORUS LINES	VOWEL TYPE	F1 VALUES	F2 VALUES	MEAN
LINE1	/ʊ/	494.730 Hertz	1183. 642 Hertz	839.186 Hertz
LINE 2	/ʊ/	662. 234 Hertz	2396.693 Hertz	1529.4635 Hertz
LINE 4	/ʊ/	571. 687 Hertz	1636.244 Hertz	1103.9655 Hertz
LINE 5	/ʊ/	407. 302 Hertz	1676.083 Hertz	1041.6925 Hertz
TOTAL		2135.953 Hertz	3446.331 Hertz	2791.142 Hertz

PRAAT VALUES FOR LADY SAW'S HIGH FRONT VOWELS IN THE CHORUS

CHORUS LINES	VOWEL TYPE	F1 VALUES	F2 VALUES	MEAN
LINE 3	/aɪ/	600. 202 Hertz	2182. 810 Hertz	1391.506 Hertz
LINE 6	/aɪ/	1039.934 Hertz	2043.558 Hertz	1541.746 Hertz
TOTAL		1640.136 Hertz	4225.368 Hertz	2932.752 Hertz

Based on the foregoing Praat analysis, the back vowels for Gyptian's F1 and F2 values are higher than Lady Saw's high back vowels, which signifies his back vowels are more back than hers, While his front vowel values for F1 and F2 are much lower than hers, which also proves that Lady Saw's front vowels are more front than his. This shows consistency with previous works by linguists Gordon and Heat (1998) who state that women tend to produce front vowels more front than men, and men lead in the backing and rounding of vowels, Milroy and Milroy (1985).

DISCUSSION AND CONCLUSION

The analysis consistently indicates that male and female dancehall artists use more low and back vowels in the choruses of their songs when specifically targeting men, and more high front and high-mid front vowels when targeting women. However, male artists have more songs with back vowels when compared to those of women in the study, and women have more songs with high front and high mid front vowels than men. This observation is supported by literature in which previous research completed in other settings find that men and women have a preference for particular vowels, high front, and low and back, respectively (Gordon and Heath 1998; Milroy and Milroy 1985; Chambers and Hardwich, 1986). Although women have more songs with high front vowels than men in the study, that target women, this portion of data is relatively small (14/32). It can be compared with the amount of songs that they demonstrate with low and back vowels (16/32), targeting men and the remaining two songs targeting a general audience. This however reveals that women target more men than they do women.

It can be argued by some that this usage of more of a particular vowel could be as a result of the rhyming scheme of the song, but the data do suggest that both male and female artists choose more rhymes with low and back vowels when targeting men and more high front and high -mid front vowels in their rhyming scheme when targeting women. If a speech feature is used more frequently by one group rather than another group, or in one speaking situation than another, it is common practice to claim that the feature has group salient or situation- salient meaning (Coupland 2007:93). According to Eckert and McConnell–Ginet (1992:469) 'variables that women use more than men through-out the different strata of a community signal female identity in that community and men who rarely use those variables thereby signal their male identity'. For example, if men use a lot of the [n] as opposed to [ ] of the (ing) variable, it seems reasonable, according to this convention to say that [n] marks maleness, or (even more contentiously); male identity' (Coupland 2007:93). Thus, in the current study it could be said that males use more back vowels and this could be a feature associated with male linguistic style, specifically within the genre of dancehall music. However, this does not account for the female artistes in dancehall.

In trying to explain the linguistic behaviour of female artists, with almost 53 per cent of their songs targeting men, it can be argued that women are more likely to pattern the linguistic norms of men because of the status of men in the industry. If women's language is considered weak (Lakoff 1975) and inferior to that of men (Coates 1998), then arguably, women will be more than likely to adopt the more powerful and presti-gious form of a language, since they are focussed on acquiring symbolic capital. The female artists' style of shifting towards the 'male' preferred vowels are significantly more represented, than are examples of male artists' willingness to shift towards 'female'-preferred vowels. Here, Gordon and Heath (1998) state that 'while 'male' adoption of 'female' pronunciation tends to be too infrequent and contextually specialized to show up in statistical sociolinguistic data, the 'female' adoption of 'male' pronunciation is more systematic' (p.426). Indeed, Eckert and Mc Connell-Ginet (2003) state that 'women's speech is lacking in authority and more tentative than men's' while, Winkler (2009) notes that men borrow discourse markers less frequently than women, (i.e. 22 per cent vs. 49 per cent). This could be explained by the concept of dominance, which relates to the fact that there are significantly more men in dancehall music than women; and since it has been argued that men dominate talk in public spaces (Herring 1992) this could mean that male phonological features may also be more dominant (in this case back and low vowels) and perceived as more prestigious. Additionally, Dawkins (2009) reveals that men are producers of songs, the studio engineers recording the songs, the owners of rhythms, the promoters of popular dancehall concerts and the DJ's on the radio who select songs for air play, and most of these songs are by men targeted at men. It is, therefore, not surprising that men appear to also dominate the linguistic norms of this industry.

It is arguable that men have what Milroy and Milroy (1992) refer to as a close knit network, which has the capacity to reinforce linguistic norms. Also pertinent to this analysis is that men have been known to form formal alliances within the dancehall industry. For example, there is the 'Alliance' which consists of only male artists, such as Bounty Killa, Busy Signal, and Mavado. These and other men in other dancehall groups work together and support one another in direct ways, such as influencing each other as well as others, performing at the same concerts, and sometimes penning lyrics for each other. It is common for a community or a close knit network group of speakers to have the same or similar linguistic norms and patterns, and thus it can be hypothesized that this phenomenon appears to reinforce a particular linguistic norm, such as vowel usage. To date, there are no known, similar female groups or alliances in dancehall.

Additionally, where the issue of dominance is concerned, Coates (1998) also argues that women are at greater pains to prove that they belong in certain prestigious occupations, so they use language as a means to success, generally the standard variety, because they are talking for success. In a relared vein, Patrick (1989), states that women's place in society makes them more vulnerable to criticism, therefore they use more of the standard variety of language as this can be seen as a way of being 'beyond reproach.' Jamaican Creole is the 'prestigious language' of the dancehall industry, and the occupation as an artiste is also deemed prestigious, since it comes with fame and financial benefits. Therefore, the observation that women within this industry not only use the vernacular language, but appear to adopt the more prestigious phonological norms of the dominant forces within the industry, those being men, is consistent with the literature. Trudgill (1974), posits that marginalization in the local market will lead to women producing more of the non-standard variety or the vernacular. Coates (1998), states that 'we also know that in all known societies it is the way men speak that is held in high esteem, while women's ways of talking are compared unfavorably with men's' (p.2).

Accommodation theory can also be used to offer an explanation of female linguistic behaviour in dancehall music. The women in dance-hall music are aware that men are the rulers of the industry, therefore, women will accommodate the norms of the industry which is male dominated and will be more likely to converge rather than diverge to male linguistic norms (such as vowel use) that seem to attract the audience. For example, in an interview on Television Jamaica's popular entertainment program, 'Entertainment Report,' reggae/dancehall artist Queen Ifrica told the host that a promoter will more than likely book 'a Movado (a popular male dancehall artist) for a show than a Queen Ifrica, because the audience will prefer to hear a Movado over a Queen Ifrica, because of what he is saying and how he says it.' She also stated that male artists are paid more than women.

It has also been observed that female artistes like Queen Ifrica and Tanya Stephens demonstrate a number of common linguistic features in that they use more back than high-front and high-mid front vowels within their songs, are more aggressive on rhythm sound tracks than other females artists within the dancehall industry, and do, in fact, generally target more men than women. These female performers are praised for this approach to music and performance and seemingly garner a little more respect than the average woman within the industry because they do not sing like the 'typical' high- pitched female (Queen Ifrica sings with a husky male-like voice). Here, dancehall stands out as a culture of 'roughnecks,' oozing masculinity and machismo (See Hope 2010). Contrary to popular belief, I argue that women are not expected to be polite in terms of the language they use in dancehall as the industry is rough, the shows are rough, therefore the artists are expected to look and sound rough.

On her album *Gangsta Blues* Tanya Stephens states that for a woman to be considered half as good as a man in this industry she has to work twice as hard, and points out that she herself has worked a hundred times harder and states explicitly that she does not want to be compared to any other female within the dancehall industry. In an interview in Belgium Stephens stated that when she goes onto the stage, she goes on as one of the guys, 'I really don't think about being female at all when I work.... So I just go on as one of the guys, I'm just working' (Tanya Stephens, Rotterdam Reggae Festival 2011). Her album *Gangsta Blues* was very successful, yet Stephens complained publicly that she was not being paid enough for concerts, charging that men who did not have a hit album at that time were being paid more for the same shows that she did. Junior 'Heavy D' Fraser, one of the leading promoters of the annual dancehall stage show *Sting* (arguably the greatest one night dancehall/reggae show on the globe) confirmed quite passionately in an interview that a woman can never get more money than a male artist. Fraser stated that he will never pay a female more money than a male, even if she has the 'hottest' tract out because, 'ʊman kjɑn dʒɹɑ dɪ kɹoʊd wɛ man dʒɹɑ' *(women can't attract the crowd men attract)* at an event. Gender-biased attitudes such as these and the social and economic dynamics associated with them further reinforce male dominance, not just in terms of the presence of men in the business but also in terms of the choice of target audiences.

Finally, as it relates to a community of practice, it could be that low and back vowels are the linguistic norm for the dancehall community of practice and by that I mean the artists who record dancehall songs. This may be so because it stems from a culture of machismo, masculinity and toughness, and back vowels are usually associated with a culture of toughness as seen earlier on in the literature (Habick 1991; Eckert 1989, Peirrehumbert et al 2004). Therefore, participants will demonstrate the linguistic norms of this particular community and in doing so continue the linguistic norms of this community of practice. This goes back identity theory, in which participants who join this community are trying to identify with this particular community, and thus conform to this particular community's identity. Since the dancehall community is male dominated, women who become a part of this community will use the language associated with it, or accommodate by identifying with this community's linguistic identity, because this is the prestige language variety of the community and they want to establish an identity with the prestigious form. Here, Boves (1992) states that the imitation of the speech of the powerful, those having some form of status, is done by others in order to adopt some of their social esteem. Kloeke (1927) considers this type of social process as the essential/main source of language change where 'In any group, some persons receive more imitation than others, they are the leaders in power and prestige. The humble person is not imitated; the lord or the leader is a model to most of those who hear him' (Bloomfield 1933:476). In this same regard, Eckert and McConell-Ginet (1992) states that gender is constructed in a complex array of social practices within communities, practices that in many cases connect to personal attributes and to power relations.

In the final analysis, relevant sociolinguistic literature suggests that men show a preference for back and low vowels, while women show a preference for high front vowels. In the performance of Jamaican dancehall lyrics, however, vowel choice appears to be influenced more by the target audience and in some respect the particular community of practice than the biological sex of a particular singer. In short, both male and female dancehall artists tend to use more low and back vowels in the final syllables of choruses of their songs when they are targeting a male audience, and more high front and high mid- front vowels when targeting a female audience. This work also suggests that gendered patterns in targeting can be discerned in Jamaican dancehall where both male and female dancehall artists tend to target more men than they do women. This trend might be expected of male artists who demonstrate 'normal' masculine behaviors and associations especially within this particular community of practice, but it is also significant in the cases of female artists. It suggests that the tendency for female artists to target the opposite gender is linked to the male dominance in the music industry in Jamaica.

REFERENCES

Baldwin, J. R. & Michael L. Hetch. 'The Layered Perspective on Cultural (In)tolerance(s): The Roots of a Multi-disciplinary Approach to (In) tolerance'. In R.L. Wisemanm(ed.) *Intercultural Communication Theory*, Thousand Oaks, California: Sage, 1995, pp. 59-91.

Bell, Allan. 'Language style as audience design' in *Language in Society*, 13, 1994, pp. 145-204.

_____. 'Styling the other to define the self: A study in New Zealand Identity-Making', in *Journal of Sociolinguistics*, Vol. 3, 4, 1999, pp 523-541.

_____. 'Back in style: Reworking audience design'. In Penelope Eckert and John R. Rickford (eds.) *Style and Sociolinguistics Variation*. Cambridge and New York: Cambridge University Press, 2001, pp.139-169.

Besnier, Niko. 'Literacy and the Notion of Person on Nukulaelae Atoll' in *American Anthropologist*, 93, 1991, pp. 570-587.

_____. *Literacy, Emotion and Authority: Reading and Writing on a Polynesian Atoll*. Cambridge: Cambridge University Press, 1995.

Best Lyrics. 22nd March 2008. Retrieved from http://www.allthelyric. com/lyics/variousartistehtml.

Borden, G., & Harris, P. *Speech Science Primer:2nd edition*. Baltimore: Williams and Wilkins, 1984.

Boves, T.L. *Speech Accommodation Theory In Co-operative and Competitive Conversations*. Nederlands: Trefw, 1992.

Bloomfiled, L. *Language*. London: Unwin, 1993.

Chambers, J. K. & M.F. Hardwick. 'Comparative Sociolinguistics of Sound Change in

Canadian English' in *English World-Wide*, Vol, 7,1, 1986, pp. 21-46.

Coates, Jennifer. *Language and Gender: A Reader*. UK: Blackwell , 1998.

Collins, Miguel. Personal Interview. 31st Mar. 2008

Cooper, Carolyn. *Noises in the Blood: Orality, Gender and the 'Vulgar' Body of Jamaican Popular Culture*. Durham: Duke University Press, 1993.

_____. *Sound Clash: Jamaican Dancehall Culture at Large*. New York: Palgrave McMillan, 2004.

Coupland, Nikolas. *Style: Language Variation and Identity*. New York: Cambridge University Press, 2007.

Dawkins, Nickesha. 'Gender-based Vowel Use in Jamaican Dancehall Lyrics'. In *Sargasso*, I, 2009, pp. 95-114.

Deuchar, Margaret. 'A pragmatic Account of Women's Use of Standard Speech' in J. Coates and D. Cameron (eds) *Women in their Speech Communities* pp. 27-32. London and New York: Longman, 1989.

Devonish, Hubert. *Electronic Orature: The Deejays*. BAmsterdam, The Netherlands: John Benjamins Publishing Company, 1998.

_____.'On the status of dipthongs in Jamaican: Mr. Vegas pronounces' in Simmons-McDonald, Hazel and Robertson, Ian (eds.) *Exploring the Boundaries of Caribbean Creole Languages*. Kingston: University of the West Indies Press, 2006, pp. 73-95.

Eckert, Penelope. *Jocks and Burnouts: Social Categories and Identity in the High School*. New York: Teachers College Press, 1989,

_____. *Linguistic Variation as Social Practice*. Maldon, Massachusetts and Oxford: Blackwell Publishers, 2000.

Eckert, Penelope and Sally McConnel-Ginet. 'Putting Communities of Practice in their Place' in *Gender and Language*,1.1, 2006, pp 27-38.

Farquharson, J.T. 'Faiya-bon: The socio-pragmatics of homophobia in Jamaican (dancehall) Culture' In S. Mühleisen and B. Migge. (Eds.),

Politeness and Face in Caribbean Creoles. Amsterdam, The Netherlands: John Benjamins Publishing Company, 2005, pp. 101-118.

Fraser, Junior. Personal Interview, February 26, 2009.

Giles, H., Mulac, A., Bradac, J.J., & Johnson, P. 'Speech Accommodation Theory: The first Decade and beyond'. In M.L. Mc. Laughlin (Ed.), *Communication Yearbook 10*. Beverly Hills: Sage, 1987.

Giles, H., & Powesland, P. *Speech Style and Social Evolution*. Cambridge: Cambridge University Press, 1975.

Gordon, Matthew & Heath, Jeffrey. 'Sex, Sound, Symbolism, and Sociolinguistics.' In *Current Anthropology,*39, 4, 1998, pp. 421-449.

Habick, T. 'Burnouts versus rednecks: effects of group membership on phonemic systems,' in *New Ways of Analyzing Sound Change*, (ed) P. Eckert. San Diego: Academic Press, 1991.

Herring, S. C. Sex of LINGUISTs: Results of survey in *LINGUIST List Vol. 4.517*, June 30, 1993. http://www.linguistlist.org/issues/4/4-517.html - 1

Higgins, E.T. The 'Communication Game: Implications for social cognition and persuasion'. In E.T. Higgins, C.P. Herman, & M.P. Zanna (Eds.) *Social Cognition: The Ontario Symposium* (Vol.1) Hilsdale: Erlbaum, 1982.

Hindle, D. M. *The Social and situational condition of phonetic variation*. Ph.D. dissertation, University of Pennsylvania, Philadelphia, 1979.

Hope, Donna P. *Man Vibes: Masculinities in the Jamaican Dancehall*. Kingston: Ian Randle Publishers, 2010.

_____. *Inna Di Dancehall: Popular Culture and the Politics of Identity in Jamaica*. Kingston: University of the West Indies Press, 2006.

Irvine, Allison. 'A Good Command of the English Language: Phonological variation in Jamaican Acrolect' in *Journal of Pidgin and Creole Languages*, Vol. 19, 1, 2004, pp. 41-76.

Jones, Deborah. 'Gender trouble in the workplace: 'Language and gender' meets 'feminist organizational communication.' In Janet Holmes (ed.).

Gendered speech in social context: Perspective from gown and town. Wellington: Victoria University Press, 2000, pp. 192 – 210.

Joseph, John. *Language and Identity: National, Ethnic and Religious.* New York: Palgrave McMillan, 2004.

Kloeke, G.G. *De Hollandsche expansie in de zestiende en zeventiende eeuw en haar Weerspiegeling in de hedendaagsche Nedelandche dialecten.* Gravenhage: Nijhoff, 1927.

Labov, William. *The Social Stratification of English in New York City.* Washington DC: Center For Applied Linguistics, 1966.

_____. 'The intersection of sex and social class in the course of linguistic change', in *Language Variation and Change,*Vol, 1, 1990, pp. 205 – 254.

_____. 'The unobservability of structure and its linguistic consequences'. Plenary address, New Ways of Analyzing Variation (NWAVE) 22, University of Ottawa, 1993.

Lakoff, R. *Language and Woman's Place.* New York: Harper & Row, 1975.

Le Page, R., & Tabouret-Keller. A. *Acts of Identity: Creole-based approaches to language and Ethnicity.* New York: Cambridge University Press, 1985.

Milroy, James and Milroy. 'Social Network and Social Class: Towards an Integrated Sociolinguistic Model', In *Language in Society,* Vol. 21, 1, 1992, pp.1-26.

_____. 'Linguistic change, social network, and speaker innovation' in *Journal of Linguistics* 21, 1985, pp. 339-384.

Pierrehumbert, J., Benjamin, T., Bradlow, B., Munson. T, and Bailey, J. 'The Influence of Sexual Orientation on Vowels Production' *Acoustical Society of America,* Vol. 43,70, 2004, pp. 1905-1908.

Popular lyrics. 22 March 2008 - http://www.lyricsandsongs.com/lyricslady-sawhtlml.

Romaine, Suzanne. *An Introduction to Sociolinguistics*. New York: Oxford University Press, 1994.

Schilling-Estes, Natalie et al. *The Handbook of Language Variation and Change*. USA: Blackwell, 2002.

_____. 'Investigating 'self-conscious' speech: The performance register in Ocracoke English' in *Language in Society*, Vol. 21, 1998 pp. 53-83.

Stephens, Tanya. Video Interview, April 24, 2011 - http://www.youtube.com/watch?v=8EDUHk4LoqM

Street, R.L., & Giles, H. 'Speech Accommodation Theory. A social cognitive approach to Language and speech behavior'. In M.E. Roloff & C.R. Berger (Eds.) *Social Cognition and Communication*. Beverly Hills: Sage Publications, 1993.

Trugill, P. 'Sex, covert prestige and linguistics change in the urban British English of Norwich' in *Language in Society* 1, 1972, pp. 179-195.

Trudgill, Peter. *Sociolinguistics: An Introduction*. Harmendsworth: Penguin, 1974.

_____. *On dialect*. Oxford: Blackwell, 1983.

Winkler, Elizabeth. (2009). 'A Gender-based Analysis of Discourse Markers in Limonese Creole' in *Sargasso* I, 2009, pp. 53-72.

NOTES

1. In this paper, the term sex will be used to refer to categories that are overtly biological, while gender is used for those that are generally said to be more social in nature.

2. Phonetics is a branch of linguistics that studies the physical property of speech sounds. Phonology, on the other hand, is concerned with factors rooted in language as a system, that is, phonology is the study of the sound system of a language (the distribution of sounds in a language).

3. This is represented thus in the Cassidy LePage Writing System (a system used to represent Jamaican Creole):

(Buju Bantan's 'How Maasa God Worl a Run)

	Chorus in Jamaican Creole (Mesolectal variety)	Translation in English
EXAMPLE 1:	*Soma`di pliiz tel mi nou ou` maasa gaa`d worl a ro`n*	*Somebody please tell me now, what is going in God's world*
	Pu`t di waar a ba`k an priez Gad ya mi so`n	*Put the war behind and praise God my son*
	Tel mi nou` ou` pupa Jiizo`s worl a ro`n	*Tell me now, What is going on in the Lord Jesus' world*
	Mek wi ko`m tugeda` kaa di faa`da suun ko`m	*Let us come together because the father will be coming soon*

(Devonish 1998, 46)

4.   Explaining front and back vowels for the non-linguist

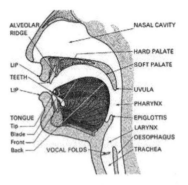

Front vowels are pronounced in the front of the mouth with the front part of the tongue or the tongue tip, using the front muscles of the tongue. The tongue is arched high in the mouth and moves up toward the teeth ridge otherwise known as the alveolar ridge. Examples of words containing high front unrounded (unrounded means that during production of these vowels the lips are spread apart) vowel sounds are 'sweet' and 'pick'. Examples of words containing High mid front vowel sounds are 'face' and 'peck'. The tongue lowers slightly during the production of each front vowel. The tip of the tongue remains low and behind the lower front teeth for each front vowel. Low vowels are produced with the back of the tongue placed low in the oral cavity (mouth) and high back vowels are produced with the back of the tongue placed further back in the mouth. High back rounded (rounding means that the lips are pursed or rounded during the production of these vowels) vowels sounds are represented in the following words 'cool' and 'book'. An Example of the high mid back vowel sound in a word is 'go'. Examples of the low mid back vowels are 'caught' and 'love'. Examples of low vowels sounds in words are 'ball', 'hat' and 'got'. The International Phonetic Alphabet represents the following vowels in the above words as:High front unrounded tense vowel [i] > [swit] 'sweet'; high front unrounded lax vowel[ɪ] > [pɪk]'pick'. High mid front unrounded vowel [e] > [fes] 'face'; low mid front unrounded vowel [ɛ]>[pɛk]'peck'; high back rounded tense vowel [u] > [kul]'cool', high back rounded lax vowel [ʊ] > [bʊk] 'book'; high mid back rounded vowel [o] > [go]'go', low mid back rounded vowel [ɔ] > [kɔt] 'caught'; low mid back unrounded vowel [ʌ] > [lʌv]; low back unrounded vowel [ɑ] > [bɑl]'ball', low front unrounded vowel [a] > [hat]'hat', low back rounded vowel [ɒ] > [gɒt] 'got'.

5. Stress is the relative emphasis that is be given to certain syllables in a word, or to certain words in a phrase or sentence. It is a property of syllables and not individual phonetic segments.

6. A diphthong is the production or pronunciation of two vowel sounds in one syllable or two tones. The diphthong is also called a gliding vowel, this refers to two adjacent vowel sounds occurring within the same syllable. Technically, a diphthong is a vowel with two different targets: That is, the tongue moves during the pronunciation of the vowel. In most varieties of English, the words *hide* [haɪd], *beer* [bɪəɹ] *how* [haʊ], *boy* [bɔɪ] and *cow* [kaʊ] contain diphthongs. Diphthongs contrast with monophthongs which are single vowel sounds in syllables. Examples of some English monophthongs are *bad* [bad], *bed* [bɛd], *pin* [pɪn], *steel* [stil], *shape* [ʃep], etc.

7. Monophthongization is the process of becoming a monophthong, this process usually occurs with diphthongs and triphthongs.

8. Interlocutors are persons who take part in a conversation.

9. These songs were obtained from VP records from their Simply the Best and Reggae Gold album charts stemming from the period 1990 – 2006 and builds on the data from Dawkins (2009).

10. This is a useful representation of the uneven distribution of men and women on the reggae dancehall charts and in the dancehall music industry itself.

11. The International Phonetic Alphabet (IPA) is an alphabetic system of phonetic transcription / notation based primarily on the Latin alphabet. It was designed by the International Phonetic Association as a standardized representation of the sounds of oral language. The IPA is used by linguists, lexicographers, foreign language students and teachers, Speech-Language Pathologists, singers, actors, constructed language creators, and translators. The IPA is designed to represent only those qualities of speech that are distinctive in oral language: it has only 1 symbol to represent a specific sound in

any oral language; it eliminates silent letters and double letters in words such as 'palm' [p m] and 'little' [l tl] respectively.

12. Information about the target audiences was obtained directly from artist where possible; and in other Instances, was determined through textual analysis and careful interpretation of the song's chorus. Popular dancehall and reggae artist Miguel Collins, (stage name Sizzla Kalonji), and dancehall promoter Junior 'Heavy D' Fraser both provided information about the target audiences in question.

13. When this song was released, it was rumored that the mother of Sizzla's child (his babymothr) had ended their relationship and that, in response, he wrote, recorded and released the song. In the second verse of the song Sizzla states, 'Margo I love you so, I really hate to see you go.' 'Margo' is the actual name of his child's mother.

14. In her song *Belly Rob a Dub*, which targets men directly (see Table 2), she uses more of the close mid back vowel [o] than high-front or high-mid front vowels.

15. Hertz (abbreviated: Hz) is the standard unit of measurement used for measuring frequency, for example, sound frequency. Since frequency is measured in cycles per second, one hertz equals one cycle per second. Hertz is most commonly used to measure wave frequencies, such as sound waves, light waves, and radio waves. The average human ear can detect sound waves between 20 and 20,000 Hz. Sound waves close to 20 Hz have a low pitch and are called 'bass' frequencies. Sound waves above 5,000 Hz have a high pitch and are called 'treble' frequencies.

PART 3
MUSICAL
CONVERSATIONS

6 RHYTHM, RHYME AND REMIXING

DAVID KATZ IN CONVERSATION WITH SLY DUNBAR

INTRODUCTION

In this session, I shall be embarking on a dialogue with one of the most exceptional figures of Jamaican popular music, a true pioneer whose stylistic innovations have been crucial determinants in the music's evolution, and whose work has gone on to influence many other forms of popular music around the world. As we shall see, his developments often involved a reinterpretation of overseas styles through a transformative process of Jamaicanisation, matched by his own creative ingenuity, the resultant innovations later filtering through to other prominent forms of popular music on the other side of the Atlantic. To better illustrate the proceedings, we shall play some musical extracts to make plain what we are referring to.

There are a few other thoughts I would like you to keep in mind during this session: throughout the course of this conference, we have heard countless examples of the ways in which reggae music has made a significant international impact during the last few decades. In an era of increasing globalization, we are now at the point where some form of reggae is being made on virtually every continent, and the conference speakers here have brought home the realities of Jamaican music's influence, as heard through their direct testimonies of reggae's global importance, not only through explorations of the reggae and dancehall scenes that exists right here in its Jamaican homeland and throughout the broader Caribbean region, but also by providing fascinating insights into the reggae scenes of Latin America, Asia, the South Pacific islands, and perhaps most importantly, the continent of Africa, which is not only the point from which most Jamaican directly trace their lineage, but is indeed the very cradle of Mankind itself.

Reggae music is now made and played everywhere, from Accra to Amsterdam and Beijing to Bombay, from Sao Paulo to St. Petersburg, and from Tallahassee to Timbuktu. And as the dancehall style is a growing force on every Caribbean island and large swathes of Central and South America, Jamaican music is clearly one of the most influential forms of popular music on the planet. Yet reggae is still somehow viewed as a specialist form of outsider music, labeled with a symbolic stigma that renders it supposedly less worthy than the more recognized forms of American music, such as rap, jazz, or even heavy metal. About eight years ago, when I was putting together my book *Solid Foundation: an Oral History of Reggae*, I interviewed Winston 'Pipe' Matthews of the esteemed Trench Town harmony group, the Wailing Souls, and at that time, Pipe described reggae as a 'rebel underground music,' which he saw as both positive and negative: positive in the sense that it is good to rebel against an unjust, racist and unequal system that perpetually penalizes the oppressed, but negative in the sense that the music is not being given its due recognition or exposure, despite being, in his words, 'just important as any other music, and maybe even more so'. The situation remains sadly the same nearly one decade later; which is why the scholarship here at UWI is so important, and I would like to salute the ongoing reggae research that is taking place here, as well as to salute each presenter at this conference for helping to illuminate some of the complexities that are inherent in reggae's creation, dissemination and consumption, as well as for raising broader issues about the relationship between Jamaican culture and overseas culture.

Before moving on to the heart of the matter of what we shall celebrate in this special session with our very special guest, I wish to remind you that we live in strange and paradoxical times. Thirty years ago, Earl Sixteen sang of a 'Changing World,' and over twenty years ago, Admiral Tibet warned of 'Serious Times,' and in the present, the times are that much more cantankerous and dangerous, this being an era where the past wrongs of colonialism have been replaced largely by forms of neo-colonialism and cultural imperialism, and when advances in new technology mean that it is potentially easier for all of us to access music and to be connected to beings on the other side of the Atlantic, yet at the same time, we feel less connected to the actual communities in which we live, and the music industry as we knew it has virtually collapsed, meaning that music is much more readily available, yet music sales have almost completely dried up. And this is a highly problematic situation for the performers and producers of the music, to say the least. To borrow a phrase from a record that the ace producer Niney the Observer once recorded with the Morwells harmony group, it is safe to say that 'everything mix up,' since so much reggae is made and consumed by Europeans, and by others located outside of Jamaica, some of whom even wear dreadlocks, perform in Jamaican language instead of Standard English, and even purport to be followers of Rastafari; such developments can be seen as positive or negative, or perhaps both at the same time, depending on one's point of view.

In pondering on such contradictory questions, we are fortunate to have one of reggae's wise sages in our midst. As I am sure all of you are already aware, Sly Dunbar has been at the forefront of significant changes in Jamaican popular music during the last forty years or so. He has brought about many stylistic shifts, has been the driving engine behind countless hits, and has an astounding array of recordings under his belt. He has not only been one of the most outstanding musicians of the 1970s and 80s, but has also been the key element in a production team that is probably responsible for more hits in Jamaican music than anyone else. With his partner, bassist Robbie Shakespeare, Sly has been one of the first to help bring reggae to the attention of the outside world, and their intense and wide ranging collaborations with musicians active in other genres has brought reggae music greater renown all over the planet. He has also been one of the driving forces in dancehall production in the last two decades or so, innovating with computerized drum forms, despite being widely recognized as one of the greatest drummers of all time. We are thus extremely fortunate to benefit from his first-hand testimony to guide us through the many changes he has helped bring to bear on Jamaican popular music, as well as to comment on its changing relations with the musical cultures of the rest of the world.

CONVERSATION

DAVID KATZ: *I would like to begin this session by asking, in your early days of growing up, what kind of music where you exposed to?*

SLY DUNBAR: I would listen to a lot of Motown, a lot of Beatles recordings, a lot of Skatelites, and a lot of mento.

Where were you exposed to the foreign music, like Motown and the Beatles?

My mother had a Rediffusion,[1] I don't know if a lot of people know [of] that. It was locked on RJR, and I was sitting on top of the Rediffusion and listening to all the music when I come home from school.

Where were you exposed to mento? You were living in Kingston, but mento is more associated with the countryside?

We used to go down to Victoria Pier, and there was a guy down there by the name of Count Owen,[2] and we used to stop and listen to him sing, and we used to listen to [mento on] the radio.

Can you tell the people a bit about where you were growing up? Are you a Kingston native?

I was born on Windward Road, and then I move to Waterhouse, and I was kind of in love with music; I attended Trench Town High School and when we get free period at school, a group of us would be in the back, singing all these songs...I realized that I wanted to do music, so I told my mom I don't feel like going to KC [Kingston College]; I was suppose to go to KC, but I wanted to do music, and she said, 'OK,' just like that, so I didn't go to KC. [Bassist and vocalist] Lloyd Parks[3] was at the studio one time, and he come by my house with a big tape recorder; he would come every day and I would play on some pans, like the drums, and he would listen to what we were doing. And then I got introduced to Ranchie McLean[4] – he was a guitar player, but he met in an accident, and he made me start playing guitar, because there was no guitarist. Then I got introduced to a band called the Yardbrooms; Mikey Boo,[5] one of the best drummers in Jamaica, was playing [in the band] at the time, and then Mikey left, and I was playing; we did out first show at Tinson Pen. A little after that, I went to check Ranchie McLean; I was playing in a group called the RHT Invincibles, and the drummer there was a great drummer by the name of Tin Legs,[6] but he had to go somewhere, so [keyboardist] Ansel Collins[7] said to me, 'Play,' and I was playing, and he said, 'I like how you play.' The next week, Ansel called a session and [asked] if I want to come and play, and I said, 'Yeah.' So I went to the studio, and the first time I played; I was fifteen years old, and it was 'Night Doctor.'[8]

Had you shown musical aptitude at this point? When did you become aware that you had a talent for rhythm, and how did other people become aware of it?

I think Ansel Collins was the one who started me. I was like his little key person; anywhere he's going, he would call me and say, 'Come with me.' I was like his sidekick. I remember the next song I was going to play for him was called 'Double Barrel.'[9] When I was like sixteen years old, he called me and said, 'Come and listen to this piano part,' and I said, 'Wow, wicked!' And I said to him, [simulates drum rhythm and bass line], then he said, 'Oh, that's wicked!' So we went to rehearsal at RHT Invincibles, Father Gooden's place. Then we started to put it together, myself and him; we rehearsed that song for like a week and we got all the parts [together] for everybody, so we booked some time by Dynamics studio, and we recorded the song. But when we recorded the song that night, the bus had stopped running; him say we have to walk home, so I said to him, 'It's a million seller,' and they laughed at me and said, 'You're joking, this is not going to sell.' In 1970 I was at home, and I heard *Solid Gold*,[10] and ['Double Barrel'] was number one in England, and it went to number twenty-two on the Authentic chart in *Billboard* magazine. So that was my second song, at sixteen years old, and form there on, I just started playing, and take it serious and go for it.

Those tunes already have a very distinctive style of drumming, but you are saying they are the first two recordings you made, and you were still in your early teens?

Yeah, the first two. I always listen to a lot of the Jamaican drummers, people like Mikey Boo, Winston Grennan,[11] Lloyd Knibb,[12] Joe Isaacs,[13] Fil [Callender][14] from Studio One, and Carly [Barrett][16] from the Wailers... so I just put my one and one together, and try to see where it pan out; one of these days I would find a sound for myself, so I start working on it by listening to a lot of stuff from Philadelphia, a lot of stuff from Stax, and with the help from Channel One and Ernest Hoo-Kim,[17] I developed a sound.

Did you have an instrument of your own?

No. At the time, we used to borrow a drum set, but I'm a sound person—I love sound, so I would try to remember sound as I go along; I would go to a drum set and choose the way I want to tune the sound I want to hear. So whenever we rent a drum set for a session, I would just do it the way I think it should be for me.

You are saying basically that Ansel Collins more or less discovered you, and began to record you?

Yes, he's my Godfather.

You said at that time Ansel was active in a group called the RHT Invincibles, but you initially had been playing in a smaller group called the Yardbrooms?

Yes, and then I went to join the RHT Invincibles.

What does the name mean? Why was it the RHT Invincibles?

It's a man named Father Gooden, I think it is the Rainbow Healing Temple.

Father Gooden had a bakery?

Yeah, he had a bakery, and we used to go there at rehearsal, and as the bread come out of the oven, we just take the butter and drop it right inna the bread. So we used to make sure everyday we go [to] rehearsal, fi get bread.

A little after you were in the RHT Invincibles, you were also moonlighting with Tommy McCook and the Supersonics?

One Christmas, Tommy McCook was playing and didn't have a band, so we decide say we gonna jump at it; we went and audition for Tommy, and he asked, what I'm doing here? I say, 'I come to play,' and he said

I should go back to school, but I said, 'No, no, I want to play.' Father Gooden had fired us at the time, because he heard that we went to play with Tommy; it was Christmastime and Tommy had all these big gigs coming up, and we wanted to make some money, so we went with Tommy...we played with Tommy McCook for a while.

Tommy McCook and the Supersonics was of course the defining band of the rock steady era, but you were playing for them a little later, after rock steady had waned. Did they still have high status at that time?

Well, I want tell you something, playing with Tommy McCook, the first time I signed an autograph, we went to play somewhere in the country, and a man said to Tommy, 'Where you get this juvenile playing?' And Tommy say, 'Is a new musician,' so he asked me if I knew something called 'Black Santa,' which I knew, so the band said to Tommy, 'I'm gonna request Black Santa, so cut it off,' and we started playing; its like a ska tune and [the man] said, 'Juvenile, young drummer, you good you know,' and he give me a cigarette box and say, 'Sign it.' So it's the first time I sign my name on something.

Did you actually record with the Supersonics?

I think I did one song with Tommy McCook; we had booked some time up by Studio One, and we did one song for him.

Who did you begin to play with next?

I left Supersonics and went to join a band called the Volcanoes; we used to play at a club called Tit for Tat, and the leader for the band was a man called Mr. Harvey. There was Ranchie playing guitar, Jimmy playing bass and Mr. Harvey playing guitar; I think there was one other guitar player. Mr. Harvey got this job in the country to play at this hotel, so we left the Tit for Tat club and we went there for a month; the hotel closed down, so we [were stuck] there. At that time we used to listen to a lot of Sly and the Family Stone records, so Mr. Harvey looked at me and say, 'Everything is Sly. Sly, Sly.' I said, 'I like Sly and the Family Stone,' so him say, 'Alright, we a go call you Sly from now,' so everywhere I go, they say, 'Sly, Sly, Sly'; I came back to town and everybody saying, 'Sly,' so the name just stuck on me like that, and I just took the name. Then we formed a band in Kingston called Skin, Flesh and Bones; we used to play at the Tit for Tat club, played there for about five years, and we were doing recording at Channel One at the same time, but after that, I went on a tour with Jimmy Cliff in '75...

Before we get to the Jimmy Cliff period, I want to clarify a few more particulars about this era. Your given name is actually Lowell Charles Dunbar?

Lowell Philmore Dunbar.

You ended up with this nickname Sly, because you were listening to Sly and the Family Stone?

Yeah.

Where did you hear Sly and the Family Stone?

Well, I used to hear Sly and the Family Stone on the radio in Jamaica, and when we go to a club or a party...like 'Thank You (Falettinme Be Mice Elf Agin)' and all these songs.

Were those songs big hits in Jamaica, or only underground?

Normally underground. Once you go to clubs, you will hear it playing.

What appealed to you about those records?

It's the groove. If it don't got swing, it's not gonna work.

Is there any song that you remember that particularly inspired you?

A lot of songs: 'Thank You (Falettinme Be Mice Elf Agin)' and 'Sing a Simple Song,' and they had a song called 'Family Affair' that was wicked, and there was a song name 'Hot Fun in the Summertime' which was wicked.

I believe you were involved in a cover version of one of those songs.

'Somebody's Watching You' by Black Uhuru.

That's quite a bit further down the line. Why was the band named Skin, Flesh and Bone? Where did that name come from?

We were looking at Earth, Wind and Fire, and then I was skinny, and the bass man was sort of stout, so we just say, Skin, Flesh and Bones.

So is this another funky club link? Is that where you had heard Earth, Wind and Fire?

We used to listen to that on the radio, and I go to clubs and hear all these stuff.

So you were heavily inspired by American music back then?

American music, African music, every kind of music. When I really start taking the drum serious, I was watching a movie called *Soul to Soul*[18] with Roberta Flack and all these people, and I saw them singing just to percussion, and I say, 'Well, if we can play dub, if we can get a drum with the dance semi-tone, I think we're into something else.' So when I got to Channel One, I start talking to Ernest [Hoo-Kim] about the idea. It took us two years for Channel One to come up with the drum sound and everything like that.

With Skin Flesh and Bones, you did a cover of Al Green's 'Here I Am Baby,' with a dub version on the B-side. When we listen to both the vocal and the dub version, you are doing a cover version of an American song, but you're not just doing a cover version; you are Jamaican-ising the rhythm and you're turning it into something else, which was part of when dub began to evolve into an art form in the early 1970s—Jamaican artistry at work. What can you tell us about that process?

Skin Flesh and Bones was like a dance band, so we use to play Al Green's version; when Dickie Wong, who owned the club, decided he wanted to record something with the group, [and] we said this would be the best song to cover, so we immediately transformed the song, just using some elements from the guitar that Ranchie is playing that wasn't in Al Green's version—Ranchie sort of created that himself. We learned from Studio One, where [keyboardist and musical arranger] Jackie Mittoo[19] would take a foreign song and scale it down and turn it around and let it sound like they are the ones that created it, so we learn from Studio One people.

Before I interrupted you, you were telling us how you ended up on Jimmy Cliff's album, around 1975.

Jimmy Cliff came into town, looking for musicians to play on his album *Follow My Mind*, and then I went with him on tour, but after that, I was fired, because Joe Higgs[19] wanted us to do a performance somewhere, and Ranchie and myself decided not to go, so Jimmy fired us. Later, he came back and asked me if I wanted to go play with him when the Channel One stuff started happening, and he asked me to go with him to Africa, so I went back with him to tour.

Around that same era, in Jamaican popular music there was a new style that developed, which I believe initially comes from the Soul Syndicate band, known as the 'flying cymbal' style, or 'flyers.'

The flying cymbal style wasn't created by the Soul Syndicate band. I first heard that flying cymbal in a song called 'Moonlight Lover';[20] I don't know who was playing that drum, but if you listen to the Skatelites stuff, Lloyd [Knibb] is playing something like that. And when I heard 'Moonlight Lover,' the first time I tried to play it, I played it in 'Double Barrel', and it was a hit. Then, after a while, we didn't play it [any more], so I played it on 'Here I Am Baby' with Al Brown, and it was a big hit. Then Bunny Lee[21] realized that the style was working, and he took it and started calling it the flying cymbal, so that's it for flying cymbal.

The way Mikey Boo described it, he was trying to emulate 'The Sound of Philadelphia,' aka 'TSOP,' the theme song from Soul Train, recorded by a studio band from Philadelphia [called MFSB].

Well, 'TSOP' got it from us, personally. Our songs came out before 'TSOP'; 'Moonlight Lover' was out before, and 'Double Barrel' was out before.

The time when the 'flying cymbal' style really took off is around the same period when you and Robbie Shakespeare started to play together. Can you tell us how you first became aware of each other as musicians, and what happened from there?

I used to play at the Tit for Tat club, Robbie use to play at the club called Evil People, that was next door to Tit for Tat...in North Parade, where Randy's record store is, we used to call it Idler's Rest, and all musicians would meet there in the daytime, like we punch the clock and everybody come work, but because there is no work, we looking work. So I remember Robbie was giving me a lift in his green Escort to Channel One, so I tell him to come check me tomorrow, because sometimes a whole heap a sessions run. But prior to that, he used to come over to the club where I was playing at and watch us play, and I used to go over to his club, and he called a session with Bunny Lee, and I think the first song we played together [on] was a song for John Holt named 'I Forgot to Say I Love You Till I'm Gone'—a Chi-Lites song. We did that first song, and Bunny say, 'Wow, this is wicked,' and Robbie asked me to join him with Peter Tosh, because I had just did a tour with Dennis Brown, and I did one also with the Mighty Diamonds for Virgin, so I said, 'No problem,' and this is where the whole development starts, we trying to put a show together with Peter Tosh. Robbie and myself, we used to share rooms, so we start to come up with ideas; we start playing the dub live with Peter, because after Peter sings, we didn't know how to end the songs, so we play a long dub, and the people would love it. We start developing all these things, night after night, and we took the idea to the recording studio, and try and capture everything.

So it was really through this shared experience of playing with Peter Tosh that you began to develop your ideas together?

Yes.

Peter Tosh is obviously one of the most iconic figures in reggae, but he is also someone who is largely misunderstood. What was it like working with Peter, and what was Peter Tosh like as a person?

Peter Tosh as a person is cool, he just stand up for what he believes in, and he always believe in equal rights and justice. [And when] we are on tour, he is a cool person to work with. I can remember when we were making 'Buk-in-hamm Palace,' we were just playing the rhythm, Robbie and myself, and he took his guitar and start playing, lighting a spliff, and it was wicked. He's just a jovial person, and he's serious about certain things, but he's cool.

There comes a time when you were no longer active with Peter Tosh and then you began to concentrate on your own productions. What happened exactly?

We were doing our productions and we had just done the 'Pull Up to the Bumper' rhythm for Grace Jones, and it was a big hit, and we were trying to guide Peter in a certain direction, but he refused. So we left Peter's band in Germany and we went straight to Nassau, called Gwen Guthrie,[22] and did her first hit song, which is 'It Should Have Been You,' and we just take it serious from there and start making our own productions. But Peter was good for us, because he was the one that took us out there, so people could actually see us playing live together as a unit.

We'll discuss the Compass Point era in a moment, but I want to play a slightly earlier record that you produced, one of the earlier records you did with Black Uhuru, a version of the Wailers' 'Let Him Go.'

This was like a trial record we put out, an experimental record to get the sound.

There's a lot happening in that record and I want you talk us through it. First of all, tell us about the rhythm, because it's a very distinctive rhythm.

Well, the original version was by the Wailers, and we were just trying something with Black Uhuru to get their sound on the marketplace, so [that] people would react to them, so we tried to shift the rhythm a little bit; we were playing an original drum pattern that I created, and Robbie was playing something different that was made for Black Uhuru, and after that, we realize that Black Uhuru was accepted, so we started going into the regional stuff. But this was like one of our original kind of rhythms, on one of the songs by [the] Wailers.

Where does your connection with Black Uhuru start?

Michael [Rose]'s brother and I were good friends, and there was this little studio in Waterhouse on Scarlett Avenue, owned by a guy named Newton,[23] and Michael was actually a deejay before he started to sing, so we would go around there and record; there was a song called 'Woman a Ginal fi True,' it was recorded around there, so this is where Michael Rose started doing his first recording.

You formed a very solid partnership with Black Uhuru later in the decade, and they ended up becoming the biggest reggae act following the death of Bob Marley, but I want to remind that in addition to the productions you were doing for your Taxi label, you were also the mainstays at Channel One studio, working on a lot of other material that you weren't producing, like the Wailing Souls' 'Back Out With It.' What can you tell us about records like those?

When I went to Channel One, we never had any money at the time, so we used to spend some time in the studio, [and] we used to beg Ernest [Hoo-Kim] some studio time, so [if] we had four musicians in the session, each musician would do one song, and give the engineer a song for himself. So I say to Ernest, 'This song is your song, which is not [on] this rhythm, it's the rhythm that [the Mighty] Diamonds came up with, 'When the Right Time Comes'.' And he couldn't believe [it]. I say, 'This is your rhythm, because you gave us some time [but] no money, so this is your own.' So when Joe-Joe [Hoo-Kim] come [in] the evening, Ernest played it for him, and Joe say, 'This is really your rhythm?' And [Ernest said], 'Yes, it's mine; [Sly] made it for us and give it to us,' and from then, Ernest and Joe, they start[ed to] look at me different, and say I must just go out and play whatever I want to play, and take everything into control. They had a version of ['Back Out With It'] called 'Tings and Time,' so we played the drum pattern and make it two different mixes, so this is where I really got my go-ahead in the recording business from Joe-Joe, because he give me the freedom. Because one of the times, when you're doing a session, you couldn't play what you feel, because the producer would tell you, 'No.' But Joe-Joe would give you the freedom to do anything, and this is why my songs came out of my head how they are sounding today.

In this same era, you were also collaborating with overseas artists, for instance you made some records with Serge Gainsbourg from France, Manu Dibango from Cameroon, and Chris Hinze, a German artist, and I think some people from Japan. Tell us a bit about how those collaborations started to take place, and what they were like for you as a musician.

The collaborations started taking place because people heard the sound that was coming out of Channel One, and they wanted a piece of it; they came to us, so we gave them a piece of it, and we collect some money from them. When everything started, and other people start coming to us from all over, saying they want a piece of this stuff, we always try to get the rhythm on a certain groove, [to] let it feel like a hit song; we didn't just play it like that. And after that, Serge Gainsbourg came in and I think he has one of the biggest albums ever in France, up to this day, which is a reggae album.[24] And from there on, Chris Blackwell hook up those jobs, and then he called us and said he had this Jamaican girl, her name is Grace and she lived in Paris and he wants to do an album with her, so he gave us some records with her, which, up to this day I haven't listened to them yet, and he called a session in Nassau, and we went to Nassau, start listen[ing] to the track, start playing, and Grace Jones was just off the hook and running from there.

What can you tell us about Grace Jones? Another iconic figure, with a reputation...

She was singing 'My Jamaican Guy' in a kind of Jamaican dialect of Patois. So what we did at that time was mix mento and r&b together for her, and she would just flow. And we were grooving with Wally Badarou[25] around the keyboard; Chris Blackwell was just looking for something fresh, but he wanted to keep the element of Jamaican music in there also, so we have to find a way to keep that [element], so Robbie and myself was responsible to lock that end down. We had [guitarist] Mikey Chung,[26] [percussionist] Sticky Thompson[27] and...who[ever else] would be around doing other things.

Chris Blackwell had said that he put that band together to try to meld the Jamaican rhythm section with a new wave feeling from some European players.

Yeah, that's true. It was an English guitarist, African keyboard player, Jamaican guitar with Mikey Chung, Sticky from Jamaica on percussion, and Robbie and myself. That was it, that was the band.

And you were recording in the Bahamas in a custom-built studio for Chris Blackwell. What were those sessions like?

It was cool because we stay down there for a month; I would record every day, cutting tracks for Grace, and there was this big picture of Grace in the studio, so you look at her and you just play the music like how the picture looks, and she was there in front of you. She felt so comfortable, because she was amongst Jamaicans, so she was free to do anything. I think that is why this record came out so good.

She also has something of a reputation of being a difficult person to work with.

I haven't seen that in her, because I worked with her the other day, when we did this Island 50th [anniversary concert],[28] and she's cool. When she's amongst Jamaicans, I think she is cool. But I think other people sometimes sort of drive her nuts, so she gets mad.

Tell us about the song 'Don't Stop The Music,' another of your hit productions from Compass Point, credited to Bits and Pieces. First of all, who is doing the vocals?

We were in Nassau, and it was a Saturday, and Grace Jones took the day off, so we decided to use the time [ourselves]. There was this American record by Yarbrough and Peoples which was there, so we say, 'Let's just do a reggae version of the song,' so we played the rhythm. [Then] I went inside the studio, fooling around the microphone, so [engineer] Steven Stanley[29] press 'record' and say, 'Boy, oonu sound good,' so we went back in and start fooling around, deejay and rap, and they decided to put [it] out [as] a record; Tyrone [Downey][30] is singing background harmony, and Robbie, and I was doing the deejay-style thing. It never came out as Sly and Robbie, it came out as Bits and Pieces, because we were hiding our names, and I think [it was] the first deejay recording that went on the charts; I was just fooling around, [and] it wasn't a great record, because I couldn't do it again. That Saturday was just a day like today; you know, just going on, and it work.

So it was your rapping debut, but you decided not to pursue it?

No. We were just joking around, and we just captured that moment.

The rhythm sounds like it started to have some mechanical effects.

Yes, Steven Stanley started doing some reverse stuff, just to make it different from the r&b version. And we sold probably like 300,000 copies of this version in the clubs, so it was good.

From your time at Compass Point, there are a number of other international collaborations, like with Ian Dury, a punk balladeer; Joe Cocker, an English blues singer; Joan Armatrading, a British woman of Caribbean origin; the Rolling Stones, and perhaps the most infamous of all, a James Brown session that didn't really come off. Then, following your tremendous success with Black Uhuru, you started discovering some young talent. For instance, you made an important record that had a lasting effect with the vocalist Ini Kamoze, called 'World-A-Music.'

A lot of people know this song as 'Welcome to Jamrock.' Well, this is the original song, and it was done in 1984. But how I got to meet Ini Kamoze was, Newton [aka Sipho Merritt][31] was a cousin of Jimmy Cliff; he gave me a cassette. At that time, we used to go to [the] studio like six o'clock in the morning to record, and by two o'clock, we finish we day work, and go on some corner and link a little while, and I give Robbie the cassette and I say, 'Don't play it until you get home.' And the next day he said, 'Yes, it's wicked.' So we called Ini and he came to the studio and he did six songs in half an hour, and he voiced in half an hour. And we put out a record, [on] Island Records, and he was a part of the whole team. Twenty years later, Stephen Marley sampled it, and it was called 'Welcome to Jamrock,' but this is where it came from.

You then started to collaborate with people like Herbie Hancock, and you've also made some records with Bob Dylan, and you formed this interesting partnership with New York-based producer Bill Laswell, when it sounds like things are getting a lot more technological, on tracks like 'Make 'Em Move.'

This was a record when we wanted to work with a producer, to produce our record, so we worked with Bill Laswell and he got Manu Dibango to play saxophone, and Herbie Hancock to play keyboard. So we make this record, and I think it was [used] in a movie [soundtrack], so it's called 'Make 'Em Move.' It's sort of a Sly and Robbie experiment: we go outside of reggae, but we still combine it with it. We did it to go into the American market, and it work.

There was a follow-up record you did with Laswell that also had some big hits in the States, like a version of 'Fire' by the Ohio Players.

We also did a version of 'Fire' called 'Boops'. 'Boops' was a top-ten record in England.

Around the same time, correct me if I'm wrong, but Sly and Robby started to get criticized in Jamaica for spending too much time abroad, and for maybe being out of touch with predominant styles.

Well, they use to quarrel that we are spending too much time abroad, but we were still working; we were making hit records at the same time. [But] I figure they were right in a sense, and when we came back and start settling down in Jamaica, that's when [Chaka Demus and Pliers'] 'Murder She Wrote' came along.

Then you set down your drumsticks and started to make computer rhythms?

Well, I didn't really put it down, but because everybody was...nobody wanted me to play drum machines, but I [was] forced to. So I start using it too, because at the moment, most of the drummers that used to do all the recordings in Jamaica, none of them would be programming machines, and they wouldn't get any jobs. I wanted to make some money, so I learn the machine, so I could program. Up to this day, I am the only recording drummer who is programming. None of the stalwarts like Paul [Douglas],[32] Mikey Boo, Horsemouth,[33] none of them programming.

The dancehall productions that you made using drum machines were quite innovative, like 'Murder She Wrote' and 'Alms House' by Capleton; they both used bhangra[34] beats.

That's where the bhangra stuff came from.

Where were you exposed to bhangra, and why did you decide to use it?

I was listening to a lot of Indian stuff when going to England, and I decide that I'm going try some of that stuff. But my job is really, I take everything that I can find and take it to reggae. So the next thing is that I can take a Brazilian music, I can take everything to reggae [and] fuse it. Because I defend the Jamaican culture.

Let's take a listen to a later track that you made in dancehall, again with quite an innovative approach to rhythm and music production. This is Innocent Kru's 'Impossible Train,' what can you tell us about putting that together?

We had done a cover version of [the] 'Mission Impossible' [theme song], which I [didn't] think we could do a good version of, but Gitsy [guitarist Lloyd Willis][35] said we had to; I had a CD of the original version, and I checked the tempo and I realize that we could do it, so we did it. I was looking for a dancehall group with a certain sound, and [manager] Yoland [Knight] took Innocent Kru to us and I listen [to] them and I said, 'Wow, I like the sound, let's re-cut 'Mission Impossible' and you guys can sing the song to it.' So they did just that, and it was a big hit for them.

So the same way that you had discovered new talent, like Ini Kamoze at the time was an unknown; so you still continued to work with relatively unknown young talent?

Yeah man, definitely. We still looking for talent; we don't care if you have a hit record before, once you have the talent.

Let's take a listen to one final track, Beenie Man's 'Foundation,' which again was a huge hit and another innovative production. And once again it's a Jamaican reinterpretation of an original American record, although this time with an additional Jamaican reference. The original track is a jazz saxophone track by Ernie Freeman...

Yeah, and the Skatelites did a version of it also.[36] But this Beenie Man track...when we did 'Mission Impossible,' Beenie Man wanted to go on the rhythm, but I tell him, 'No, no, no, this rhythm is going be an instrumental.' So when we are mixing this song now, Beenie Man rode up on a bike and say this one is not going to miss him; everybody was in the studio and they say, 'Here comes Beenie Man,' and we went inside and him turn on the mike and he tries something, and it wasn't working – nobody said anything to him, and he said, 'One more time again,' and he started saying, 'A jus Selassie-I send them,' and everybody start saying, 'It sound wicked...the hard section is gonna be coming up, so let's see how he do this part,' and he just back up and say, 'Die, die, da-da-da-die,' and it was the first time he's hearing the record, and we say, 'Wicked!' and we just leave him alone – a just watch him till the song finish, and that's it. Him just went on the bike and ride out and say, 'Later.' And it's one of his biggest songs to date.

In a moment, I'm going to open things up for contributions from the audience, and questions for Sly, and so forth, but just to bring us a bit more up-to-date, after that, you did some more esteemed collaborations with international artists like No Doubt, and perhaps more controversially, with Irish singer Sinead O'Connor's Throw Down Your Arms, an album of reggae cover versions...so when you are on the road, you are still behind the drum set, but in Jamaica, you're making computer rhythms?

I'm both. I'm behind the drum in Jamaica, and also making computer rhythms. But on tour, just [drum] kit; I can't use any drum machine, nobody don't want to see that.

Are you still recording live drums in Jamaica?

Yeah man.

What can we expect in the future? What do you want to alert us to right now, of any projects you are working on?

I don't know, I just try and make some music for the people. Sometimes you don't know what's gonna happen; we just go inside and make a beat. But we have good beats in store that is there, but we have to time the music with the people, if they are into this or not. We can't just...like now, they're into different things, so we have to watch until they get tired of this, and try and slip in. That's how it goes [in] the music business.

QUESTIONS AND ANSWERS

MICHAEL BARNETT: *Sly, I'm very interested in what inspired you to collaborate with the 'Irish Siren,' as some people would know Sinead O'Connor, recently with her reggae venture, a few years back? How did the collaboration come about? Did she approach you and Robbie?*

SLY DUNBAR: She called us, and she was the one who picked the songs. She said she wanna cover some Jamaican records; she said she want to come to Jamaica and make a total[ly] Jamaican record. So she came to Jamaica and we did it at Tuff Gong studio with her; she picked all the songs them, and she picked some tough songs, songs sung by male groups, and she did it. We did a tour with her, and she was great, and we were supposed to continue, but she got pregnant, and that's it. But we [are] still in touch with her, because there is some concert coming up and she wants us to [play] for her, [but] I'm not sure how that will work out. We have to do some rehearsal with her again.

DAVID KATZ: *I'd like to add a comment that in England, one day I was tuning in to a community radio station, and a Jamaican-born disc jockey was playing a few tracks from the album, back when it was first released, and he did a little competition for his listeners, where he said, 'I want you to phone in and tell me who is singing.' And it was very intriguing to hear the loyal listeners to this*

Jamaican community station phoning in and saying Marcia Griffiths[37] and Phyllis Dillon.[38]

PERSON TWO: *Sly, there's a great story of, I think the time and place [was]... where you were when you received your first Grammy with Black Uhuru. It was 1984, right? Where were you when you found out about that?*

When we heard that we won the Grammy, we were in Manhattan, in the studio with Bob Dylan, recording his album, and he came and told us that, 'You guys won a Grammy.' I said, 'Really?' That's how I knew we won a Grammy; he was the one who came to us. We were not looking to win; we were just making records and it happen that that was the first one, and we say, 'Well, thanks!'

H. DENNIS: *Sly, you've worked with Half Pint, Ini Kamoze, Black Uhuru, Gregory Isaacs, and you've managed to give every one of them a particular sound; when you hear a song that you produce with any of these artists, it is distinctive, yet different. How do you manage that?*

OK, first, everybody have a different personality, right? [So] I need to sit with the artist and look at them, and see how they move, and see what they're like; it's like making a movie: you try to tailor the music to sound like them. Like Half Pint, we see like he's fidgety, so you make the music like [that]. Gregory now is a cool person. So you set the rhythm like how they look. So, for example...an r&b soul group [sounds] just like how they look or how they play, but everything is in the singing or the vocal. A singer will come on and sing to you, and you try and fit that groove behind the song. Like today someone will build a rhythm and the artist goes on it, sometimes it work and sometimes it don't work. You have the coloring of the music to match the artist's vocals sometimes for it to really work. And I think this is what we [are] really missing in the music today. There's a lot of things working, but we missing that.

PERSON THREE: *Sly, I have a memory of the One Love Peace Concert, when you played behind Peter Tosh, and somewhere in the middle of the set, a man* *jumped up on the stage, and came up and started [to] salute on the stage, and started [to] praise you...what do you recall about that? What are your recollections? Because I know from us, all like we in the audience...afterwards, when Bob [Marley] came on, it took us a little while to...the rhythm section had just torn up the place.*

We didn't know Peter was going to talk,[39] because we didn't want to do the concert; they sort of force him to, and he did it, and I remember that night, Bubbler [keyboardist Franklyn Waul][40] came to me and asked me what I did to the drums; I say, 'I wet up the drums.' We were using a transparent kit, and I had a bottle of water, so I wet up the drums; what I really wanted was the wet skin, so the water would splash into the sky and the light would pick it up, and it would look like starlight coming from the drum. It worked, I mean yesterday we were talking about it: the sound of the drum from the wet skin was [so] dangerous that they say, 'Everybody came to look. Sly was playing just two drums and the [beat] was so heavy that we could not believe how it sound.' So I guess we discovered something new, the wetting of the drum to get a great sound from it with water.

PERSON THREE: *I think the whole 'rockers'[41] era, that impact...I remember some songs like John Holt, 'Have You Ever Been In Love.'*

Well those songs, Joe-Joe, Ernest and Channel One, that would give me the green light to just create anything, but not out of the blue. So [Ernest] say, 'Just create some drum pattern, different kind of style.' So I started just creating anything as I go along, like 'Have You Ever Been In Love' was one of the songs that took us four hours to record, because I was playing it a certain way, and it wasn't sitting down...so I switched, and then started playing 'Kang, kang, kang, kang,' and the studio went crazy!

PERSON FOUR: *Greetings to the I, could you tell me which school you went to as a youth, started out in Primary school?*

I went to Trench Town Primary and Trench Town Comprehensive.

PERSON FOUR: *So you were born in Trench Town?*

No, I was born in Windward Road.

PERSON FOUR: *You can remember in the 60s, Trench Town was like a Mecca everybody come to, [from] Uptown, all East, all round...*

I was there every day, so I used to go down and check Delroy Wilson.[42]

PERSON FOUR: *You remember a sound name Soulmate? It used to be top side Trench Town Comprehensive and Greenwich Street.*

Well, I probably used to pass and hear them playing sometimes.

PERSON FOUR: *The Mighty Diamonds, they use to hang out over that sound, that's why I really ask you.*

See, where I went to school, the Primary and the Comprehensive, I use to go to Boys Town every day, just to see Delroy Wilson...

PERSON FOUR: *Yeah, a great era, man. So tell me now, who [do] you think are the five best drummers in Jamaica?*

The five best drummers in Jamaica: Lloyd Knibb is one, Mikey Boo is one, Joe Isaacs is one, Fil Callender is one, and Carlton Barrett is the other.

PERSON FOUR: *What about Horsemouth?*

Horsemouth come after that. That would make it about six, right?

PERSON FOUR: *So what about you, how you don't include yourself in that?*

Well, I don't consider myself...

PERSON FIVE: *You talked about being a drum programmer, and we all felt like reggae was a natural music. How [do] you feel [about] how computers and electronic devices can be incorporated, without interfering with the natural feel?*

Well, I'm a drummer, so when I sit behind the drum machine, I look at the drum machine and I start playing it like how I would play the drum; it's very simple...a keyboard player probably would do it different. But then again, to use the thing, like to make it sound natural, it can work. Like for example, we're in the digital world and a lot of people think that ProTools can make a hit record. But if you don't have that groove to put to the ProTools, it can't happen. So even if you go to the drum machine, or you're playing it live, you have to know the molecules of beat—how much volume on this I'm going to use, bring down this, bring down that some more, to let the whole thing flow. It's something that you have to study, you know, just like going to school every day, to see which thing can push up a bit louder. Because I can make a mix now, and I push the high-hat up too much, and it's out of place; you have to pull it down, because you have to know the molecules of sound—which one high, which one low—so the people will take it, will understand it much more and feel it much better. So it's just understanding. But I don't think the digital thing...the digital thing couldn't take away something, because the real soul is you playing it live. And the drum machine is all right, but the drum machine cannot play that real soul that a drummer would play. So it's cool, and it's technology, and they making money from it, so if you can use it, you use it.

DENNIS HOWARD: *I just want to greet you first of all. Mr. Katz, congratulations. I don't know if the audience knows that when Lee Perry gave you that ring with the skull on it and appointed you his ghost writer, and after that, so many beautiful volumes came out of that association. But Sly, this conference is supposed to be about current and future trends in the music, and I would just like to find out what you see in the future for Taxi Records?*

In the future for Taxi Records, all Taxi Records wants to do is just keep people dancing and just making hits, anything the people groove to, because I believe in dance records. When I say dance records, it must have the groove. If the record is danceable, then the dancer has to listen to it, but if it's not danceable, he won't hear it, so he won't move; I want them to move, so it has to be danceable, the groove, so as Duke Ellington say, 'Every day, Taxi swing; if it ain't got the swing, it don't have nothing.' So we have to get that groove in it to make it work. So that is what Taxi Record is all about—just groove.

NOTES

1. Launched in 1950 as Jamaica's first commercial radio station, Radio Jamaica Rediffusion, known as RJR, was initially a cable subscription radio service that supplied radio signals to household receivers via wired relay networks.

2. Mento singer Count Owen, aka Owen Emmanuel, was one of the first local artists to be recorded in Jamaica, cutting 78s for producers Ken Khouri and Stanley Motta during the mid-1950s; recordings for Dada Tewari were licensed to RCA in 1960, while his association with Khouri subsequently yielded several albums. He also recorded sparsely for Studio One during the early 1970s, and continued to perform on the north coast into the new millennium.

3. After getting his start in a vocal harmony duo called the Termites, Lloyd Parks became one of Jamaica's most highly rated bass players during the early 1970s. He has since played with countless acts, and was notably Dennis Brown's bandleader during the singer's peak period of popularity.

4. An expressive guitarist, Bertram 'Ranchie' McLean would later become a key member of the Revolutionaries house band, established by Sly Dunbar at Channel One studio during the mid-1970s.

5. One of Jamaica's master drummers, Michael Richards, aka Mikey Boo, later became the chief drummer with the In Crowd, one of Jamaica's most popular acts during the mid-1970s, and was also the studio drummer with the Now Generation, a sophisticated group featuring brothers Mikey and Geoffrey Chung.

6. Tin Legs, aka Lloyd Adams, was a very talented drummer with a dynamic style that often made use of non-standard timing. After passing through various session bands, he would eventually rise to prominence with Inner Circle.

7. Top-ranking keyboardist Ansel Collins is best known overseas as half of the hit-making duo, Dave and Ansel Collins; creator of the legendary 'Stalag' rhythm, he has worked with countless performers, and was a key member of Jimmy Cliff's backing band during the 1980s and 90s.

8. The instrumental 'Night Doctor' was a chart success in Britain in 1969. Although produced by Ansel Collins, the song was credited as a Lee Perry production after Collins licensed it to Perry's Upsetter label, since he was unable to release the record himself, due to a lack of ready finance.

9. Dave and Ansel Collins' 'Double Barrel,' recorded for producer Winston Riley, was another significant chart success in Britain in 1970.

10. S*olid Gold* was a syndicated American television music charts program that broadcasted during the 1980s; Sly is probably thinking of *Top of the Pops*, a British television music charts program that broadcasted weekly between 1964 and 2006.

11. Sometimes credited as the originator of the 'one drop' style, Winston Grennan was a top drummer during the rock steady period. After moving to the USA in 1973, he played drums for a range of notable performers, including jazz giants Dizzy Gillespie, Herbie Hancock, Herbie Mann and Robin Kenyatta, and iconic singers Marvin Gaye, Aretha Franklin, Paul Simon, the O'Jays, Minnie Ripperton and Garland Jeffreys, as well as an early version of Kid Creole's Coconuts. He died of cancer in 2000, recording and performing right up until the end.

12. Lloyd Knibb became the Skatalites' drummer in 1964 and still plays with the band. He is credited as the first drummer to interpret the rhythms of buru hand drumming on a drum kit.

13. One of Jamaica's unsung musicians, Joe Isaacs is best known as drummer for the Soul Vendors, formed at Studio One in the mid-1960s.

14. As well as being a talented vocalist that fronted the In Crowd band, Filberto Callender played a key part in the development of the Studio One sound as a drummer during the late 1960s.

15. Getting his start in the Hippy Boys during the late 1960s, ace drummer Carlton Barrett backed the Wailers as a member of Lee Perry's Upsetters and remained the group's rhythmic backbone from the formation of their Tuff Gong imprint in 1971. A gifted musician whose command of the snare gave the Wailers' work a particular texture, Carly was murdered in 1987, the horrific result of a plot hatched by his wife and her lover.

16. Channel One studio, established by the Hoo-Kim brothers on Maxfield Avenue, became the most important studio in Jamaica during the mid-1970s, particularly after Sly established the Revolutionaries as the in-house band.

17. The documentary film *Soul To Soul* covered a concert of the same name held in Accra, Ghana, in 1971, featuring American soul stars such as Wilson Pickett, the Staples Singers, Ike and Tina Turner, Roberta Flack, and gospel group the Voices of East Harlem, as well as jazz stars Les McCann and Eddie Harris, and Latin-influenced rock act Santana, along with several local performers, such as drummer Guy Warren and highlife pioneer Kwa Mensah; portions of the concert featured local percussionists collaborating with the overseas artists, such as calabash player Amoah Azangeo, who was featured during Les McCann and Eddie Harris' set.

18. One of the most important musicians in the history of Jamaican popular music, Jackie Mittoo was a supremely talented keyboard player that became in-house arranger at Studio One during the mid-1960s. Although he moved to Canada in the early 1970s, he remained an active component of the diasporic music scene, producing exciting sounds in Toronto, New York, London and Jamaica into the late 1980s, but ultimately succumbed to cancer in 1990.

19. Singer Joe Higgs, a vocal coach to the young Wailers, was part of Jimmy Cliff's live act during the mid-1970s. After cutting two critically acclaimed albums, he moved to Los Angeles in the mid-1980s, and died of cancer in 1999.

20. 'Moonlight Lover,' a massive hit by American singer Joya Landis, was recorded in Jamaica with the Supersonics for Duke Reid in 1968.

21. One of the most successful Jamaican record producers of all time, Edward 'Bunny' Lee probably issued the largest number of hits records featuring the 'flying cymbal' style.

22. During the 1970s, New Jersey-based singer-songwriter Gwen Guthrie co-wrote hit songs such as Ben E. King's 'Supernatural Thing' and Roberta Flack's 'God Don't Like Ugly,' as well as several songs on Sister Sledge's debut album. Collaboration with Peter Tosh brought her into contact with Sly and Robbie, who seriously elevated her solo career through a series of dub-influenced dance records. Remaining active into the mid-1990s, she died of cancer in 1999.

23. Newton Simmons ran a recording studio in Waterhouse, known as SRS.

24. The album, *Aux Armes Et Caetera*, was recorded with Sly and the Revolutionaries at Dynamics in 1978.

25. Born in Dahomey (now known as Benin), West Africa, innovative keyboardist Wally Badarou was raised in Paris, where he became active in funk and zouk outfits, and backed African stars like Hugh Masakela and Miriam Makeba. He was drafted into the Compass Point All Stars after playing on M's spectacular hit, 'Pop Music,' and his mastery of the Prophet 5 synthesizer became a big part of the Compass Point sound.

26. A gifted musician and musical arranger, Mikey Chung was a key member of the Now Generation, one of Jamaica's leading bands of the mid-1970s.

27. Uziah 'Sticky' Thompson got his start as a deejay before being directed to percussion by Lee 'Scratch' Perry in the late 1960s. Since the mid-1980s, Sticky has been an active percussionist with several of Bob Marley's sons.

28. Held at London's Shepherd's Bush Empire in May 2009, the Island 50th Anniversary Concert saw the reformation of the Compass Point All Stars, who backed Grace Jones, Aswad and others.

29. Forward-thinking engineer Steven Stanley played an important role in helping Compass Point to yield a futuristic sound.

30. Wailers keyboardist Tyrone Downey was also involved in some of the material Sly and Robbie created at Compass Point, including 'Don't Stop The Music.'

31. Newton 'Sipho' Merritt co-founded the Mogho Naba and Selekta labels with Ini Kazome.

32. A veteran of the Beverley's All Stars and several other session bands of the late 1960s, Paul Douglas has been the regular drummer for Toots and the Maytals for several decades.

33. Star of the film *Rockers*, Leroy 'Horsemouth' Wallace is an innovative drummer that first made an impact on Burning Spear material at Studio One. He went on to join the Soul Syndicate and Black Disciples bands, and made lover's rock music in England with Sugar Minott in the early 1980s, after touring with Prince Fari. Since the late 1990s, he has been an active member of French artist Pierpoljak's band.

34. Based on the fusion of traditional Punjabi folk music with rock and other contemporary forms, the bhangra style became a popular component of the British music scene during the mid-1980s.

35. A former member of the Mystics, Lloyd 'Gitsy' Willis has been an active session guitarist since the early 1970s.

36. The Skatalites' version is titled 'Beard Man Ska,' recorded in 1965.

37. 37. In addition to being a member of the I-Three, Bob Marley's backing vocalists, Marcia Griffiths has enjoyed a thriving solo career since the ska era.

38. A popular singer during the rock steady years, Phyllis Dillon migrated to New York in late 1967, but continued to sporadically record on return trips to Jamaica. She died of cancer in 2004.

39. The One Love Peace Concert was held at Kingston's National Stadium on April 22nd 1978, as a symbolic means to stop partisan violence between street gangs, linked to the nation's two rival political parties. During Peter Tosh's performance, he repeatedly harangued the leaders of both parties in very direct language, and later received a savage, life threatening beating by police for his efforts.

40. Franklyn 'Bubbler' Waul is a highly talented keyboardist that was a prominent member of the Professionals house band at Joe Gibbs' studio during the late 1970s, where his percolating rhythms and sweeping synth effects brought greater depth to work by noteworthy artists such as Dennis Brown.

41. The 'rockers' style took Jamaica by storm during the mid-1970s, sweeping away the popularity of the 'flying cymbal' in the process. The style was driven by aggressive, militant drumbeats, largely pioneered by Sly Dunbar at Channel One studio.

42. Emerging as a child star, Delroy Wilson's emotive tenor scored him countless hits during the 1960s, 70s and 80s. He succumbed to cirrhosis of the liver in 1995.

7 JAMAICAN MUSICAL GENRES

INNOVATION AND TRANSFORMATION

Jamaica has contributed more musical genres to the world than even the country that gave us jazz, blues and rock and roll. In a brief five-decade span Jamaica has given us ska, rock steady, pop and roots reggae, dub, dub poetry, the dj style and dancehall. Each distinctive genre has gone on to inspire international variations and taken root in other parts of the world as Jamaican music itself continued to innovate and transform.

The ska music of the early sixties, celebrating a time of liberation for Africans and Jamaicans, held sway for about five years on the island of its origin, but returned in successive waves in England and the United States and remains a vibrant rite of passage for many young people today. Original ska musicians and singers, many of who went on to record in successive later styles returned to the form in later years to greet new generations of fans. Somewhere in the world right now—Europe, Japan, America—a new generation of young musicians are playing ska. Ska itself incorporated jazz, R & B, blues, country, even a hint of rock and roll. The musicians who formed the core of studio players were schooled in jazz and in many cases played in Jamaican big bands of the forties and fifties, entertaining in hotels, on cruise ships, and in clubs. Many of the early ska singers were heavily influenced by rhythm and blues. The early Jamaican Sound Systems relied heavily on American R & B and jazz records with artists such as Fats Domino achieving great popularity in Jamaica.[1] But ska was always more than a combination of the Western styles that influenced it.

Early groups like Carlos Malcolm and his Afro-Jamaican All Stars and Don Drummond's Skatalites drew heavily from African and Caribbean rhythms and song structures. Ska was not alone in reaching across the Diaspora for inspiration. Much of American blues is rooted in Africa. The connection is strong in the music of New Orleans where it can be heard in songs like 'Iko Iko' by the Dixie Cups. Many of the Jamaican ska musicians like Tommy McCook and 'Bra' Gainer, though steeped in American popular music, played regularly at Wareika Hill with Count Ossie, rooting Nyahbingi rhythms to freestyle solos. Mento, Jamaica's homegrown calypso or folk music, carried over into ska, rock steady and reggae in its earliest and later forms.

Afro-Caribbean roots and Latin and pop influences helped direct ska into the mainstream. In its earliest manifestations ska was instrumental music, played with an uptempo shuffle beat and dominated by horns. But as the Jamaican recording industry grew hundreds of young singers pushed their way to the fore, seeing an opportunity to advance themselves with music. Producers and Sound System operators recognized the demand for homegrown Jamaican music and a veritable flood of recordings emerged. Among the top producers of the ska era were Clement S. 'Coxsone' Dodd (Studio One), Duke Reid (Treasure Isle), Ken Khouri of Federal Records, King Edwards, Prince Buster, Justin Yap (Top Deck) and Byron Lee. As the decade proceeded many new independent producers such as Lyndon Pottinger surfaced and dozens of record labels sprang up. Like the rock steady and reggae that followed it, ska was dance music. 'The Ska' was a dance every bit as much as The Twist or The Hully Gully. Some of the earliest international releases of ska came complete with dance instructions or photos so that neophytes could learn the steps.

Ska was Jamaica's dominant musical form from around 1961 to 1966. Although there was middle class resistance to the music, which was born in the ghetto, there was also pride in a purely Jamaican form of music that was born at the same time as Jamaica declared her independence from England. Some of the great Jamaican musicians of the ska era include the members who formed the core of The Skatalites and also worked under names like 'The All Stars' for producers such as Duke Reid and Prince Buster. Guitarist Jah Jerry Haynes, drummer Lloyd Knibbs, bassist Lloyd Brevette, trombonist Don Drummond, sax players Tommy McCook and Roland Alphonso and Johnny 'Dizzy' Moore on trumpet were among those who helped to lead the charge.

At Studio One, headquarters for some of the greatest innovations of Jamaican music, Clue J. and the Blues Blasters scored one of ska's first hits—some say the first ska record—with 1959's 'Shufflin' Jug.' Cluett Johnson played bass and the group included Roland Alphonso on sax, Rico Rodriguez on trombone, Theophalus Beckford on keys and Drumbago on drums. Roland Alphonso led the core group of musicians called The Soul Brothers who served as one of the earliest 'house bands' for producer C.S. Dodd and Tommy McCook's Supersonics filled a similar role for Duke Reid. As happened in Hollywood and London in the 1960s, a group of about twenty-five players joined forces in various combinations to supply nearly all of the musical backing for the classic ska recordings. In various combinations these musicians might record as The Skatalites, Duke Reid All Stars, Prince Buster All Stars or (for King Edwards) The Upcoming Willows. No matter what name they performed under or in what combination these seasoned musicians (joined now and then by up-and-coming players like Monty Alexander) secured a legacy for Jamaican music. Other musicians of the ska era include Arkland Parks ('Drumbago') and Hugh Malcolm (drums), Theophalus Beckford, Jackie Mittoo and Gladdy Anderson (piano), Lloyd Spence (bass), Lyn Taitt, Hux Brown, Ernest Ranglin, Bobby Aitken and Harold McKenzie (guitar), Carl 'Cannonball' Bryan, Lester Sterling, Bobby 'Big

Bra' Gaynair, Deadly Headly Bennett, Val Bennett and Dennis Campbell (saxophone), Rico Rodriguez, Vin Gordon (aka 'Don Drummond Jr') and Ron Wilson (trombone), Raymond Harper, Baba Brooks, Percival Dillon, Frank Anderson and Dave Madden (trumpet), Count Ossie (percussion) and Charlie Orgainaire and Roy Richards (harmonica). Many of the 'backing' players like Roland Alphonso also had big hits of their own.

Among the singers who stepped forward in the ska era were many who went on to rule in the rock steady and reggae eras, including Jimmy Cliff, Stranger Cole, Ken Boothe, Alton Ellis, Desmond Dekker, Delroy Wilson, Prince Buster, Laurel Aitken, Lee 'Scratch' Perry, Joe Higgs, King Sporty, Larry Marshall, Bob Marley, Cornell Campbell, Eric 'Monty' Morris, Carl Dawkins, Derrick Harriot, Vernon Allen, Basil Gabbidon, Ken Parker, Kentrick Patrick, Amos Clarke and Slim Smith. Some like transplanted Trinidadian Jackie Opel, early dj Honeyboy Martin, Shenley Duffus, Lord Tanamo, Lloyd Briscoe, Ferdie Nelson, Ronald Wilson, Winston Samuels, Archibald Trott, Duke White, Jackie Estick and Lloyd Clarke, who in some cases went on to record later, are still mainly known for their work in ska. Many top musicians also took a turn at vocals in ska days, including guitarist Bobby Aitken (who, like brother Laurel, originally hailed from Trinidad) and pianist Theophalus Beckford. Female vocalists of the ska era include Doreen Shaffer, Marguerita, Millie Small and Millicent Todd ('Patsy').

The duo was a popular format in the ska era and groups like The Blues Busters, Alton (Ellis) and Eddie (Perkins), Stranger (Cole) and Ken (Boothe) and (Joe) Higgs and (Roy) Wilson were among the top. Others include Winston & George, Ewan McDermott and Primo Davidson and Clive & Naomi. Millicent Todd ('Patsy') made a career of pairing with a series of singers including Derrick Morgan (Derrick and Patsy), Stranger Cole (Stranger and Patsy) and Eddie Perkins (Eddie and Patsy). Millie Small, who went on to a successful solo career, teamed with singers Jackie Edwards and Roy Panton (Jackie and Millie, Roy and Millie). Panton also did a sting as one half of Monty and Roy with Eric 'Monty' Morris. Ken (Lazarus) and Keith (Lyn), the main singers for Byron Lee and the Dragonaires, made records individually and as a duo; the same is true of (Frank) Cosmo & Denzil (Dennis).

Other vocal duos include Andy & Clyde, Andy & Joey, Owen & Leon (Silveras), Chuck (Josephs) and Dobby (Dobson), Lloyd (Robinson) and Glen (Brown), The Blues Blenders, Douglas Brothers, Bunny & Scully, Billy & Bobby and Bobby (Aitken) and Hyacinth. Records in the duo format were recorded by John Holt and Alton Ellis (as John and Alton), Stranger (Cole) and Monty (Morris) and other one-off combinations. The earliest roots of what was to become the dj phenomenon can also be heard in ska, particularly in the earliest recordings of Sir Lord Comic, Count Machuki and King Stitt. This was a direct result of the switch-over from the live music of the Jamaican big bands to the popularity of the Sound System where selectors spun records and 'DJ's' got on the microphone to 'hype up' the crowd. Lord Brynner's 'Congo War' is a classic 'talking' style record from the ska era.

There were also original ska groups including The Jiving Juniors (featuring Derrick Harriot), The Rulers, The Valentines, The Selected Four (a.k.a. The Selected Few), The Avalons, The Dreamlettes, The Spanishtonians, The Deacons, Al & the Vibrators, The Jetts and many more. Groups who began in the ska era - often with only one tune - and went on to rock steady and reggae include The Tartans, The Paragons, The Heptones, The Flames and The Gaylads. Club bands, often featuring vocalists who recorded solo, recorded in the ska days as well, including The Vikings, Bobby Aitken's Carbbeats, Byron Lee's Ska Kings, Aubrey Adams and the Dewdroppers and The Shieks. A special case was Carlos Malcolm and His Afro-Jamaican Rhythms. Malcolm was musical director at JVC and managed to bridge the gap between popular and cultural presentations including a wicked treatment of a U.S. television theme ('Bonanza Ska').

Quite a few vocal groups who were established in the ska era — and some, like The Maytals, who preceded it — went on to score success in later eras, including The Clarendonians, The Ethiopians, Justin Hines and the Dominoes, The Techniques, The Charms, The Charmers, The (original) Upsetters (aka The Checkmates), The Silvertones and of course The Wailers. And of course many solo artists emerged from groups or formed other groups as in the case of Pipe Matthews, who sang lead with The School Boys in the ska era and went on to The Wailing Souls whose music spans several eras from ska to contemporary reggae.There were also female vocal groups in the ska era, including The Soulettes led by Rita Marley.[2]

Any treatment of this era must be constantly updated as new compilations continue to appear in the market. A couple recent releases include Ska-ing West (2010, Trojan), a double CD set that includes cuts from The Granville Williams Orchestra, The Four Aces, The Cherry Pies, Sir Percy, Rupie Edwards, Daniel Johnson, The Wong Brothers and The Mighty Avengers. Ghetto Ska: From the Vaults of WIRL & Federal Studios (Kingston Sounds) features a generous selection of cuts from Theophalus Beckford as well as obscure delights from the likes of The Tenor Twins and Shenley and Annette.

Original Jamaican ska presented hundreds of singers and players, all working out of less than a handful of studios in Kingston. Much of the music was exported to England and appeared on labels like Ska Beat and Blue Beat, the latter becoming an alternate name for the style in the UK. By the late sixties many of the original Jamaicn artists were also recording in England where a separate musical scene developed. Ska was not the only Caribbean music to be revisited by Western popular music. There is a strong Caribbean element in the music of Sam Cooke, and the late fifties and early sixties saw hits on the U.S. charts like the reworked calypso 'Man Smart, Woman Smarter' and 'The Banana Boat Song,' both later covered by Harry Belafonte. Calypso itself first invaded the U.S. through the big bands in the 1930's. In America, ska crossed over with the appearance of Byron Lee and the Dragonaires at the New York World's Fair in 1964. Their song 'Jamaican Ska' was covered by popular television personality (The Micky Mouse Club) Annette Funicello. Though not quite as popular as her big hit 'Tall Paul,' her version was one of the only ska records to reach American ears. Two of the others were Millie Small's 'My Boy Lollipop' which became a staple of oldies radio, and Prince Buster's 'Ten Commandments' issued on RCA.

When ska faded most of these players went on to play in the later styles and genres. But just as Jamaicans continued playing rhythm and blues when rock and roll took over in America, many music fans in England (where Jamaican music served in much the same capacity as Motown and Soul in the U.S.) stuck with ska. As ska faded from popularity in Jamaica, it continued to be produced in England. In the early eighties when a 'second wave' of ska took hold in England, some of the original players like Rico Rodriguez (who migrated to the UK in the sixties) played on those records too. Many of the UK studio groups utilized some immigrant or second generation Jamaicans. They backed second generation ska groups in the studio or cut instrumentals, sometimes adding their own vocals. These groups include The Pyramids (who also manifested as Symarip), The Rude Boys, The Invaders, The Jubilees, The Maroons and The Mopeds. Expatriate Jamaicans in England kept ska alive, among them Dandy Livingston whose 'Message To You Rudy' combined elements of ska and rock steady. Among the groups who charted in England in this era were second generation ska outfits like Madness, Selector, Bad Manners and The Specials. The Beat, known in the U.S. as The English Beat, were among the groups that melded ska with pop and post-punk. Often they first gained attention by covering an original ska tune, as in the case of Madness' eponymous cover of Prince Buster's tune 'Madness.' This tradition, which brought revivals of classic tune's like Andy and Joey's 'You're Wondering Now,' continued into the reggae era with covers such as Blondie's version of The Paragons' 'The Tide Is High' and entire albums of covers from UB40, who themselves established with a cover of Tony Tribe's 'Red Red Wine' (itself a cover of a Neil Diamond tune).

Many of the ska revival groups either continued in some form or have experienced a series of revivals over the years. Almost all of them released new music again in the nineties as ska achieved a new popularity in the U.S. One of the best things about the ska revival was that it breathed new life into original Jamaican ska. Reissues of classic material from

Studio One, Treasure Isle and Top Deck were followed by the reunion of the surviving members of the original Skatalites who have continued to record and tour in one form or another in the succeeding decades, adding a huge body of work to their already burgeoning catalog. As early members passed on other players who first established in that era have stepped forward to front the band (led for many years by the indomitable Tommy McCook) including the late Roland Alphonso, who died of a heart attack while performing onstage with the group. 'Cannonball' Bryan and 'Im' Brooks are among the players who have served a stint in the reformed version of the band.

Known as the 'Third Wave,' the U.S. ska revival lasted throughout the nineties and many of these bands are now experiencing revivals of their own as another wave of interest returns. American ska has taken many forms, from 'traditional' to punk ska, heavy metal ska, acoustic ska and pop. Perhaps the best known artist to emerge from the post-ska movement at this point is Gwen Stefani, who has gone on to have major pop international hits but the list of U.S. ska groups is truly amazing.

During the two decades from 1989 to 2009, as Reggae Update columnist for *Beat Magazine*, I reviewed full-length ska revival CDs from groups and artists including The Adjusters (two CDs), After Hours, The Aldermen, The Allstonians (who backed many original ska artists such as Eric 'Monty' Morris' in concert), The Allentons, The Articles, Attack of the Planet Smashers, Brent Barry (two CDs), The Bluebeats, Bim Skala Bim, Bop Harvey (two CDs), The Busters, Coyabalites (with original ska guests including Justin Hinds) and Crazy Baldheads. The post-ska proliferation continued with groups such as Dancin' Mood, Deal's Gone Bad (three CDs), The Drastics, Dr. Ring Ding (two CDs), The Eclectics, Eastern Standard Time, Eat at Joey's and The Exceptions. Many of these releases were on independent labels and a few on established U.S. labels like Shanachie. Producer Joe Ferry released two cd's titled 'Skallelujah' and 'Big Ska.' More music came from Filibuster, First Grade Crush (two CDs), Flashlight, Freetown, Go Jimmy Go (three CD's and counting), Isaac Green and the Ska-lars, Greenhouse, Heavy Step, Hot Stove Jimmy (two CDs), The Insteps, The International Beat, The Israelites,

Joe Kenny, King Chango, King Django, The Kingpins, Let's Go Bowling (two CDs), Los Hooligans, The Mighty Mighty Bosstones, Mobtown and Mr. Review. Some of the groups, like The New York Ska-Jazz ensemble, were steeped in the sounds of original ska masters The Skatalites, who broke up in the sixties but revived after the 'new ska' movement and returned to recording and the road. Others presented a more pop, punk or lighthearted approach. These include Orangetree, Buford O'Sullivan, Out of Line, The Parka Kings (three cd's), Peacock, Pressure Cooker, Prime Time, Pure Amphetamines, The Robustos, Ruder Than You, Run For Your Life, The Scofflaws (two CDs), The Secondhands, The Skalatones, The Skandalous Allstars, Skanic, Skapone, Skavovie (three CDs), speed metal ska enthusiasts Skinnerbox (three CDs), The Skoidats, The Slackers (four CDs), Spring Heel Jack, Stalking Roxy, Stand So Tall, Steady Ernest, Steady Ups, Stiff Breeze, Still Standing, The Stingers and Suspect Bill.

And it doesn't end there. Something in the high-energy uptempo beat of ska has continued to inspire young artists to pick up guitars and horns and return to the wellspring time and time again. Groups like Telegraph, The Toasters (four CDs), Thumper, Tricia and the Supersonics, Westbound Train and the Zyooks continue to pour out of America. From England new groups like Spunge mix punk and ska, traditionalists like Jazz Jamaica touch up the classics and offer new original works and offer new origianl works. The Tokyo Ska Paradise Orchestra is only one of a number of Japanese ska bands. The U.S. Shanachie label, which established itself with traditional Irish Music and branched out in reggae, released a number of ska anthologies, including *Freedom Sounds: A Tribute To The Skatalites*, two-volume ska covers of pop songs titled *SKAndalous*, two volumes of *Women In Ska* (second generation), and two volumes titled *Ska: The Third Wave*. In Los Angeles, groups like Hepcat, See Spot and the Kingston Ska Collective helped keep ska alive. Entire labels such as Stubborn Records, Beatsville, Steady Beat and Stomp issued catalogs and anthologies include *The West Coast Chronicles* featuring groups like The Upstarts and The Titans. *Skaliente* from the Grita label gathers bands like Mephiskapheles and Todos Tus Muertos. Two CDs titled *Everything Off-Beat* gathers ska from Chicago, including The Ska Beatles and Luke Ska Walker. The label specializes in Mid-West ska and has also issued four separate volumes titled *American Skathic* and one called *Ska American Style*. New York Beat on the prolific Moon Ska label catches up the East Coast action with three volumes titled *Skarmageddon* and three dedicated to Latin Ska featuring bands from Spain, Italy, Argentina and beyond. *Land Of the Rising Ska* from the same label puts the focus on Japanese ska bands. One of the most recent — and most welcome — additions to the ska revival is the release of Skatroniks' *Jamaica Skalsa #1* on the Skajam Records in 2009. Steeped in the sound of original ska with tight arrangements and driving 'riddims,' this eight-piece holds aloft the tradition that inspired the various tributaries of the ska revival. After hearing all the scattered stylings of the various influences that fed into the third wave, Skatroniks' straight on approach is like returning to the source.

From Ska to Rocksteady

Many of the later ska groups also branched out into rock steady and early reggae. Rock steady lasted less than two years as a dominant style but served as a crucible for many of the groups and artists who laid the foundation for reggae. It also heralded the advent of the independent producer and today enjoys a revival celebrated most recently in the documentary *Rocksteady: The Roots of Reggae* (directed by Stascha Bader, 2009, Hessegruttert Film AG).[3] Dozens of anthologies of classic rock steady productions from Duke Reid's Treasure Isle and Coxsone Dodd's Studio One, as well as productions from Bunny Lee, Phill Pratt and others are available from a variety of producers including new gatherings released for the first time in just the last few years. Since the publication of my book, *The Small Axe Guide To Rocksteady* (2009)[4] several new anthologies, a few of which include tunes not previously available, have been issued showing a revived interest in this classic style. Previously unavailable material from producer Bunny Lee includes a four-CD anthology and the new compilation *Rocksteady Hits the Town* (Kingston Sounds, 2010), which offers selections from Ann Reid, Glen Adams, Cynthia Richards and the Sensations among others. Many singers who established in the ska era flowered in the rock steady era (and came to full bloom as reggae artists). Alton Ellis, Ken Boothe, Stranger Cole and Desmond Dekker are among the singers who moved to the fore in rock steady.[5] Many of the same players who recorded in the ska era helped to create the backing tracks for rock steady classics, including particularly Lynn Taitt, Hux Brown, Tommy McCook and Gladdy Anderson. But rock steady also brought an influx of new blood into the studios of Kingston, Jamaica. Players like Dwight Pinkney, who went on to fill lead guitar duties for the long-running Roots Radics, first stepped forward in the rock steady era. Among the crucial players of the day are bassists Boris Gardner and Jackie Jackson, drummer Winston Grennan, keyboardists Jackie Mittoo, Leslie Butler and Winston Wright, and hornsmen Bobby Ellis and Jo Jo Bennett.[6] A whole new set of independent producers emerged in the rock steady days including Joe Gibbs, Bunny Lee, Leslie Kong, Ken Lack (Caltone), Alvin Ranglin, Sir J.J. and Jamaica's first great female producer, Sonia Pottinger. New singers emerged, like Phyllis Dillon, whose entire career is virtually rooted in the rock steady recordings she did for Duke Reid, and her label-mate Hopeton Lewis. Some, like Hemsley Morris, Austin Faithful or Johnny and the Attractions, may forever be known as rock steady artists for one or two great recordings. Others, like singer (and later producer) Clancy Eccles, Errol Dunkley, vocal duo Lloyd (Robinson) and Devon (Russell) and the soulful Winston Francis went on to solo careers in reggae. As with ska, some artists who began at the tail-end of that era went on to greater success in the next. This is the case with Horace Andy and Dennis Brown, each of whom recorded one late rock steady tune before establishing themselves among the greatest of reggae singers.

The rock steady era saw the emergence of hundreds of new vocal groups such as The Termites, The Pioneers, The Federals, The Rulers, The Tennors, The Uniques, The Jamaicans, Soul Leaders and The Melodians. Two of rock steady's biggest influences were American soul music and particularly the vocal group Curtis Mayfield and the Impressions. As reported in an interview with the members of The Meditations, all the groups of this era (including Bob Marley, Peter Tosh and Bunny Wailer, core members of The Wailers) wanted to 'be' The Impressions and included at least a few of their tunes in their repertoire. Indeed, both Burning Spear's 'People Get Ready' and Bob Marley's 'One Love' show the influence of Curtis Mayfield's early work with The Impressions.

Many established artists like Derrick Morgan and The Ethiopians, prospered during the rock steady period and, like Toots (Hibbert) and the Maytals, went on to even greater success with reggae. The duo Keith and Tex sit astride the two eras with reggae tunes that have a solid rock steady root. Deejays also took a giant step as the tempo slowed to rock steady. U Roy 'woke the town' with a string of hit records voiced over rock steady classics from The Paragons, Melodians, and others. Swiftly followed by Dennis Alcapone and Scotty, the new style opened the floodgates for what was to become one of the staples of the reggae and dancehall eras.

Establishing a tradition that continued into the 21st Century, with the success of the style came radical change. As groups like The Soul Brothers and Soul Vendors achieved success and went on tour new youths stepped up to become studio house bands, as was the case with Sound Dimension in the rock steady days at Studio One. Sound Dimension can be credited with some of the classic 'riddims' that not only bedded rock steady hits but went on to be re-worked for decades fueling hits not only from Studio One (which re-used the classic backing tracks with new young singers) but were 'updated' in succeeding years by Channel One, Penthouse and other studios and still bed many of today's dancehall hits. Artists as disparate as Aretha Franklin and No Doubt have paid tribute to this enduring musical style (both with songs title Rock Steady). Here, it is worth noting that rock steady—like ska and reggae—began life as a dance. 'Jamaican Ska' by Byron Lee and the Dragonaires,'Do the Rock Steady' by the Termites, and Toots and the Maytals' ground-breaking 'Do the Reggay' were all dance instruction records. Even dancehall's name reveals its origin. But the dances have not always fared as well as the songs they inspired—or which, in some cases, they were inspired by. Very few of today's reggae fans can actually dance the reggae.

Rock steady has seen recent revival in England as Bunny Lee to Pickering have incorporated original rhyt Treasure Isle and Studio One, voicing over the 'riddim: porary singers. Two recent albums from UK-based Bitty strong new melodies and lyrics over classic backing tra albums of rock steady have also been released by The Blackstones, a British vocal trio who have had many great singers pass through over the years. The rock steady beat morphed into a popular form of reggae known as Lover's Rock which survives on the British Charts to this day. It has also been given a new twist in the U.S. on anthologies like *Punk Steady* from Skandalous All Stars and *United Front* from David Hillyard and the Rocksteady Seven. Other Jamaican musical forms have been treated by a wide range of artists in the U.S. including Venice Shoreline Chris, Lord Mike's Dirty Calypsonians and the group called Mento Buru.[7]

As with all musical genres and categories, Jamaican music is really too amorphous to be squeezed into conceptual boxes like ska and rock steady. There are ska tunes that prefigure rock steady, rock steady tunes that hark back to ska, and tributaries that never turned into rivers along the way. One clearly defined 'sub-genre' that bridged rock steady and reggae is the style I have always known as 'chargers.' The Scorchers, Maytones, Ethiopians and Maytals all recorded songs in 1967 and 1968 that are neither rock steady nor reggae and this is what we used to call them 'chargers' - uptempo romps at the speed of ska that have elements of rock steady and reggae but really are in a style all their own. Interestingly, this style too has been revived, most recently by the L.A. based group, The Aggrolites, in a style they have dubbed 'dirty reggae.'

AND ON TO REGGAE, DUB AND DUB POETRY

The tendency of Jamaican producers to utilize new combinations of musicians to get new sounds fed into the stylistic innovations that birthed reggae music. Drummers Joe Isaacs and Paul Douglas, guitarist Ronnie 'Bop' Williams and saxman Dennis Campbell were among the players who helped shaped the sound in the studio. New young players,

...king with established practitioners, helped open up the sound. Reggae contains elements of pop and from the earliest days there have been pop reggae records from cover tunes like Bob and Marcia's 'Young Gifted and Black' to reggae-fied hits such as 'Don't Worry, Be Happy.' But reggae made its biggest score internationally with roots. The soundtrack to the film, *The Harder They Come,* starring Jimmy Cliff, introduced viewers and listeners around the world to ska, rock steady, reggae and roots and the popularity of Bob Marley and the Wailers, Toots and the Maytals, and later Black Uhuru ratcheted up the case for reggae music.

The diversity of roots music as it entered the international market-place in the mid-1970s was astounding. Peter Tosh, Bunny Wailer, The Gladiators, The Twinkle Brothers, Culture, The Abyssinians, U Roy, I Roy, Prince Far I, Burning Spear, Dennis Brown, Big Youth, Ras Michael and the Sons of Negus, and Max Romeo opened the floodgates and out poured Doctor Alimantado, Althea and Donna, Joe Higgs, Owen Gray, The Mighty Diamonds, Pat Kelly, Marcia Griffiths, Judy Mowatt, Jah Lloyd, Prince Hammer, Lee 'Scratch' Perry, Delroy Wilson, and dozens of other artists. Following closely behind were groups like Steel Pulse, Black Slate and Aswad, Dillinger, Trinity, Lone Ranger and startlingly innovative albums by King Tubby, Scientist and more. A new world of music was available and the reverberations are still being felt. Reggae music captured the minds and hearts of young people around the world in the 1970s, and today it continues to inspire feelings of hope and revolution around the world. Wherever a liberation movement springs up—in Belgrade, Belfast or Belmont Shore—reggae and images of its leading light are seen and heard. As the roots rock reggae style took hold internationally groups like Steel Pulse and Misty In Roots in England helped spread the word. In the U.S. labels like Bullwackies and Jah Life, both formed by Jamaicans living in New York, helped keep it alive. Less well known were early American reggae groups like Juice, Killer Bees, The Terrorists and Blue Riddim. But as the 1980s and 1990s advanced, more and more U.S. reggae bands began to get the feel and groups such as Inka Inka, steeped in the original roots music of Jamaican outfits such as The Itals, began to proliferate. These early groups forged a style that drew on reggae as it was heard in the U.S. and therefore developed a style that drew as much from rock as it did from reggae.

One of Jamaica's greatest musical innovations is dub. Born in King Tubby's studio in the Waterhouse district, this creative remixing of recorded tracks took on a life of its own in Jamaica but fell out of favor at the dawn of the digital age. Nonetheless, the plethora of releases in the 1970s and 1980s inspired new generations in England where new dub works continue to be released from artists like Mad Professor, Alpha and Omega and Jamaicans like Jah Shaka and (in the U.S.) and Scientist, who have gone international. The U.S. dance remix movement can be traced directly to dub's door. Among those working actively in the field of dub today are Canada's Mossman and Ryan Moore's Twilight Circus Sound System based in The Netherlands. The Japanese group Mute Beat was equally adept at ska and dub both live and on record. Some who have taken dub in new directions include U.S. groups Dub Addxx, Dub Station and Dub Trio. Internationally, dub beds work by groups such as Double Standart, Sevendub, Up Bustle and Out, as well as the work of Per Tjernberg. The pop group Gorrilaz released a dub version of some of their best-known tracks, and the 'dance single' extended mix offers 'versions' of work from the likes of Paul McCartney and Madonna.

Dub poetry, an offshoot of dub, brought artists like Mutabaruka to the fore. In England, Linton Kwesi Johnson held sway (often backed by Dennis Bovell, a UK reggae artist in his own right and founding member of the group Matumbi) and Canada's Lillian Allen, was at the forefront of a group of female dub poets. Carrying the style forward, artists like Yasus Afari kept to the roots and culture themes of Rastafari. Today, a bit of the dub poet can be heard in the contemporary artist, D.Y.C.R., and in the explosion of groups from beyond Jamaica like Midnite and Bambu Station. One of my favorite contemporary dub poets, Inubia, is a graduate of the University of the West Indies at Mona, in Jamaica.

Several international artists have scored hit records covering Jamaican tunes. Eric Clapton with Bob Marley's 'I Shot the Sheriff,' Blondie and The Paragons' 'Tide Is High' and Johnny Nash with 'Stir It Up.' Nash were among the artists who, like Paul Simon, recorded in Jamaica scored hits incorporating rock steady and reggae riddims. Jamaican music has served as an inspiration for many hits, and this cuts both ways—many of Jamaica's great singers were inspired by international artists and Jamaica has had her share of hits covering U.S. and British artists from Ken Boothe's 'Everything I Own' to some of today's radio fare. Yet, the biggest international influence has been and will continue to be the song catalog of Bob Marley and The Wailers. I've often wondered why if you grow sideburns and sing 'A-well-A-well-A' you are tagged as an Elvis Imitator, but if you grow dreadlocks and sing 'A Woah Yo Yo' you are known as a reggae singer. Nonetheless, artists around the world continue to be directly influenced by the look, sound and style of the man who has become reggae's leading ambassador. Watching a high spirited dance across the stage at a reggae festival a friend asked me 'why do they all do that?' It took only a moment of reflection to answer, 'Because Bob did.' But the reason for Marley's influence goes far beyond style. His songs stand as anthems of struggle against oppression, rebellion against wrong and upliftment. Whether they inspire you to chant down Babylon or take pride in your own achievements, make a commitment to create a better world or simply ('Three Little Birds,' 'Everything is gonna be allright') make you feel good, these songs provide hope and inspiration for downtrodden people around the world. Whatever else stands—ska, rock steady, dub, dancehall—the songs of Bob Marley innovated and will continue to transform.

The classic roots music of the late seventies and early eighties has spawned successive generations of roots singers and artists and producers in Jamaica like Luciano, Beres Hammond, Tarrus Riley and Richie Spice. Groups such as Morgan Heritage, originally based in New York, have joined the ranks of Bob Marley and the Wailers, Peter Tosh, Jimmy Cliff and groups such as Culture, The Gladiators and Israel Vibration, who have continued to keep a positive vibration emanating from Jamaica. First and second generation DJs such as U

Roy, Dennis Alcapone, Big Youth and Lone Ranger, inspired both the English MC style and the next generation 'bobo dread' chanters such as Sizzla, Anthony B and dozens of others. The reggae era also brought a whole new set of producers onto the scene. Some who began in the rock steady era, like Joe Gibbs and Bunny Lee, came to rival Studio One. The studio Channel One with (for it's time) technologically advanced recording equipment to get a clean, crisp sound, began to dominate — ironically utilizing reworked versions of original studio one 'riddims.' Ernest and Jo Jo Hookim opened the door to other producers, including artists turned producers like Jah Thomas and Jah Woosh. Linval Thompson and Junjo Lawes were among the producers who got a new sound from the studio. Succeeding waves of musicians were waiting at the studio gate and old hands like Tommy McCook were joined by a new generation of players. Glen Adams, Augustus Pablo, Bo Pee and dozens of others stepped up. Lloyd Parks, who originally sang alongside Wentworth Vernal in rock steady's Termites, took over bass duties for hundreds of sessions. Horsemouth Wallace, The Lewis Brothers, The Barrett Brothers, 'Wire' Lindo, 'Touter' Harvey and many many more made their mark in the roots era.

In time-honored tradition the top studio players gained success and moved on, making room for a new generation. Skin Flesh and Bones made way for The Revolutionaries.[8] Soul Syndicate began as new kids on the block and also served time as members of The Aggrovators and The Ark Angels. With Fully Fullwood on bass, Santa Davis on drums, Earl 'Chinna' Smith playing lead and Tony Chin rhythm guitar and Keith Sterling on keyboards (as with many studio outfits the lineup fluctuated from session to session) they brought a fresh approach to a constantly changing music. By the time The Roots Radics (with guitarist Dwight Pinkney, bassist Flabba Holt and Ansel Collins on keys) became house band at Channel One, a new generation of DJ's like Yellowman steered the music in the direction we would eventually know as dancehall. The paradox here is that the Roots Radics were also Gregory Isaacs — and sometimes Bunny Wailer's — band. They went international with a deal with RAS Records (much as Sly and Robbie had done before them with

Island and Black Uhuru), playing behind dozens of artists from Israel Vibration to Peter Broggs on albums and international tours. This of course freed up the studio again—only this time, as had happened in America in the preceding decade, the musicians were replaced by keyboards wired to computers as the new digital age of recording hit Jamaica.

The explosion of singers and DJ's continued as reggae hit the town as well. Bob Andy, Don Carlos, Keith Poppin, Claudius Linton, Junior Delgado, Sugar Minott, Bim Sherman, Cornell Campbell, Leroy Smart, Barry Brown, Al Campbell and dozens of others, each with a unique approach, made names for themselves. Groups like the Maytones, Morwells, Royals, Slickers, Cables, playing bands such as inner circle and DJ's galore including Jah Stitch, Jah Lloyd, Prince Jazzbo and more, made reggae seem a never-ending parade of talent. New studios seemed to be opening every day with fresh young producers such as Donovan Germain and Mikey Bennet, scoring new triumphs. King Tubby's protégé, Jammy, issued a series of popular dub albums and went on to produce his replacement in the studio, Scientist, who soon had a string of albums of his own. Engineers like Errol T, percussionists like Sticky, Scully and Bongo Herman and artist/producers such as Yabby You, kept reggae moving at a pace that seemed unstoppable.

INTERNATIONAL REGGAE

In the meantime, hundreds of homegrown reggae outfits around the world helped keep the spirit of roots reggae music alive. I have reviewed reggae groups and singers from nearly every country in the world—from Belfast, Berkley and Bombay to Israel, through to the former Iron Curtain, and India. Perhaps you never heard of The Ulsterfarians, FC Apatride (from Belgrade), Soul Vibrations from Nicaragua, Chile's Gonwana or Brazil's Skank, but they have been played on my radio show, alongside Jamaica's Chuck Fenda, Junior Kelly and Jimmy Riley. Today, there is hardly a town or city in America that does not have a little reggae shop, a club with 'local' reggae bands (often featuring members originally from Jamaica, Belize, Barbados or Africa) and venues for Jamaican artists and groups on tour. International reggae includes Cidade Negra from Brazil, Canada's Pressure Drop, Cuba's Arawak Jah, Free Joseph and Nasio Fontaine from Dominica, No Explanation from Finland, Three Dimensions from Germany, Haiti's Papa Jube, Roots Africa from Israel, Japan's Highest Region, Tierra Sur from Peru, The Ganglords from Switzerland, and Crucial Bankie from the Virgin Isles. Burgeoning reggae scenes abound from France and The Netherlands to South America and Guam. Truly, reggae has gone international.

Reggae took another turn in the UK where singers like Maxi Priest, Peter Hunnigale and Bitty McLean mashed up the roots and lover's styles. A new generation of DJ's took root in the UK as well, where artistes including Pato Banton, Tippa Irie, Papa Levi, and others inspired a new generation of artists like Top Cat, Dominique and many others who gave the MC a new spin. In America as well singers and DJ's with Jamaican roots like Sister Carol, Scion Sashay Success and Glen Washington moved up. Over the years, the American reggae bands have developed more of a 'yard' feel, incorporating elements of ska, rock steady, roots, the dj style, dub and even a sprinkling of Hip Hop into their style. Among the reggae groups I've written about in *Beat Magazine* are Boom Shaka, a group that issued an album each on nearly every American reggae label. From Ababa and The Ark Band to The Woodwellas and Zion Train, American reggae bands include Rising, Roaring and Whispering Lion, Jah Eye, Jah Moon, and Jah Roots, Roots Natty Roots, Roots Rock Society, Roots Foundation and Roots Syndicate. One Foundation, One Tribe and One World, Native Elements, Native Roots, Urban Roots and Native Sun as well as Collective Security, Foreign Exchange, Lambsbread and Local Hero, with stops along the way for nearly every Bob Marley song title from *Buffalo Soldier* to *Uprising*. The latest crop of U.S.-based reggae groups has achieved a sound that is dynamic, innovative and forward. Groups like Grounation, Soja, Soul Majestic and Ten Foot Ganja Plant have large internet followings and fill venues in America and Europe. Many of the groups in the Los Angeles area, such as The Aggrolites, The Lions, The Expanders and Chapter 11, have incorporated early Jamaican styles and contemporary recording techniques to create a soulful sound all their own. As much of the great early Jamaican music was inspired by rhythm and blues and jazz, with singers like Fats Domino, Brook Benton and Sam Cooke imitated and revered, these groups have taken their own approach, while tipping their tams to Bob Marley and others. One of the most interesting manifestations of reggae has taken place on the island of Hawaii. Turn on your radio in Hawaii and you'll swear everything you hear is reggae, although it is almost all recorded by homegrown Hawaiian (some say 'Jawaiaan') singers and bands. Even on the mainland most Hawaiian shops offer Bob Marley T-shirts alongside the 'traditional' Hawaiian shirts, and even those might be emblazoned with the words 'Jah-Loha'. Hawaiian reggae leans toward the pop sound of UB40 but often the lyrics are as militant as the roots music of old.

In the philosophy of Marcus Garvey, the writings of Walter Rodney, and the music of Bob Marley, Burning Spear and other Jamaican singers, the African root is paramount. The Nyahbingi 'riddims' that underpin roots reggae hark to pre-diaspora origins. Reggae came full circle with the music of African artists like Alpha Blondie, Majek Fashek and the late Lucky Dube. Although they emulated the Jamaican sound of the 1970s, they brought a fresh approach to reggae. Today, Africa continues to utilize the reggae beat as recent releases like African Reggae on Putamayo reveal. New African voices include Takana Zion, Victor Deme and Niominka Bl and Ridiaxas Band.

INNOVATION AND TRANSFORMATION: DANCEHALL, TECHNOLOGY AND BEYOND

But Jamaica refused to stand still while its music captivated the rest of the world. Within the context of reggae continued innovations such as dub, dub poetry and the DJ style that created entire new genres of music, with hundreds of album-length releases leading to direct imitations including techno, the dance remix, rap and hip/hop. In many cases, these reactions fed straight back into Jamaican music which had earlier assimilated R & B, country and Latin elements and continues to absorb international components into the original mix of African roots, Caribbean rhythms and that uniquely Jamaican element, patois. As at every change in style and tempo in Jamaican music, new young musicians, artists and producers were waiting at the gate to jump into the fray. Dancehall singers and DJ's—the line between the two approaches began to blur from this point on—honed their skills on Sound Systems in the time-honored tradition, then made their way into the studio to record. Cocoa Tea, Charlie Chaplin, Brigadier Jerry, Sister Nancy and Early B, are but a few of the first wave of artists who made their name in dancehall. New young roots singers like Yami Bolo, Half Pint, Ras Shiloh and Jah Mali followed the lead of Admiral Tibet and Garnett Silk in returning conscious themes to reggae in this time. It is well known, though not always acknowledged in the U.S., that Hip Hop was inspired by and grew directly out of the Jamaican DJ style. Early proponents of Hip Hop like Cool Herc were themselves transplanted Jamaicans and many of the early Hip Hop artists like Heavy D and Notorious B.I.G. were born in Jamaica or of Jamaican heritage. Certainly their music and the concept of reworking pre-existing rhythms was inspired by the fast-chat style that took root in Kingston decades before it reverberated around the world in rap.

All the earlier Jamaican styles of music fed into dancehall, which brought still more innovation into the mix. A new generation of artists and producers came with a new sound that grew up alongside the international roots rock reggae approach, again sweeping first Jamaica and then the world. The rise of the female DJ, DJ duos and digital technology led to a whole new style dubbed ragga, and once again Jamaica continued to alter the elements - the music we call dancehall today is as different in sound from that of the late 1980s, as rock steady was from ska, or reggae from rock steady. Though influenced by American Hip Hop in an ongoing cycle of cross-fertilization, dancehall's own influence has been felt internationally—witness the crossover success of Matisyahu as only one instance. An entire sub-genre of music from Latin America (Reggaeton) stems from the influence of just one dancehall tune—Shabba Ranks' 'Dem Bow.' Even more impressive are the post-dancehall chart achievements of a new generation of Caribbean artists including Rihanna and Sean Kingston, as more and more top selling releases dip into the wellspring of reggae.

I first began playing reggae music on the radio in Southern California in 1982. On my show Reggae Central on KPFK in LA I play ska, rock steady, pop and roots reggae, dub, dub poetry, the DJ style and dancehall, trying to give a glimpse of the depth and breadth of reggae music in each installment.[9] I have shared reggae music with listeners on the West Coast for over twenty-five years and both Reggae and radio have both changed a lot in that time. There is one school of thought that the glory days of Jamaican music are in the past—and there is so much great music from the past I can understand why they feel that way—but reggae is a living, breathing entity and some of the best new music to my ear is equal to anything that came before it. In addition, the concept of local radio has changed significantly. For example, you can now go online to KPFK.ORG and hear my show live anywhere in the world (each show is archived for two weeks so you can tune in anytime you like). Through a couple of links—www.myspace.com/reggaecentralkpfk or google Reggae Central Facebook—you can view photos and video clips of guests in the studio. In short, radio is now available everywhere anytime and you can see as well as hear it.

New technology has also made the modern recording process even sweeter. Gone are the days of the 'computerized' riddim that sounded tinny and mechanical. With Pro Tools and other affordable technological advances in software and hardware a plethora of home studios now dot the island of Jamaica, pumping out good music. An entire new generation of young singers, deejays and singjays are utilizing these developments to speak their own minds much as an earlier generation had the chance to speak theirs. The music business itself has changed, and independents rule. Each producer or artist can set up his or her own website and make their music available without the middleman— the corporate labels and the corporate chains that once controlled the industry. These changes require innovation—they represent transformation—and they can be used to create in a way that has never been possible before.

CONCLUSION

Reggae music and dancehall culture serve a unique function in Jamaica, empowering the young and disenfranchised just as ska did for their grandparents more than fifty years ago. It is their music, and nothing can or will take that away. Reggae fills a great void for fans around the world as well, as anyone who has ever attended a festival or a dance can attest. Jamaican music has served as a unifying force signaling the possibilities of freedom, justice and equality and it is no wonder you see flags with Bob Marley's face adorning them flying wherever in the world people demonstrate for human rights.   One thing that has kept Jamaican music vibrant (though initially criticized as destructive to it) has been the continued revisiting of it's own roots versions and the re-use of 'riddims,' often reworked and updated but continually referencing earlier approaches. Thus, we have Buju Banton deejaying over ska tracks, new singers covering rock steady tunes, classic reggae riddims from Studio One and Bob Marley utilized to bed new songs and a whole new generation of artists who are as at ease in the deejay style as they are in singing. In fact, I believe we have entered a post-dancehall era in which artists like Fantan Mojah, Lutan Fyah and Italy's Albarosie have combined the roots messages of the 1970s with the contemporary riddims of today. A new generation of deejays have eschewed 'slack-ness' (identified with dancehall) and returned cultural messaging to the forefront of their music.

No one can say with any certainty what is next for Jamaican music, but it is clear that a worldwide music industry that has been battered by hard times and changes in the way music is captured and controlled, continues to look to Jamaica for ideas and inspiration in innovation and transformation. Jamaica has proven herself equal to the task, feeding new artists, approaches and forms into an ever-changing industry. There is a very good chance that whatever lies on the horizon in the world of music, its origin will be traced back in time to the island of Jamaica.

NOTES

1. For example, listen to Fats Domino's groundbreaking 'Be My Guest' from 1959, where virtually every element of what we came to know as ska is present.

2. This is by no means intended as a complete list of Jamaican artists and groups who recorded ska.

3. I treat the rock steady era in depth my book: Foster, Chuck. *The Small Axe Guide To Rocksteady,* Muzik Tree, 2009

4. This book features artist, musician and producer profiles of the period, plus a full discography on albums on vinyl and CD.

5. My first book, Foster, Chuck. *Roots Rock Reggae: An Oral History of Reggae Music From Ska To Dancehall,* Billboard Books, 1999, features in depth career-spanning interviews with Desmond Dekker and Ken Boothe.

6. For a more complete review of musicians of the rock steady era see *The Small Axe Guide To Rock Steady,* 2009.

7. I recently produced a tune called 'Rock Steady' for Zema, an artist now based in Kingston.

8. Sly Dunbar drummed for both groups but new combinations were formed first with bassist Lloyd Parks then Robbie Shakespeare.

9. KPFK has the strongest signal west of the Mississippi, 112,000 Watts (over twice the power of the strongest commercial signal in LA) covering San Diego to Santa Barbara and Inland. I have been blessed to have some of the great Jamaican artists of all time—including artists like Alton Ellis, Joe Higgs, Phyllis Dillon, Lucky Dube and Dennis Brown who are sadly no longer among us—as guests on my radio show.

8

PUTTING
UP
RESISTANCE

INDIGENOUS RADIO SERIAL DRAMA
AND REGGAE MUSIC

> *To live is to choose. But to choose well, you*
> *must know who you are and what you stand*
> *for, where you want to go and why you*
> *want to get there.*
>
> **Kofi Annan**

BACKGROUND

Based on earlier research in oral culture, this paper attempts to establish interconnectivity between reggae music and indigenous radio serial dramas in that both seek to document, through the gaze of the marginalised, aspects of Jamaican oral tradition that are influenced by Europe and rooted in the Black Great Tradition of Africa. Additionally, the major inner city ghettoes of Western Kingston stand

as sources of inspiration for the contents and performance of indigenous radio serial dramas and reggae music. This area provided shelter
for the steady trek of thousands of 'country come a town' young men
and women who, from as early as the mid-19th century, continued to
migrate from rural to urban Jamaica to eke out a livelihood.

Among the main causes for this migration from rural to urban Jamaica
was the decline in agricultural production as well as the persistence
of other socio-economic conditions in postcolonial Jamaica. Illustratively, there was the collapse of the plantation economic structure and
a continual decline in sugar production. The *Report of the Economic
and Social Survey of Jamaica* (1973) documented the decline in sugar
production from 383,000 tons in 1969 to 326,000 tons in 1973. The
quantity exported also showed a decline from 302,000 tons (1969) to
261,000 tons (1973). This downturn resulted in the massive dislocation
of rural persons from their traditional sources of income. The pull to
the metropolis, Kingston, was attributed to its commercial functions
and embryonic industrial development. The Labour Department's 1954
Annual Report stated that of the 722 registered factories in Jamaica, 357
were located in Kingston. The 1954 Registrar General's Estimate also
showed that twenty-six per cent (26 per cent) of the island's inhabitants
lived in Kingston and St. Andrew.

Maunder's (1960) survey findings revealed that the Kingston labour
force represented a concentration of persons with no formal education
or training; and that this group was largely comprised of semi-skilled
persons, who either worked as manual labourers or provided personal
services. Though many of the unskilled migrants gravitated to occupations such as farming, fishing, street vending and higglering in the
markets, their aspirations for social and economic amelioration in the
city remained largely unrealised. The situation that unfolded as a result
of the economic uncertainties was one of masses of disenfranchised
Jamaicans trying to eke out a living from their positions on the periphery of mainstream society, without being able to penetrate the borders.
This expanding reservoir of under-utilised migrants from rural Jamaica
generated numerous problems to society in that there were no official/

structured measures in place to absorb them in the production cycle. These persons used numerous coping mechanisms, including the development of a common language, to ensure their survival; and in so doing created Homi Bhabha's notions of 'hybridity' and the 'third space' from which insiders projected their shared experiences and aspirations (Bhabha 1996). The improvement in mass communication and the intensification of nationalist fervour gradually shifted the traditional boundaries to centre the margins.

RADIO AS AN EFFECTIVE MEDIUM OF MASS COMMUNICATION

Although the popularity of radio as an effective medium of mass communication intensified after the Second World, initially this reali-sation was missed by many members of the listening public. However, the entrepreneurship class recognised the popularity of this electronic device so in order to maximise its potential, radio companies built networks and sought content to fill their allotted airtime. Initially, music and drama programmes were imported and represented a stable diet for radio listeners. Although these imported programmes were well-received in Jamaica, their contents were unfamiliar to the masses and were possibly embraced because of the technological novelty that radio represented or because of Jamaicans' familiarity with orality and storytelling and the diversification provided by this innovative way of communication.

Thus, given this predisposition to orality, radio provided a convenient, far-reaching and cost-effective medium for transmitting reggae music and indigenous serial drama. The airing of both genres not only contrib-uted to the development of radio broadcasting in Jamaica but provided the impetus for its use in national development. One of the obstacles identified was the level of literacy among the Jamaican masses. The editorial in *The Daily Gleaner* on May 4, 1954 reported that:

'Complete illiteracy is the miserable lot of about one person in four over the age of eleven in this Island... the remaining

three-quarters of the population can be classified as semi-il-
literate, reading without facility or any real understanding of
what they read and writing only as a result of a major physical
and mental effort.'

Some policymakers in the post Independence era who recognised
that the English associated with broadcasting was incomprehensible
to most Jamaicans advocated for and encouraged the use of Nation
Language, although *The Great Tradition* of Europe continued to be the
signifier of progress and social acceptance. Kamau Brathwaite's (1993)
discourse on *nation language* speaks of a submerged language coined
by the enslaved Africans for communication among themselves. This
was an Africanised version of the English Language imposed by the
colonial masters. Thus, the choice of Nation Language proposed by
policy makers to communicate with the masses was opposed by the
Eurocentric minority group. However, its resonance among the masses
reinforced the appropriateness of using Nation Language to communicate issues of national concern. These issues included agricultural
development, family planning and cultural integration.

THE JAMAICA BROADCASTING CORPORATION (JBC) AND NATIONALISM

During the 1950s, as Jamaica prepared to embrace its political Independence, the fervour of nationalism manifested itself in the advocacy
of indigenous media programmes to foster civic pride. To reiterate,
Jamaica had established a tradition of transmitting radio serial drama,
but the popularity of this genre of programming heightened with the
emergence of the Jamaica Broadcasting Corporation (JBC) radio station
in 1959 as a public communication entity with a specific mandate to
promote Jamaican arts through the fostering of home-grown talents.
John Maxwell stated that the JBC was responsible for exposing Jamaican musicians such as Count Ossie, Bob Marley and Toots Hibbert. He
posits that:

'It was the JBC whose attention to the mento, jankunnu, kumina and rastafari cultures brought them to the notice of their own people and the world. It was the JBC that created the market for Jamaican musicians and producers where none had existed before' (Maxwell 2009).

To enable this fostering of local talent, the JBC introduced a number of facilities. This included the construction and equipping of a recording studio to develop local talent and the employment of staff to facilitate this training and broadcasting. For example, Bradley (2000) posits that during this thrust of nationalism, radio broadcasting increased the popularity of downtown Ska music from the urban centre of Kingston to Jamaica in general.

The introduction of local radio broadcasting triggered ambivalent reactions from Jamaican society. This generated tension between those who supported the written word as opposed to orality as a preferred means of communication. This bias is evident in early media reports. An article in an issue of the *Public Opinion* Weekly Newspaper in January 1954 stated that:

'Some readers complain that too much space is being given to radio; but when one considers that this medium reaches a larger audience than any publication in Jamaica, including the daily papers, one must agree that radio, good or bad, deserves some notice'.

Radio programming of *Folk* culture in oral narrative performances represents a paradigm shift from the colonial era when music and drama programmes were imported from overseas. The transmission of live ska music was one of the indigenous programmes provided by JBC radio during its fledgling stage. Keeble MacFarlane recalls the work of Sonny Bradshaw in staging the *Jamaican Hit Parade*. According to McFarlane, this programme:

'tracked the sales of locally produced records and gave them extensive exposure on the air. Bradshaw also devised and produced the landmark *Teen Age Dance Party*, a programme which ran in the later afternoon five days a week and which showcased local music' (2009).

Both genres of oral narrative performances had the misfortune of being categorised as mere entertainment. The tendency was for media houses to air these programmes routinely and discard, if not physically then through scant regard for how they were preserved and stored. Consequently, many of these early recordings have been lost to posterity because the radio station's policy seemed to have omitted a retention aspect for these oral narrative performance productions.

BACKGROUND TO INDIGENOUS RADIO SERIAL DRAMA

Initially, canned soap operas were imported from areas such as the USA and Australia by the only radio station, ZQI. These were used as fillers. With the emergence of the new nation and the thrust towards national development, indigenous programming provided an engaging alternative to imported programmes which were popular but disconnected from the reality of most people's existence (Mock Yen, 2002). Experimentation with developing indigenous programmes appropriated *edutainment* strategies for effecting positive behavioural changes. Persons were able to look at themselves introspectively and be guided by some of the solutions communicated through the use of indigenous language, storyline and messages. As the popularity in both genres increased and programme ratings excelled, reggae music and drama serials were repositioned in the programme schedules. By the 1980s the radio drama serials had become an important feature of primetime programming.

This official thrust of national development to create indigenous programmes, was considered an essential exercise to dissipate what earlier Eurocentric Jamaicans regarded as the masses of uneducated people's propensity to civil disturbances and unrest (Handbook of Jamaica 1887). Among the early indigenous programmes were the productions of radio serial dramas. My research to date has shown that approximately 18 radio serial dramas had been produced over a 27 year period. The appropriation of this genre in Jamaica was embraced to interpret and communicate national agricultural, economic and cultural development plans to the masses.

Another expression also used in the literature for radio serial drama is the term 'soap opera', which was coined by the American Press in the 1930s to denote serialised domestic radio dramas. By 1940, this genre represented approximately 90 per cent of all commercially-sponsored daytime broadcast hours in the USA. The 'soap' in soap opera alluded to their sponsorship by manufacturers of household cleaning products. The defining quality of the soap opera form is that it is a serial oral narrative. That is, a story told through a series of spoken individual and narratively linked installments.

Jamaica's experimentation with developing indigenous radio serial dramas began in the 1950s. Among the earlier productions was *Life with the Morgan Henrys*. According to Mock Yen (2002), this was the first radio programme scripted and spoken on air in the language spoken by most Jamaicans most of the time. This radio serial drama offended the sensibility of some middle class Jamaicans and generated a great deal of controversy because of the use of Nation Language instead of the English associated with *learned* society and broadcasting. This production was aired on Sunday evenings and featured Alma Hilton (now Mock Yen) and Ranny Williams who played multiple roles. Williams was its scriptwriter, producer and director. Mock Yen recalled that the airing of the programme at 6:00 p.m. on Sundays reportedly was blamed for the decline in the number of church-goers who normally attended evening worship, but then opted to stay home to listen to the programme.

POSITIONING PERKINS' PERFORMANCE NARRATIVES

Elaine Perkins, Jamaica's renowned scriptwriter, producer and director of indigenous radio serial drama began her experimentation with this genre in 1959. In an interview (2010), she reported that her success could be attributed to her ability to submerge *Self* to project *Others* in developing her scripts. Her intrusion on this *in-between* space enabled her to listen to people and write about their stories. Additionally, her cast members were amateurs whom she identified while *eavesdropping* on people's conversations. This approach to storytelling represented a paradigm shift from the norm in which others wrote as experts and used professional actors to perform. Perkins' strategies also reflect some of those used by reggae lyricists as sources for writing songs. In her works, Perkins exposed the space occupied by the marginalised masses, through her use of the contestations with which they grappled and the survival strategies they implemented. These issues provided the organic framework in which Perkins interjected the desired messages.

Between 1959 and 1985, Perkins wrote and produced six multi-episode radio drama serials in which she promulgated people's lived experiences as follows:

Raymond the Sprayman (1959) which showcased the government's mosquito eradication campaign;

Life in Hopeful Village (1963-1976) which promoted integrated rural development. This was the most popular radio show in Jamaica for four years;

Stella (1967-68) which focused on some social issues that were important to the middle class;

Dulcimina: Her Life in Town (1967-80) which addressed problems faced by rural-to-urban migrants. It retained the number-one spot on the radio ratings for 13 years. The real-life nature of the characters made them seem familiar to listeners;

Life at Mimosa Hotel (1984) which exposed some of the issues that were affecting the tourism industry in Jamaica; and

Naseberry Street (1985) which addressed family planning issues.

Perkins's indigenous radio drama serials were well-received and outperformed the imported ones. They consistently received high audience ratings in that category as well as overwhelming support from government broadcast entities, the Jamaica Information Service and Jamaica Broadcasting Corporation radio stations. For example, in 1973 *Dulcimina: Her Life in Town* attracted 97 per cent of the available radio audience.

CHAOTIC KINGSTON

The exponential growth in population in urban Jamaica and the limited state resources that were available in a skewed society posed numerous challenges for policy makers and urban dwellers. Robotham, in defining what he calls 'our urban blight' (2003) posited that the current social and human decay among inner city residents in Jamaica is as a result of the sub-human living conditions of those thousands of rural Jamaicans who came to Kingston and settled in inner city locations such as what is now known as Tivoli Gardens (that is the area near to the old Tivoli cinema); and along the Spanish Town Road, beyond Cockburn Pen. As successive generations of rural dwellers drifted to the city in search of gainful employment they brought with them a wealth of cultural practices and expressions that provided them with safety valves when the rigours of urban living conditions and the accompanying disappointments began to overwhelm them. Many of the coping mechanisms used in putting up resistance to a system of governance that failed to provide for the masses of marginalised Jamaicans have been memorialised in Jamaica's indigenous music genres, especially reggae. The sentiments communicated through these songs have been further endorsed by some scriptwriters of indigenous radio serial dramas. Research has shown that effective communicators of indigenous cultural expressions are those who remain connected to the true sources of information – the people themselves whose lived experiences provide organic resources for the development of edutainment docudramas. Feature programmes of interviews with reggae artistes have also revealed how their connections to the customs and practices of rural Jamaicans have infiltrated the lyrics and music of their songs.

As the growing numbers of rural migrants who mostly became the urban marginalised masses continued to compete for scarce resources their disappointment often manifested itself through expressions of militancy and resistance to the established system of governance. These expressions which were often transmitted through their performances included the urban *Rude Boy* phenomenon, alternative religious practices, Rastafari Movement, music, dance and the use of Nation Language to communicate with *insiders*. The messages of resistance that were communicated orally include the Wailers' lyrics such as 'Get up, stand up: stand up for your rights!' and 'Slave driver, the table is turned' (Stolzoff 2000). These songs communicate the plight of the marginalised masses and have served to document the militancy of our people in ways that resonated with that group of disenfranchised young Jamaicans who were classified as 'Rude Boys'.

ORAL NARRATIVE PERFORMANCES AND THE AESTHETICS OF SILENCE

Reggae music is indigenous to Jamaica and is now a defining factor in the conceputalization of Brand Jamaica. According to Reggae artiste, Patrick Barrett, (also known as Tony Rebel), *You no see it reggae music a positive vibration and that's why it deh inna the four comers of the earth.* Barrett also reminds us that: *A nuh coke or crack, reggae music put Jamaica on top...* One plausible worldview is that Reggae evolved from the fusion of the local folk music form known as Mento, coupled with outside influences, especially from the USA. The external music forms that have influenced reggae include jazz, bebop, rhythm and blues, and rock 'n' roll. Lyrically, although some music critics regard Reggae music as a form of protest, to cultural practitioners it effectively chronicles the often difficult socio-economic conditions of persons living on the periphery of mainstream society both in Jamaica and what was then called Great Britain. It is through the oral narrative performances of both Jamaicans at home and in the Diaspora that the construction and liberation of Black identity is facilitated.

Many Jamaican Reggae artistes emerged from a position of *nothingness* and *invisibility* to give the disenfranchised people a voice and in so doing they have documented aspects of Jamaican oral culture in their sound and video recordings that have both local and universal appeal. Some themes used by these artistes are derived from the Bible, Jamaican folklore, their environment, Duppy stories and Obeah (White, 2000). Additionally, the cultural signifiers embedded in reggae music support the motif of liberation in that this genre serves to defy the tenets of mainstream society with its entrenched systems for enforcing compliance and conformity. The exponential growth in reggae music and the global acceptance of its messages which are rooted in oppression and disenfranchisement, represent a counter-discourse to the established order and its intolerance of non-conformists. When reggae music is combined with moving images the scope for interpretation is enriched, especially for research scholars whose range of interests tend to be multifaceted. According to Hebdige, 'The music always sounds sweet, even when the lyrics include scathing attacks on the colonial system.' He further adds: 'In effect, Marley was making the Western world dance to the prophecies of its own destruction' (1990, 81).

The urban *Rude Boy* phenomenon had its genesis in the 1940s when the squalid social conditions and abject poverty in western Kingston generated a criminal underworld that threatened to erode the established order. The *Rude Boy* phenomenon has been memorialised in a Jamaican dance-song genre known as Rock Steady. This genre emerged during the mid-1960s, that is, during the early years after Jamaica had been granted political independence from Britain. Jamaica's independent status did not provide the panacea anticipated. Hardships persisted and the jobs anticipated did not materialise. The *country come a town* phenomenon escalated and the number of new internal migrants resulted in exponential growth in the urban population. This meant more persons vying for the few available jobs. The political directorate had no ameliorative systems in place to diffuse the mounting tensions. Instead of encouraging dialogue, they intensified the forces of oppression and imposed sanctions that only served to further fragment the fledgling unity that was evident in the aftermath of Independence.

It was against the background of levels of hopelessness, alienation and disillusionment among the disenfranchised masses of young people that a subculture began to develop, which manifested itself in delinquency and rowdy behaviour. Vincent 'Ivanhoe' Martin, popularly known as 'Rhygin', was among those young people who came to Kingston to seek employment but resorted to a life of crime. He was a hero among the oppressed people but a security risk to the authorities. His exploits were legendary and indicated a rejection of authority. They were the inspiration for the movie and hit song 'The Harder They Come,' which feature internationally recognised reggae artiste, Jimmy Cliff. The song's profound lyrics encapsulate the indomitable spirit and resilience of the masses:

> *Well, they tell me of a pie up in the sky*
>
> *Waiting for me when I die*
>
> *But between the day you're born and when you die*
>
> *You know, they never seem to hear even your cry...*
>
>
> *Chorus:*
>
> *The harder they come*
>
> *The harder they'll fall*

> *One and all*
>
> *And I keep on fighting for the things I want*
>
> *Though I know that when you're dead you can't*
>
> *But I'd rather be a free man in my grave*
>
> *Than living as a puppet or a slave*
> *(The Harder They Come, 1972)*

Elaine Perkins also immortalised the symbolic Rude Boy, *Rhygin*, in the context of an evil spirit used by the obeah man to induce acquiescence from his disruptive clients. Rhygin was murdered on Lime Cay in Jamaica. Perkins' use of this information could be viewed as a source of intimidation to prevent some inquisitive characters from visiting the island.

Although Rock Steady as a music dance form only lasted for a few years, many aspects of its *Rude Boy* culture are still evident both in Jamaican music and in the general society. Prahlad views 'the rude boy as an aspect of the warrior/priest persona' that later evolved into reggae artistes, who eventually became Rastafari. He further explained that 'the rude boy posture is defiant, tough, rebellious, and sometimes lawless'. (Prahlad 2001, 34) Prahlad cites Rowe's discourse on Rastafari to make the connection between *Rude Boys* and Rastafari. According to Rowe:

> 'The open defiance and opposition to the state linked the rude boy phenomenon to the Rastafari movement, where rudie tended to seek refuge when fleeing from the authorities' (1998, 34).

The Rastafari Movement intensified as increasing numbers of Jamaicans identified with the issues explored by this group. State coercion did not eliminate this movement and its members continued to explore options for expressing dissatisfaction with the Establishment. The interconnectivity between Rastafari and reggae music is recognised internationally. Reggae music emerged towards the end of the 1960s as a fusion of the jubilant Ska with its promises of hopefulness and the contemplative Rock Steady with its reality check. Among the distinct features of reggae music is the application of African drumming techniques and the influences of the United States' Rhythm and Blues (R&B), soul, gospel and rock music.

Some *Rude Boy* expressions and posturing associated with the Rock Steady genre were utilised in Elaine Perkins' radio serial drama by certain characters who objected to the system of governance. The *Rude Boy* discourse is evident in reggae songs such as Peter Tosh's 'I'm the Toughest' and Max Romeo's 'Smile Out of Style'. Both discourses represent a continuum in the subaltern's attempts to negotiate a space for identity affirmation.

RELIGION: RITES AND ROUTES

Religion, which has been regarded as fundamental to Jamaican life and a panacea for the masses, is central to their coping mechanisms and therefore factors prominently in their daily lives. What is observed in both reggae and indigenous radio serial drama performances is that there is a tendency within the marginalised group to embrace a holistic and Afro-centric approach to religion. This approach to worship is referenced in biblical sources and tends to focus on a central figure whose dominance is validated by the persona's knowledge of African belief systems, traditional stories and also of healing practices that can relieve the sufferings of the afflicted. Consequently, alternative religious practices to the westernised tenets of the established orthodox churches have been embraced by grass-roots Jamaicans and have been documented in both genres of oral narrative performance.

The Bible has been an inspirational source for the construction of context and content in our oral tradition over the years. The tradition of using references from the Bible is rooted in our colonial past where slaves used this civilizing tool of their masters to deconstruct the hegemonic stranglehold of the imperialists. Biblical references are also evident in Negro Spirituals such as: 'Didn't My Lord Deliver Daniel?', 'Go Down Moses' and 'Little David, Play on Your Harp'. In the context of music, a number of artistes have used biblical references in the development of their narratives. For example, Bob Marley who is accepted as one of the greatest reggae artistes is renowned for his unique blending of narratives in slave songs with Jamaican music to develop a special genre of music songs. In 'Redemption Song,' which is reminiscent of Negro Spiritual songs, Marley transposed himself to the time of slavery when he sang:

> *Old pirates yes they rob I, Sold I to the merchant ships,*
>
> *Minutes after they took I to the bottomless pit.*
>
> *But my hand was made strong by the hand of the Almighty.*
>
> *We forward in this generation triumphantly.*
>
> *Won't you help to sing these songs of freedom.*
>
> *'Cause all I ever had, redemption songs ...*
>
> *Emancipate yourself from mental slavery*
>
> *None but ourselves can free our mind...*
>
> (This song was performed at a show in Pittsburgh, Pennsylvania on September 23, 1980, was Bob's last concert.)

Aspects of Elaine Perkins' work are rooted in Western religious practices and also in African cosmology. This syncretism is appropriated by the subaltern in their development of coping skills. The following performances represent this syncretism. When Dulcimina lamented that her money was stolen her friend, Baby G, said: 'Try Bible and key to find out who took your money'. Baby G also told Dulcimina to say: 'By St. Peter, by St. Paul, by the true and living God, is _____ (name a person) *tek* (stole) the pound' (British currency). There is a Balm Yard scene in which persons from the tenement yard travelled to rural Jamaica to visit a Mother (clairvoyant). On approaching the gate the visitors were told to '*tun* roll (spin around) three times' before entering the premises to join the queue to await the *healer's* 'read up' (predictions). The next ritual was that the visitors were asked to sing a religious song, 'The Life Boat Rescued Me,' prior to the performance of healing rites. Each person was instructed to 'raise a hymn when going through the door for diagnosis by Brother Emmanuel, the healer man. At the end of each session he would dismiss the client in the name of the 'Father, Son and Holy Ghost' (Episode 100). Melva's response to Dulcimina's concern that the healer man had travelled with them to rural Jamaica on the truck from Kingston was that he was a 'transfiguration' – a spirit visiting them en route to protect them. Among this group of persons who visited the Balm Yard were adherents of the Christian faith who often gave testimonies in their Church and sang 'Just as I am without One Plea'.

There are instances when reggae artistes have defied traditional biblical teachings in their quest to develop a counter-discourse to validate the need for the struggling classes to assert their right to liberation from the oppressive system that keeps them in bondage and poverty. One such song is the well-known 'Get Up, Stand Up'. This was jointly written by reggae luminaries Bob Marley, Peter Tosh and Bunny Wailer. In this work, the writers challenged the notion that freedom for the ordinary Jamaicans meant a reward in the other life. They also challenged the teaching that heaven is *in the sky*. They regarded these statements as attempts to brainwash the sufferers into subservience. In defiance, the iconic warrior/priests wrote:

> *Preacher man don't tell me*
>
> *Heaven is above the earth.*
>
> *I know you don't know*
>
> *What life is really worth*
>
> *We know and understand*

> *Almighty God is a living man*
>
> *You can fool some people sometimes*
>
> *But you cannot fool all the people all the time.*
>
> Get Up, Stand Up', 1973

Perkins' radio serial dramas also have messages for persons seeking self-employment and educational pursuits as avenues for liberation from oppression and poverty. The landlord's wife commented that the tenement yard in which Dulcimina lived was inhabited by 'smugglers, whores and thieves'. Roxy, her boyfriend, complained about how Dulcimina had settled in this environment instead of trying to improve her status by pursuing the correspondence course that he recommended. Roxy tried to convince her that improving her education would enable her to leave the area and 'get *even a typist job'*. He told her that her stubbornness was stifling her growth. (Episode 206)

Perkins uses the context of a conversation between Dulcimina and her boyfriend, Roxy, to convince her audience about the benefits of engaging in educational pursuits as a route to self-improvement. This strategy of using a 'soft-sell' approach to communicate this message of responsible living is similar to the didactic approach of the reggae trope that through their lyrics encourage advancement in education and self-help to be able to benefit from the limited economic opportunities available to them. Some characters in *Dulcimina: Her Life in Town* also complained about the difficulties they encountered when they approached the banks to get loans to finance business ventures.

At times in Perkins' stories, a character's quest to become self-sufficient resulted in the pursuit of illegal activities, under the pretext of legitimate business operations. When such illicit dealings are revealed, Perkins tends to creatively use the instances of illegal economic transactions to communicate how these can retard and not advance the anticipated intent. Daisy Deep Sea, another character in *Dulcimina*, who was ostensibly a fish vendor but allegedly a smuggler, assaulted a police officer who attempted to arrest her to continue the investigation about the theft of a pair of earrings from a jewellery store. As a result of this incident, Deep Sea had to make a hasty retreat to rural Jamaica to avoid being detained (Episode 27). Prior to her disappearance, Daisy Deep Sea advised Dulcimina that, 'No matter what we have among ourselves do not bring in the police'. Another character, Babes the owner of *Babes Haberdashery*, stocked his shop with goods stolen from the homes of affluent Jamaicans. When he realised that the police was on his trail he also sought refuge in rural Jamaica. Both incidences demonstrate the lyrics of the reggae song 'Badness Nuh Pay' (Leroy Smart, Ballistic Affair 1977).

HIS/STORY

Historically, it is observed that when telling stories, the griots often added examples from the Christian religion into which they had been indoctrinated. Ironically, the Bible which initially served the colonisers as a tool for invoking conformity to the established social order by the enslaved masses, became the ultimate reference source for the dispossessed in the vocabulary of both the Revivalists and the Rastafari community that are represented in the productions. The Bible, in postcolonial Jamaica, enabled the creation of a space for the development of a counter-discourse to validate the existence of a Jamaican identity. By challenging what has been described by some Africana philosophers as preconceived notions of invisibility, anonymity, absence and evasion, the people's appropriation of biblical references is instructive. These references provide legitimate and acceptable options for undermining the locus of the presence/absence dichotomy in which the Black majority's presence is ignored and the ruling classes' presence is acknowledged. They also provide communal empowerment by centring the margin to give a voice to the subaltern.

One possible effect of up-rootedness on the internal migrants is a disconnection from their roots in Afro-Jamaican folk culture. As happened during slavery, the memories of life in rural Jamaica are kept alive through oral performances such as songs and storytelling. The messages communicated tend to be codified and the intended inter-pretations can only be deciphered by younger generations who have been socialised to identify with this aspect of folk culture. For example, Perkins' main character 'Dulcimina,' when faced with the dichotomy between rural tradition and the urban practices prescribed for her integration in the inner city ghetto, often relayed stories and reverted to practices and sayings that were used in her rural community, but which were unfamiliar to her audience. Eighteen-year-old Dulcimina resented being called 'damn idiot' (Episode 193) by those who misun-derstood her utterances. This was usually done as a strategy to re-nego-tiate her self-identity. When her friend's youngest child died suddenly, Dulcimina hung black cloth at the window and placed a glass of pure water and burning candles in the house where the child died. She also rebuked Roxy for 'speaking loudly in the yard of the dead'. (Episode 168)

INSIDER/OUTSIDER DICHOTOMY

The contestations within the Jamaican space for power and control often result in the marginalised having a distorted and contradictory sense of self and identity. An investigator to a crime was told by an inner-city resident in Perkins' *Dulcimina* that: *We don't live down here we survive and those who survive are envied by others.* (Melva: Episode 47)

Here, oral performances provide stimuli for the reconstruction of a collective consciousness that can buffer the prevailing economic, spiritual and mental devastation. Reggae songs such as the Melodians 'By the Rivers of Babylon' and Marley's 'Exodus' resound with double consciousness and diverse meanings. In instances there is evidence of open defiance tempered with biblical references that provide a variety of benefits that include: to the underprivileged, a glimmer of hope for improvement in their status in life; solace to the respective hearers (insiders) that their experience is shared by the community of dispos-sessed young people; and distraction for those representatives of the privileged/authority group. Illustratively, there are many examples of the Warrior/Priest motif in the Rastafari worldview communicated by Bob Marley in the lyrics of the song 'So Much Things To Say':

> *But I never forget, no way,*
>
> *They crucify Jesus Christ...*
>
>
> *I no come to fight flesh and blood,*
>
> *But spiritual wickedness in high and low places*
>
> *So while they fight we down*
>
> *Stand firm and give Jah thanks and praises.*
>
> Exodus, 1977

Marley's liberation message resounds in his interpretation of the collapse of imperialism in Ethiopia. To him, this event symbolised a rejection of Babylon and freedom for the Black race. Thus, Marley composed the song 'Stiff-Necked Fools' in which the lyrics state:

> *Stiff-necked fools, you think you are cool*
>
> *To deny me for simplicity.*
>
> *Yes, you have gone for so long*
>
> *With your love for vanity now.*
>
> *Yes, you have got the wrong interpretation*
>
> *Mixed up with vain imagination.*
>
> *The lips of the righteous teach many,*
>
> *But fools die for want of wisdom.*
>
> *The rich man's wealth is in his city;*
>
> *The righteous' wealth is in his Holy Place.*

There are many dialogues in Perkins' works that support this Rastafari worldview communicated by Bob Marley and other reggae artistes. One such example that readily comes to mind is at the *Nine Night* for a child when the adults were trying to justify what had happened and to console the young, homeless mother of four fatherless boys, who was weeping inconsolably. This situation exemplifies Marley's lyrics 'No Woman, No Cry'. The narratives in this scene may seem humorous on the surface, but in reality they make a profound statement about hardships in the inner city. This young mother openly lamented her inability to provide for her fatherless children and the consequent loss of her youngest. During her lamentations, the mourners sang a popular mourning song that was intended to comfort the bereaved. Its lyrics speak of a better life after death and offer encouragement to the surviving relatives to take solace in God's supreme love for the deceased. The song, 'Wipe Your Weeping Eyes,' as performed resounded with musical discord, but its profound lyrics expounded the African worldview of the circle of life and liberation from this physical body to another life after death. Parallels can be drawn with Bob Marley's 'Zion Train' in which he encourages his audience to keep focussed on their spiritual consciousness in order to attain the ultimate goal of liberation and in 'Could You Be Loved' Marley warned:

> *Don't let them change you*
>
> *Or even rearrange you, oh no!*
>
> *We've got a life to live*
>
> *They say ...*
>
> *Only the fittest of the fittest shall survive.*
>
> *Stay alive.*

The lyrics of many other reggae songs are noted in Perkins' works. In instances when some of her characters are faced with challenging situations, such as in-equality at work or the denial of basic amenities, they can be heard mumbling the lyrics or humming the tunes of appropriate lyrics such as 'Oh, Oh poor me Israelite'. Esta de Fossard

(1996, 109) explained that in order to avoid blurring the messages being communicated in radio drama serials the inclusion of popular songs should be discouraged.

The tradition of the drum as a means of communication is pivotal to the observance of alternative religious practices; and also in the performances of reggae music and radio serial dramas. Elaine Perkins understood the significance of the drum to dissipating the pain of disillusionment and has interwoven this medium of communication into many scenes in her works. One instance is a case in which a former sex worker, who is faced with serious but undisclosed health issues, is taken to a Revival meeting. Here, in response to the beating of the drum she is revived enough to claim and proclaim her healing to others, who marvelled at her sudden restoration/restitution of health. This worldview is endorsed in the lyrics of Bob Marley's song 'One Drop' which states:

> *So feel this drumbeat*
>
> *I tell you what: it's beating within*
>
> *Feel your heart playing a rhythm.*

OTHER CULTURAL SIGNIFIERS

Gesticulations, other non-verbal expressions and naming are integral aspects of Jamaican oral culture. Prior to widespread application of technology to communication, there were griots in the villages, who mentally archived and disseminated traditional information to their respective audiences. These storytelling sessions were much anticipated and endorsed community social events. The success of the messages communicated was dependent on the griot's techniques and delivery skills. The involvement of the audience through the *call and response* technique and the naming of characters in these stories are among the strategies that have been appropriated by reggae singers and radio serial drama scriptwriters. Many reggae singers have stage names that communicate some aspect of the persona's motif. Examples include 'Tuff Gong', 'The Wailing Wailers', 'Tony Rebel', 'Burning Spear', 'Beenie Man', 'Elephant Man', inter alia.

In the area of radio serial drama, Perkins uses the technique of naming her characters as a motif for endorsing their role in the story. For example, in 'Naseberry Street', *Scattershot* is the name given to the young man who engaged in irresponsible partnering that resulted in the impregnating of many unsuspecting young ladies. He failed to support either the mothers or the children. In 'Dulcimina: Her Life in Town', *Wood Root* is a naturalist/Rastafari; *Six Foot Deep*, also known as *Axe Man*, is a merciless contract killer and *Daisy Deep Sea* is a fish vendor and smuggler. Three of Baby G's four children, *Billy Eckstine*, *Stewart Grainger* and *Errol Flynn*, were given the names of popular movie stars or singers of the time. This is in contra-distinction to the colonial era in which slaves were forcibly re-named by their masters. Baby G chose to give her children the names of celebrities in defiance of the sub-human conditions of her existence and in anticipation of a better life for them. Bunny Goodison recalls that Billy Eckstine, an American singer, was a 'fashion' icon for the males during the mid-1900s (Stolzoff 2000).

Historically, dance has been an expression of resistance. The dance movements that accompany reggae music tend to reflect the state of mind of the performer and advance the liberation motif. Similarly, in radio serial dramas characterisation is used to communicate bodily expressions of resistance. Perkins is an excellent storyteller who under-stands the need to use appropriate spoken words to communicate the intended messages/meanings in her stories. She uses what she calls 'soft sell' methods, as well as the stories of people's daily life experi-ences to create the desired messages. There are scenes set at juke boxes when persons become immersed in the lyrics and tunes to forget their problems. Onlookers involve the audience in these bodily expressions of the unseen characters through verbal descriptions. Also, discussions in the tenement yard about what happened in the public dance space where reggae music was played helped to reinforce the impact of dance movements as resistance.

In addition, the preferred language for communicating in both reggae music and radio serial drama is Nation Language which embodies both European and African linguistic influences but its connectivity to oral traditions makes it a dynamic and community-influenced product. (Brathwaite, 1979). Brathwaite (1979) categorises this phenomenon as a 'submerged/emerged culture'. A number of verbal techniques are used to relate issues, including proverbs, local expressions and sayings, which are interjected to add credibility to the message being communicated as well as to enrich and contextualise the language used both in reggae songs and in radio serial drama. Proverbs are repositories of Jamaican oral tradition of wise sayings and document the combined experiences of our historic journey. The use of proverbs also provided a convenient vehicle for communicating inner thoughts and for negotiations. Both reggae and radio serial drama discourses have engaged proverbs in the development of their respective aesthetics. This is a useful strategy for validating the seriousness of their craft which was stigmatised as mere entertainment. *Every day the bucket go a well, /One day the bottom a-go drop out* ('I Shot the Sherriff, 1973) was used by Bob Marley to warn the political directorate of the potential danger of ignoring the pleas from the subaltern for benefits. In Perkins' Dulcimina story the saying 'it is going to be eggs or young ones' is used as a form of intimidation to solicit conformity and negotiate protection of space from invasion by the armed forces. In this same discourse, Babes, Dulcimina's employer, advised her to remain silent about his [un-authorised] visit to the Carmichael's residence; to avoid becoming involved because, 'knife wey stick sheep wi stick goat' (the same problem that befalls one person can befall another).

Perkins' exposition of the worldview 'pigs of the same sow' and the reggae lyricists' perception that 'blood is thicker than water,' and 'everyone is his brother's keeper' are used in the context of family bonding. *When goat no have nutten to do him pick up sheep* was Dulcimina's response to Daisy Deep Sea's constant harassment. There are numerous instances in both narrative discourses when proverbs and sayings were used 'fe tek kin teet kibbah heart bun', to use humour to cover painful situations.

Although the use of Nation Language underpins the development of the indigenous radio serial drama created by Perkins and is also the chosen language of the reggae artistes, earlier scriptwriters of radio drama serials experienced opposition from mainstream society. Even Jamaica's renowned cultural ambassador and icon, the Honourable Dr. Louise Bennett-Coverley (Miss Lou), who developed a reputation for telling stories about grass-roots Jamaicans in their own language, was subject to ostracism by the cynics who were offended by folk sensibility as projected in her works. In defiance, Miss Lou continued to generate works using the Nation Language. In one poem entitled 'Show-Off Speech', Miss Lou spoke about those persons from rural Jamaica who had migrated to the city and were mimicking the city-dwellers by adopting their linguistic airs. Miss Lou's 'Colonisin' in Reverse' is another of her poetic discourses that critically described the state of society then. While expressing hope that Jamaicans would do to the British what the British had done to Jamaicans, Miss Lou also addressed related issues such as displacement and identity crises.

There are several examples of the Euro-centric mindset of the literati in Jamaican society that were published in the press during the period of nationalistic fervour. For example, at the launch of Jamaica Broadcasting Corporation's Television station (JBC-TV) there was a failure in the power supply while Miss Lou was performing so many persons in the audience were unable to hear the performance. One commentator reported this mishap as a *blessing* on the pretext that many people would not have understood what Miss Lou was saying. Our linguistic ambassador also challenged her critics who were unsure of which category of literature her works fit. Miss Lou continued to give oral narrative performances using Nation Language as the agent. The potential economic benefits to be accrued because of the popularity of her style of communication was eventually recognised and her works were aired in the electronic media, both radio and television. Miss Lou's persistence in centring the margins not only served to awaken the Jamaican sensibility to her work but also served to pave the way for and validate the works of Elaine Perkins, reggae artistes and others who have sought to project the story of the ordinary Jamaicans from its true centre, the gaze of those existing on the margins of mainstream society. Initially, reggae songs were mostly sung by men and radio serial drama mostly projected issues that impacted directly on the lives of women. This gender division was soon eroded by the messages, how these were communicated, the discussions they generated and the change in the media and social landscape. Bob Marley encapsulates this shifting of the gaze of the media powerbrokers with these lyrics from 'Forever Loving Jah':

> *'Cause just like a tree planted by the river of water*
>
> *that bringeth forth fruits in dry season*
>
> *Everything in life got its purpose.*

In presenting this voice of the marginalised masses, whether through radio drama serials or reggae music, these oral narrative performances enable persons to look at themselves critically and to understand the ubiquity of their situations. The stigma associated with poverty was no longer regarded as a construct of shame. Thoughts about their plight were re-oriented as people felt liberated to discuss issues that were pertinent to their daily existence and communally to find creative outlets for their sense of displacement. These discussions within the space occupied by alienated Jamaicans continuously provided organic details for scriptwriters of radio drama serials, reggae artistes and producers, especially those who made it their responsibility to listen keenly to the people's daily discussions.

This eavesdropping agenda was actually intellectualising a diversion in the tenement yards, which provided very little privacy for the tenants. In these situations inquisitive neighbours listened to each other's conversations and watched as they pursued their daily activities. The information gleaned often became a source of empowerment. When a confrontation degenerates to a 'tracing' match the unsuspecting victim's private and often intimate conversations become public knowledge for other tenants. These internal tensions provided release valves for built up frustrations but did not create any scope for the intrusion of outsiders. Trench Town was among the popular creative spaces for communal affirmation and empowerment. The lyrics of Bob Marley's song 'Trench Town' states:

> *We come from Trench Town*
>
> *We come from Trench Town, Trench, Trench Town*
>
> *They say can anything good come out of Trench Town?*
>
> *That's what they say, Trench Town*
>
> *Say we're the underprivileged people*
>
> *So they keep us in chains*
>
> *Pay pay pay tribute to Trench Town, Trench Town*
>
> *We come from Trench Town, not because we come from Trench Town*
>
> *Just because we come from Trench Town*

Elaine Perkins' characters also had animated conversations about meal and sleeping arrangements in their overcrowded rooms in Ramgeet's tenement yard. Characters complained about their living conditions yet seemed very reluctant to relocate when an opportunity presented itself. Here, segments of the Jamaican audience that cannot identify with the situations exposed are afforded opportunities to hear and possibly understand the sensibility of the marginalised masses. By the time call-in talk show programmes became popular in Jamaica in the 1990s, persons were telephoning the radio stations to discuss their situations. It is said that some policymakers factored these reports into their policies and were able to provide cursory ameliorative measures. The absence/presence dichotomy was addressed by the political directorate, especially during the 1970s. Some of the benefits promised during the political campaigning prior to the 1976 General Elections included providing free secondary and higher education; project land lease; day care centres; a National Minimum Wage; legal status to illegitimate children; employment for the unemployed and young people through an Impact Programme and the Pioneer Corps; and implementing a state of emergency to reduce crime and disorder.

In this regard, the songs by reggae artistes and the radio serial dramas produced by Elaine Perkins share the commonality of being informed by the audience for which they are performed. To this end, they also resonate with the intended audience's lived experiences and provide scope for temporary cathartic releases from the tensions associated with notions of alienation and hopelessness. Some lyrics in Bob Marley's song 'Trench Town Rock' succinctly express this stating:

> One good thing about music,
> When it hits you, you feel no pain

Burning Spear's pronouncement further endorses the healing effect of reggae music on people's psyche. The evidence is in his lyrics:

> Reggae physician play I some reggae music.
> What went wrong you want a reggae physician?
> Reggae physician give I some meditation.

ORAL NARRATIVE PERFORMANCES AS EDUTAINMENT

A radio serial drama, also known as a soap opera, when designed for edutainment (education-entertainment) purposes, is 'informative, value specific, morally coherent, realistic and theory-based' (Singhal and Rogers 1999, 60). In the Jamaican context, Elaine Perkins represents one of the most successful writers/producers in this category. In using the language, situations, concerns and people involved in the existing circumstances she developed radio serials that resonated with people, re-affirmed their identity, and in instances the messages communicated were able to effect changes in the lives of a wide cross-section of Jamaicans and her most successful and longest running radio serial drama, *Dulcimina Her Life in Town,* was aired from 1967 to 1980. This story is based on a young girl's attempts to adjust to city life. It provides insight into the aspirations of the new internal migrants from rural Jamaica to the city of Kingston; the lifestyle of the marginalized; and how the tensions that existed between rural and urban cultural practitioners are dispelled when faced with crises. Dulcimina's observations of living in a tenement yard and the parallel drawn to residing in rural Jamaica provide the listener with useful information. One sees her looking to the past to seek solace but being contemplative about how to extricate herself from what seemed to be a life of hopelessness. Her family members chide her about her rustic disposition and values, while trying to orient her to survival mechanisms in the ghetto. She shares her frustration with her friend, Baby G, who in empathy declared: 'Poor me Black girl, life will never be better for me'.

Paralleling the temporal frame of *Dulcimina*, in 1968 Jamaica's Ska and Rock Steady music genres were replaced by reggae with its inspirational base also within the lived experiences and expectations of Jamaican youth. Reggae musicians and singers wrote and sang songs of lamentation and revolt or hope and optimism. The general distrust of the marginalized youth for authority figures resonated with both genres. In both instances the term *Babylon* is used to indicate a rejection of the established order that generated hardships for the masses. The philosophy of the inner-city dwellers was *no disclosure* to the police and zero tolerance of inner-city residents who reported on each other (informers). The youth were bonded in their despair. Bob Marley, even when he had attained success, sang: 'We come from Trench Town,' and 'I remember when we used to sit, in the government yard in Trench Town, observing the hypocrites...' One character in *Dulcimina* told an investigating police officer that 'our type of people do not inform on each other' (Jenny: Episode 133).

CONCLUSION

Historically, the branding of both reggae music and radio serial dramas as sources of comic relief is a projection of a Euro-centric worldview that regards indigenous expressions as barbaric and diametrically opposed to the civilising mission of the former colonisers. The messages communicated, how these are expressed, as well as the responses they receive, are indicators of their intrinsic value in affirming identity. Both forms of oral narrative performance provide multi-faceted reflectors, such as who we are as a people, what our aspirations are, and what obstacles have hindered the realisation of a cohesive national labour force. If all these factors are properly analysed through the gaze of the margins, they can provide valid resources to assist the state directorate for the planning and implementation of government policies. The onus is on scholars to expose the value of these unconventional information resources and to ensure that these research findings are taken beyond archival records to the offices of the decision makers.

The role of twentieth century Jamaican serial drama in effecting behaviour change in listeners has been grossly unappreciated, under-stated and neglected by academics, media theorists and writers. The success of these soap operas is affected by a wide range of factors including: the sense of social 'relevance' communicated in the storyline; how class, race, and ethnicity are represented; also the extent to which attempts are made to attract younger audience by concentrating on issues that are relevant to them as well as by using younger charac-ters. This is in contradistinction to attempting to maintain the more adult listeners by creating characters and plots that presumably interest them.

Radio audience's interest in indigenous programmes, including reggae music and radio drama serials can be attributed to the relevance of the messages communicated in these genres of edutainment. It is an accepted worldview that many of our customs and practices are steeped in oral and visual traditions. Storytelling which initially entailed a griot and an audience in face-to-face encounters has evolved. Advances in radio technology have facilitated the dissemination of orally trans-mitted traditions to larger audiences simultaneously. The modern griot, whether through music or drama productions, has documented the stories of their audience's lived experiences; and in so doing has documented aspects of oral traditions including verbal expressions, styles and movements. Consequently, both these genres have contrib-uted to the mass appeal of the local radio broadcasting industry.

Perkins, the prolific scriptwriter, producer and director of radio serial drama, is to this genre what Bob Marley is to reggae music. Her work has impact on both media and academic professionals internation-ally. Many episodes of her works have been used as prototypes for the development of similar programmes for other Third World countries. Through the narrative discourses of both genres, the plights of the masses have been exposed and ventilated from the position of insiders. The 'Hybrid Third Space' of performance has been pivotal to the engen-dering of communal living and for the formulation of coping strategies.

REFERENCES

Annual Report. 1954. Kingston: Department of Labour.

Barrett, Patrick (Tony Rebel). Personal Interview, 2010.

Bennett, Louise. 'Colonization in'Reverse', 1966.

_____. 'Show-Off Speech' in *Aunty Roachy Seh*. Ed. Mervyn Morris. Kingston: Sangster's, 1993, pp. 4-6.

Bhabha, H. K. 'Culture's In-Between'. In *Questions of Cultural Identity*. Hall, Stuart and P. Du Gay (Eds.). London, Thousand Oaks, New Delhi: Sage Publications, 1996, pp. 53-60.

Bradley, Lloyd. *This is Reggae Music*. New York: Grove Press, 2000.

Brathwaite, Kamau. 'History of the Voice.' *In Roots: Essays in Caribbean Literature*. Ann Arbor: University of Michigan Press. 1993, pp. 259-304.

Economic and Social Survey. Kingston: National Planning Agency, 1973.

Annual Report: Registrar General's Department. Kingston, 1954.

Fossard, Esta de. *How to Write a Radio Serial Drama for Social Development*. John Hopkins University, 1996.

Handbook of Jamaica 1887–8. Kingston: Government Printing Establishment, 1887.

Hebdige, Dick. *Cut 'N' Mix*. New York: Routledge, 1990.

Institute of Jamaica. 1887. *Institute of Jamaica Minute Book,* 1887.

John Hopkins University. '1986 Johns Hopkins University's Population Communication Services.' Population Reports.

MacFarlane, Keeble. 'The Roots Of Radio, Long Before Roots Radio'. *The Observer*, July 11, 2009.

Maunder, Wynne F. *Employment in an Underdeveloped Area: A Sample Survey of Kingston, Jamaica.* New Haven: Yale University Press, 1960.

Maxwell, John. 1959. Launch of Jamaican Broadcasting Corporation, 2009.http://www.nathanielturner.com/1959launchofjamaicanbroadcasting.htm.

Mock Yen, Alma. *Rewind: My recollections of radio broadcasting in Jamaica.* Kingston: Arawak Publications, 2002.

Perkins, Elaine. 2009. Personal Interview.

Prahlad, S. Anando. *2001 Reggae Wisdom: Proverbs in Jamaican Music.* Mississippi: Mississippi University Press, 2001.

Robotham, Don. 'Thinking Honestly about Values.' In *The Sunday Gleaner*, March 22, 2003, p. A8.

Rowe, Maureen. 'Gender and Family Relations in Rastafari: A Personal Perspective.' In *Chanting Down Babylon: The Rastafari Reader*, Nathaniel Samuel Murrel, William David Spencer and Adrian Anthony McFarlane. (Eds.). Philadelphia: Temple University Press, 1998, pp. 72-88.

Singhal, Arvind, and Everett M. Rogers. *Edutainment-Education: A Communication Strategy for Social Change.* New Jersey: LEA, 1999.

Stolzoff, Norman C. *Wake the Town and Tell the People: Dancehall Culture in Jamaica.* Durham and London: Duke University Press, 2000.

Webster-Prince, Maureen. 'Oral Culture and Political Campaigning for Jamaica's General Elections: 1944-2002' Paper presented at Institute of Caribbean Studies Seminar, University of the West Indies, Mona, Jamaica, 2003.

White, Timothy. *Catch a Fire: The life of Bob Marley.* Revised and enlarged. New York: Henry Holt, 2000.

PART 4
REGGAE/RASTA
INTERNATIONAL

9 RASTA-REGGAE AS A LOGIC OF INCOMPLETION

DIVISIVE UNIVERSALISM IN A GLOBALISED WORLD

Few music scholars, practitioners or fans would deny that reggae is now a thoroughly globalised cultural product enjoying a vibrant life in diverse contexts well beyond its Jamaican origins. But what has been gained and what has been lost in this complex process of cultural transmission and translation? In particular, has the radical dimension of Rasta-influenced reggae - such a potent form of cultural politics in the 1970s - been irrevocably diluted as a result of its insertion into the financial circuits and flows of globalised capitalism? In this chapter, I will draw on the recent French political theories of Jacques Rancière (1998) and Alain Badiou (2009) both to isolate the specific militant logic at the core of roots reggae within the Jamaican context, and to reflect on the tensions between particular and universal, local and global, as it extends beyond that context. Such tensions ensure that globalisation - despite a great deal of scholarship from the 1990s - is rarely a one-way process of cultural homogenisation.

It is precisely this that makes thinking about the fate of conscious roots reggae as it travels necessary.

I understand 'conscious roots reggae' to refer both to a phase in Jamaican popular music from the mid 1970s to the early 1980s, and to a musical genre transcending that time frame but broadly characterised as 'message music'. Message music has lyrical content that both criticises social injustices and appeals to an African cultural heritage in order to sustain the hope that 'better must come'. Roots reggae is often contrasted with the dancehall music coming out of Jamaica today, some (but by no means all) of which is characterised by 'slackness', which is to say, by lewd, crude lyrics frequently celebrating hyper-sexualised masculinity and conspicuous consumption - an aesthetic anathema to the roots tradition. Here however, the important scholarship of Carolyn Cooper (1993: 2004), Norman Stolzoff (2000), and more recently Donna Hope (2006: 2010) must be acknowledged. As well as foregrounding dancehall as a space of cultural distinction in the Bourdieuian sense which, in Kingston, plays itself out between 'uptown' and 'downtown' as well as 'black' and 'brown' oppositions, such scholarship also complicates any simplistic opposition between roots reggae and dancehall. Stolzoff (2000) demonstrates the longer history of dancehall which, connected to the development of sound systems in the 1940s, actually precedes reggae, while Hope presents contemporary dancehall as a contested cultural milieu in which hegemonic forms of masculinity are not simply repeated but challenged. And yet notwithstanding such important academic work, the scandal generated by the apparent homophobia of some dancehall songs has undoubtedly effected international perceptions of Jamaican music, prompting recurrent calls for a return to the *seemingly* less problematic roots tradition. This 'sound clash' then, between reggae and dancehall, is in many ways symptomatic of the tensions between local and global that characterise cultural production in the era of Spotify and Youtube.

My focus here, however, will be on roots reggae. The chapter will have three sections. In the first, I will draw on the ideas of Alain Badiou and Jacques Rancière to characterise Rasta-influenced roots reggae as

- to borrow a phrase from Oliver Feltham (2008) - a 'logic of incompletion'. Both Badiou and Rancière are interested in the ways in which groups of any kind - societies, nations, parties, collectives - attempt to define themselves as complete, as containing all their elements without remainder, which can be seen as the ideal of liberal representative democracy. But Badiou and Rancière are also interested in the ways in which political movements often reveal marginalised groups that exist, but do not count as fully belonging to their situations. The logic of incompletion of my title, therefore, refers to that aspect of radical political movements which challenge the ways in which societies or nations attempt to secure their symbolic boundaries. My main claim is that this is a very apt way of describing the intersections of Rastafari and roots reggae in the context of post-independence Jamaica.

In the second section, in order to analyse reggae's cross-cultural circulation, I will explore how this 'logic of incompletion' adapts as it traverses cultural, social and political borders through the example of British reggae poet, Linton Kwesi Johnson. Through textual analysis of his poems and song lyrics, it will be argued that Johnson takes the key aspects of rasta reggae's 'logic of incompletion' deployed in Jamaica in the 1970s, and puts them to work in the very different context of Margaret Thatcher's conservative Britain in the 1980s and early 1990s. Things both change and stay the same in this new trans-Atlantic passage.

In the third and final section, I will close by making a brief but suggestive distinction between two kinds of universalism - inclusive and divisive - with which to defend the importance of reggae even in the new millennium as a 'rebel music' that remains equipped to challenge the iniquities of economic and cultural globalization (even as it is integrated into and shaped by it in extremely complex ways). However, it is pointed out that the transnational logic of incompletion I am ascribing to roots reggae leads to a critical suspension of any simplistic or essentialist claims to a monolithic 'Jamaicaness' for reggae, something that many on the island itself might find difficult to accept.

ROOTS REGGAE AS A 'LOGIC OF INCOMPLETION'

It has been argued that the emergence of Reggae music around 1967 cannot be separated from the influence of Rastafari, the cultural, political and quasi-religious black consciousness movement that emerged in Jamaica soon after Haile Selassie's coronation as Emperor of Ethiopia in 1930 (Barrett: 1988). It has also been argued that both Rastafari and roots reggae need to be thought within the long history of counter-colonial struggles by Africans in Jamaica and, further, that this history is not finished (Bakan: 1990; Campbell: 2001). What is less frequently argued is that it is a history that can only problematically be claimed as exclusively 'Jamaican', for – and this is a key point for my argument – it has consistently been *against* the dominant constructions of Jamaican national identity that Rastafarian roots reggae has pitted itself.

Simplifying crudely, it is possible to emphasise three key motifs in Rastafari that are carried over and indeed amplified in roots reggae music: one, the cultivation of a deep historical consciousness of African civilization and also of suffering that is felt and lived in the present (see chapter 4 of Barrett: 1988); two, the deployment of this black historical consciousness against the State's attempts to narrate away the continuing injustices flowing from that history of suffering; three, the core spiritual but also political message of love, peace and unity. Because each of these contributes to what I am calling a 'logic of incompletion', I will use them to structure my discussion.

HISTORICAL CONSCIOUSNESS

Scholars of Rastafari generally agree that the insistence on the greatness of pre-European African civilizations is intended to mobilse a black history *against* the dominance of whitecentric colonial history (Cashmore: 1983; Chevannes: 1995). In the terminology I am borrowing from Badiou and Rancière, we can say that black history is reconceptualised in order to 'incomplete' the symbolic closure of colonial history. But this is far from a scholarly matter aimed at professional historians. Rasta attitudes to the Bible in particular exemplify the subjective aspect of the logic of incompletion: Christian theologians engaging with Rastafarians have long recognised that their wilfully strong hermeneutic turns the 'English' Bible into a product of the distortions of the white man (Briener: 1985), one which can nonetheless be read against itself in order to unveil hidden truths that can structure attitudes and practices in the present (Foehr: 2000). This is indeed a core element of Rasta 'reasoning' (Barrett: 1988). The historico-religious perspective within Rastafari is not about remembering or merely documenting the past greatness of Africa then, but of *living* it militantly in the now.

Religion has played a vital and complex role in sustaining a resistant black imaginary in Jamaica in several historical stages. First, there was the struggle to *maintain* African rites and rituals under conditions of slavery in the form of *Obi*, *Myalism* and *Cumina*. Then there was the influence of non-conformist British missionaries who arrived on the island in the mid-to-late Eighteenth century (Baptists, Moravians, Methodists). It was these missionaries who politicized the exploited blacks against the reigning plantocracy, as well as spearheading the campaign for the Abolition of Slavery back in England (see Hochschild: 2005). Just prior to the explosive Morant Bay Revolt in 1865, sparked by the black preacher Paul Bogle, a massive island-wide upsurge in religiosity was observed in 1860 and termed the 'Great Revival' (Turner: 1988). And then, following Morant Bay, the emancipatory dimension of religion in Jamaica came through *syncretic* native church movements that took elements of Christianity and blended them with surviving aspects of African religions, resulting in hybrid formations such as *Pukumina* and Revivalism. Rastafari too draws on this long tradition of religiously inspired resistance, and did so *musically* well before the emergence of reggae. As Leonard Campbell notes (2001), the most obvious link back to Africa was the drum, often a means of rebellious communication in the days of slavery. So-called *Nyabinghi* drumming plays a key role in traditional Rasta ceremonies. It is played on a three-piece drum set called the *akete* and it emerged in the 1950s from the ghettoes of Western Kingston. Thanks to an influx of rural peasants as well as migrant workers returning from Cuba and Central America, Kingston was a genuine musical 'melting pot' at this time: Mento, Calypso, Jazz and Rhythm and Blues mixed with residually African musical practices such as Buru (Campbell: 2001). Buru was an African form of drumming which had survived the otherwise strict controls of the Jamaican slave-masters for the same reason that slave owners in the Deep South of America had allowed work songs. Although lyrically such songs often lamented the slave's plight (an emotional tone which would feed into later Blues), or even, in the form of 'spirituals', invoked Christian redemption from slavery, the extra productivity brought about by tying the repetitive movements of labouring bodies to percussive rhythms seemingly outweighed the subversiveness of such expressive forms. Buru, then, continued to be practiced in Jamaica right up to the 1950s precisely because it had been the rhythmic accompaniment to machetes cutting sugarcane on the plantations.

After a government crackdown on rural Rasta communes in the mid 1950s, many of the displaced Rastas took up residence in West Kingston amongst one of the few remaining concentrations of Buru practitioners. Recognising its African provenance, they quickly embraced Buru and, indeed, absorbed the Buru people as a distinct social group. Buru was mixed with elements of *Cumina* drumming to form the distinctive *Nyabinghi* 'riddims' of rasta rituals. One of the key links between Buru, Cumina, Rastafarian ceremonies and reggae is the seminal figure of Count Ossie. Ossie served a long apprenticeship with a Buru drummer, gaining a virtuoso grasp of its distinctive patterns which he then adapted and elaborated as a session musician with various Kingston bands, until he played on a record produced by Prince Buster in 1960 which some music historians regard as the first ever reggae record, 'Oh carolina' (later made internationally famous by Shaggy) – although 'reggae' is here used in its generic sense, denoting simply indigenous Jamaican music rather than the off-beat emphasis of 'one-drop' which only emerged around 1967. Ossie subsequently established a reggae band called *The Mystic Revelation of Rastafari* which released the landmark triple LP *Grounation* in 1973. This incorporation of buru drumming into the Nyabinghi riddims of Rasta chants effectively resurrected an African beat that was slower, heavier, more 'dread' than other forms of music imported from the wider black diaspora such as soul and R&B. Very explicitly in the roots reggae of the 1970s, we have both a lyrical invocation of ancient Africa and a musical form that together put an African aesthetic to work within a demographic context which was predominantly African in origin, yet still socially and politically constructed as British, despite *de facto* independence since 1962.

Though it goes against the grain of what many Rastas believe, it is possible to argue that the terms 'Africa' or 'Ethiopia' are less about a profound yearning for physical geographical repatriation - in fact the history of attempts at actual repatriation, as with the Shashamane community in Ethiopia, is a rather sad one - and more about a challenge to the attempted symbolic closure of the Jamaican nation. As Leonard Barrett was already observing in the late 1980s (Barrett: 1988), the theme of physical repatriation has in fact been reducing in importance in most strands of Rastafari since the 1970s. This alternative understanding of 'Africa' as an attempt to 'incomplete' the Jamaican nation resonates with Jacques Rancière's assertion that 'the essence of politics is the manifestation of dissensus as the presence of two worlds in one' (Rancière: 2010, p. 37). For what is Afrocentrism in a Jamaican context if not the insistence on two worlds in one? What Rancière means by this phrase is that politics cannot be about a single world and an identifiable sociological category - including the 'poor', the 'sufferahs' - for whom justice would be a matter of fuller inclusion within that single world. On the contrary, politics challenges what Rancière calls the 'distribution of the sensible' characteristic of one world, which is to say, how people are seen and counted as having a place in that world, by contrasting it to another world altogether. In the case of Rastafari, an African world is exposed as internal to, but incommensurable with, a post-colonial yet fundamentally British world. The political subject - and I would argue that at bottom this is what the Rasta is - is a supplement added to, but never absorbed by, the sum of the parts of the Jamaican social structure. This incompatibility with existing mechanisms of inclusion is a crucial dimension of the logic of incompletion. Certainly, Rastas have generally remained steadfastly suspicious of inclusion in the Jamaican status quo.

CRITICISING BABYLON

This is why the critique of Babylon and the 'politricks' of which it is evidently capable is so crucial to roots reggae. The rich Biblical resonances of the term 'Babylon' enable it to encompass historical *and* contemporary forms of exploitation (see Murrell: 1998). Old and New Testament themes of exile, greed, opposition to God and imperial violence intertwine and mingle with black diasporic experiences of slavery, colonialism and also post-colonial first world hypocrisy (the impact of the IMF loans on the Jamaican economy for example). In Bob Marley's song 'Babylon System' from the 1979 album *Survival*, he compares Babylon to a vampire 'suckin' di blood af di sufferahs' against which they must 'rebel, rebel, rebel!'. Later in the same album he pithily condemns the exploitative economics of Babylon as 'Pimper's Paradise'. In an exemplary chapter in her book *Soundclash: Jamaican Dancehall Culture at Large* (2004), Carolyn Cooper not only charts the injunction to 'bun down Babylon' in roots reggae music and thus underlines its strident militancy, but also maps the continuity of this militancy into the work of dancehall artists like Capleton (and we might want to add Luciano, Anthony B and Sizzla to this list).

Among many other things, Babylon can be understood as the State that pretends to include everyone equally, but in that very same gesture of inclusion effectively excludes the real sufferers. This is where historical consciousness overlaps with political critique. So when *Burning Spear* asks, on the album *Marcus Garvey*, 'Do you remember the days of slav'ry?', he is not just asking for the school history curriculum to be overhauled, but posing a challenge to live a relation to the ongoing injustices of slavery, and indeed their contemporary forms, including Bob Marley's 'mental slavery'. Likewise, when *Burning Spear* goes on to lament the fact that 'No one remembers ole Marcus Garvey', it is crucial to see this as an intervention into a particular context when the post-independence Jamaican State *was* attempting to re-imagine national identity by, in part, re-Africanizing it. To accept the 'completed' version of Jamaican nationalism eloquently summarised in its national slogan – 'Out of Many, One People' – would be to deny the very inequalities out of which, and against which, both Rastafari and roots reggae music have emerged. The irony of branding Jamaica for the outside world with the smiling face of a friendly dreadlocked Rasta is, therefore, extremely paradoxical: 'Babylon' has always been Jamaica itself. When the first Rasta preacher – a Jamaican named Leonard Howell who had read his Marx as well as his Marcus Garvey and also been peripherally involved in the Harlem Renaissance – first declared that 'Ras Tafari is King of Kings and Lord of Lords. The black people will no longer look to George the Fifth – Ras Tafari is their king' (Lee 2003, p.64), it was indisputably a strategy of incompleting British sovereignty over the island of Jamaica. Swapping national figureheads was a metaphorical means of rectifying what was undone in the aftermath of the English Civil War: the beheading of the king. The British Colonial Office certainly understood his declaration in this way. Howell was convicted of sedition (a crucial legal category in the suppression of slave insurrections as well – see Kostal: 2005), and sentenced to two years in prison.

LOVE, PEACE AND UNITY

One of the core messages of roots reggae, in stark opposition to those elements of dancehall culture influenced by the gangsta-chic of American hip-hop, is the need for an end to 'fussin and fightin' in favour of universal love. However, here a distinction should be made between what, on the one hand, one might flippantly call a 'hippy' California version of love, one thoroughly embedded in a middle-class and predominantly white counter-cultural movement in which any radicalism was firmly connected to the anti-war movement; and on the other, something much more rooted in the experience of working-class, racialized marginalisation and thus more insistently opposed to structures of exploitation (capital, ultimately) that exist outside ostensible wars. This distinction is important to insist on precisely because the former is often used to domesticate the latter, as if Rastafarian conceptualisations of love were only ever a loose romantic gloss on pacifism.

Here, Alain Badiou's pseudo-Lacanian take on love can offer us a useful way of parsing this distinction. In a chapter entitled 'La scène du Deux' in a collection called, simply, De l'Amour (1999), Badiou insists that love is not a fusion of two individuals into an amorous One (as in the saccharine phrase 'you complete me'). Nor is it the addition of two individuals into a kind of contractual couple (as in the rather more pragmatic, 'you and I make a great team'). On the contrary, love for Badiou is irreducible to *any* worldly relation whatsoever: instead, it is the fidelity to the ruptural effects of the loving encounter (or event) that jolts one out of one's world, or the world that counts itself as One, as an encompassing unity (Badiou: 1999). Lovers are those stubborn dreamers who will not conform to the world but, with irrational devotion to one another, demand that the world conform to them. To the unifying power of the One, love opposes the power of a Two which is uncountable since it is not one-plus-one, but the product of the on-going division of the One. This is why for Badiou love and politics are closely related. Both defy the world as it is.

This distinction between romantic or hippy love and militant love, between sublative inclusion and divisive exclusion, takes on particular import in relation to the internationalisation of Jamaican roots reggae. Again, Carolyn Cooper identifies the key problem in a typically piquant formulation: 'The revolutionary Tuff Gong Rastaman has been commodified and repackaged as our 'One Love' apologist for the Jamaican tourist industry' (2004, p.180). In other words, Bob Marley's revolutionary message has been diluted into a happy-clappy, multi-culti togetherness ideal for the globalised era. And yet love in Rasta reggae is not at all this bland, race-blind inclusivity that national governments dependent on the tourist dollar end up projecting to the outside world, not despite, but because of Jamaica's problems with gun crime and gang violence (see Thomson: 2009). On the contrary, insofar as it deploys Badiou's power of the Two, I would argue that the roots notion of love has much more in common with the revolutionary practice of *satyagraha* developed in colonial South Africa and India by Mahatma Gandhi (Nojeim: 2004), in which a militant *solidarity* is built upon the recognition of a common humanity both prior to and above and beyond the differences typical of colonial 'divide and rule' tactics. Love in roots reggae, then, is the dissolution of those worldly differences by which States attempt to order societies, as well as being the trans-individual affect that holds together the form of subjectivity that puts this dissolution to work. This militant sense of love is crystallized in the iconic image of Michael Manley and Edward Seaga hand-in-uncomfortable-hand at the 'One Love Peace Concert' in Kingston's National Stadium in 1978. In the context of politically funded gang warfare, this image is both unifying and explosive, indicating to the manipulated poor that they need not fight other people's battles, and to the 'crazy baldhead' politicians that people power is more powerful than the Babylonian State system.

The logic of incompletion then confronts a supposedly inclusive symbolic system, typically a nation, with what Rancière calls the 'part of no part', with, that is, those who have no assignable place or role or mode of address in the given situation. The power of this logic comes from its fundamental challenge to the reigning doxa of representational democracy, which reduces fundamental antagonisms to mere juridical claims to inclusion in the present order. Rasta reggae's logic of incompletion has proved a powerful weapon in Jamaica's rich cultural politics, as well as a seductive aesthetic in the wider world. But how does this 'logic of incompletion' which I am ascribing to conscious roots reggae function as it travels beyond Jamaica, and circulates not only amongst the global African diaspora, but amongst the cultural flows of late, globalised capitalism and consumers of all races? Can it survive that transatlantic, transcultural translation, or, as for many captured African's enduring the Middle Passage, has it succumbed to the oceanic expanses separating distinct cultural geographies?

'INGLAN IS A BITCH': LINTON KWESI JOHNSON

To answer or at least address this I now turn to the celebrated British reggae-poet Linton Kwesi Johnson. Johnson was born in 1952 in

Chapleton in Jamaica, but moved to London, England, before his 10th birthday. It was the experience of cultural dislocation and racism in the ghettoized Caribbean communities of Brixton, Peckham and Lewisham that radicalised the young Johnson in England, leading him to join the *Black Panthers* while still a school boy, and then to involvement with the *Race Today Collective* (whose journal was edited by Darcus Howe). Around the time that other British reggae bands were emerging, such as Birmingham-based *Steel Pulse* and London's *Aswad*, Johnson also hooked up with a band utilizing nyabinghi riddims called *Rasta Love* (and despite for the most part avoiding the public eye today, he still runs the reggae label *LKJ Records*). Notwithstanding the name of this band, Johnson is not a Rasta. Yet he fully acknowledges the importance of Rastafarian images and concepts in his music and poetry. Indeed, it is my claim that his literary and musical work redeploys the three Rasta motifs I have just identified. But, as Homi Bhabha (1994) has noted of colonial identity, this redeployment in a different locale produces an all-important iterative difference which is precisely the space in which to open up the gaps between nation and narration. Close scrutiny of Johnson's output suggests that the British context in which he lives and works has led him to emphasise the critique of Babylon over and above the injunction to simply be conscious of an Afrocentric perspective on black history. Love, meanwhile, has become ciphered not through the name of the 'most high' Selassie, but through a commitment to international socialism which endows his discourse of love with an explicit egalitarian rhetoric, at once emotive and politically potent. Nonetheless, I will claim that Johnson still recognisably utilises the logic of incompletion identified above, even as he necessarily subjects it to a cultural translation that is by no means a transliteration.

HISTORICAL CONSCIOUSNESS

Johnson's verse of the Seventies is the most militant and the closest to Rasta themes. The song 'Reggae Sounds' for example declares that 'bass history is a moving/is a hurting black story', arguably playing with the double-meaning of bass as musically resonating in the lowest rumbling registers but also as de-basement, de-humanization, denigration of basic rights. In the same song, fire and brimstone imagery mixes with the sense of impending riots: 'flame-rhythm of historically yearning/ flame-rhythm of the time of turning, measuring the time for bombs and for burning'. In other works such as 'Come We Go Dung Deh', 'All We Doin is Defendin' and 'Time Come' there is a Fanon-like emphasis on the necessity of a violent tipping-point in the dialectical struggle for recognition amongst British blacks during that period. Johnson has certainly studied Frantz Fanon's writings on colonial desire and the role of revolutionary violence. Perhaps as a result, history in Johnson's poems becomes a history of pain that gathers inexorably into imminent violence, echoing Hegel's master-slave dialectic.

Far from parroting historical materialism, however, Johnson was responding to real and deep-seated racial tensions in urban Britain. Throughout the seminal 1978 album *Dread Beat an' Blood* there is a pervasive mood of simmering, barely suppressed frustration. Sometimes the poet acts as a rabble-rouser advocating the lifting of the lid from this social pressure cooker, as in the promise, in 'All We Doin is Defendin', that 'wi will fite yu in di street wid we han/ we hav a plan/ soh lissen man/ get ready fi tek some blows'. And in 'Time Come': 'fruit soon ripe, fi tek wi bite, strength soon come/ fi wi fling wi mite' and 'wi goin smash di sky wid wi bad bad blood'. However, often at the very same time, the poet is offering a warning to the wider community: 'it soon come/ look out! look out! look out!', and, in the last couplet 'it too late now: I did warn you' ('Time Come'). This use of the phrase 'soon come' is the site of a politicising reinscription. Typifying the supposed lassitude of the average indolent Jamaican, as putatively lazy as their slave forebears (in fact, non-cooperation was a militant tactic of resistance – see Craton: 1982), 'soon come' here invokes the opposite: a visceral urgency coiled like a snake in the bodies of angry British blacks, a coil which was in fact unleashed spectacularly during the Brixton and Toxteth riots of 1981, and arguably found unwelcome echoes in the more recent London riots of 2011.

CRITICISING BABYLON

Arguably, however, Johnson's approach to history is focussed less on the ancient Ethiopian past and more on a social history of the present. He is at his best in these poems of the Seventies when he is opening a poignant vignette onto the everyday realities of racist Britain. Poems like 'Sonny's Lettah' and 'Street 66' vividly document the brutality of white British police against the whole Caribbean community: in the former, a son writes home to his mother from Brixton prison, having dared to resist police aggression, while the latter recounts the random house raids that were typical for West Indian residents in London at the time. Just as Rastas in Jamaica had long endured the unwarranted attentions of the JCF, so black Britons in London, Liverpool, Birmingham and Manchester in the late Seventies were subjected to invidious stop-and-search policies, the notorious 'sus' laws. The concept of 'Babylon' and its critique of State-based exclusion was more than capable of straddling the common denominator in this transatlantic experience.

Johnson punctuates this account of racism with iconic proper names that stand for the injustices Babylon commits even as it hypocritically lauds its brand of British justice. Take, for example, the song 'It Dread Inna Inglan', dedicated in its very title to George Lindo, a Jamaican living in Bradford who was wrongfully convicted of armed robbery. Unlike the poem in its initial textual form, the song opens with the unmistakable sounds of a street protest: a crowd chants angrily and the poet's declaration comes, demagogue-style, through a megaphone. The song both documents an injustice and galvanizes a struggle for justice. As Fred D'Aguiar has argued, 'Linton's work chants back to life the conscience of a society put to sleep by greed' (Johnson: 2004, p.xii). Indeed, the cumulative repetition of proper names relating to moral outrages constitutes a leitmotif of Johnson's oeuvre. It can be understood as a form of litany, in both the religious sense of a repetitive prayer to which an audience shouts an unvarying response (like the chanting crowd in 'It Dread Inna Inglan'), and in the semi-legal sense of enumerated complaints or wrongs. In 'Time Come' two similar figures are invoked in this way: Oluwale, a 'Nigerian vagrant hounded to death by Leeds police officers' (Johnson: 2002, p.24), and Joshua Francis, a 'Jamaican worker badly beaten by Brixton police officers in the early 1970s' (*ibid.*). The graphic song 'Five Nights of Bleeding' is dedicated to Leroy Harris, identified in the footnote to the Penguin edition as '[a] victim of internecine violence' (2002: p. 6). Perhaps most famously, 'Reggae fi Peach' on the 1980 album *Bass Culture* laments the death of white New Zealander Blair Peach during an Anti-Nazi League demonstration in West London (and this name recurs in the later poem, 'Mekkin History').

Love, Peace and Unity:

As this last reference to a white New Zealander suggests, Johnson's approach to the role of race in Babylonian downpression is more nuanced than the antagonistic chromatism of his days with the Black Panthers would suggest. This, I would argue, is where the generic notion of love as a form of militant solidarity based precisely upon the suspension of differences enters into Johnson's work, though stripped of its obvious Rasta symbolism. For example, as just noted, 'It Dread Inna Inglan' emphasises the common bonds between all non-white Britons opposed to racism:

> *Maggi Tatcha on di go*
>
> *wid a racist show*
>
> *but she haffi go kaw,*
>
> *rite now, African, Asian*
>
> *West Indian an Black British*
>
> *stan firm inna Inglan*
>
> *inna disya time yah*

And again, in 'Mekkin History', Indians and Pakistanis are praised for their resistance:

> *de Asians dem faam-up a human wall*
>
> *gense di fashists an dem police shiel*
>
> *an dem show dat di Asians gat plenty zeal.*

Similarly, almost echoing Paul Gilroy's later Gramscian analysis of the class-race nexus in *There Ain't No Black in the Union Jack* (Gilroy: 2002), Johnson's wonderfully acerbic poem 'Di Black Pettybooshwa' recognises Babylonians with black skin:

> *True dem seh dem edicate dem a gwaan irate*
>
> *true dem seh dem edicate dem a seek tap rate*
>
> *dem seek a posishan af di backs of blacks*
>
> *seek promoshan af di backs of blacks*
>
> *dem a black petty-booshwah*
>
> *dem full of flaw.*

Perhaps acknowledging what John Tomlinson called the 'complex connectivity' of globalisation at around the same time (Tomlinson: 1991), Johnson's poems of the early Nineties come increasingly to situate the dilemma of diasporic black communities in the context of wider international politics. For example, the poem 'New World Hawdah' references Bosnia and Palestine as much as it does Rwanda. The 1991 album *Tings an' Times* attempts both to come to terms with the fall of Soviet Communism and to retain the egalitarian impulse behind international socialism which, it seems, remains Johnson's version of 'love' to this day. Witness the significant ordering of two consecutive songs on *Tings an' Times*: 'Mi Revalueshanary Fren' expresses dissatisfaction with the unreconstructed Marxist who responds to the fall of the Soviet Union merely with parroted orthodoxies, whereas 'Di Good Life', against a lilting calypso beat, figures socialism in Biblical terms as 'a wise old shepherd/ im suvive tru flood/ tru drout/ tru blizad', and anticipates that those of the flock who have strayed from his protection will return. This song even eschews the juridical, rights-based version of justice at the heart of liberalism in favour of the militant praxis of freedom:

> *freedam is nat noh ideology*
>
> *freedam is a human necessity*
>
> *it cyaan depen pan noh wan somebaddy*
>
> *is up to each an evry wan a wi.*

In summary then, Jamaican-born but Britain-raised-and-resident reggae poet, Linton Kwesi Johnson, moulds the logic of incompletion of the Jamaican roots tradition to the particularities of Thatcher's deeply racist, divided Britain. Historical consciousness becomes a social history of the present that documents the injustices of the day; the critique of Babylon specifically targets claims of legal legitimacy in the face of barefaced hypocrisy, especially on the part of the police and the Independent Police Commission (which, like its Jamaican counterpart, has a shockingly poor record in disciplining police for use of excessive force – see Amnesty International: 2001); and love, finally, is secularised as a commitment to international socialism that nonetheless retains the centrality of a generic humanity in order to oppose the social divisions – class, race, gender, sexuality – that enable the State to 'divide and rule' the population. Rather as Kwame Dawes has argued in his anthology of reggae poetry *Wheel and Come Again*, however, I would argue that there is a coherent aesthetic (although I prefer the word 'logic') discernible beneath these iterative differences. Indeed, Fred D'Aguiar recognises the continuity of this logic of incompletion when he writes of Johnson: 'he tests the civility of the nation by its capacity to co-exist with the other: those who are in it but thought to be not of it' (Johnson: 2002, p.xiii), with, in other words, Rancière's 'part of no part' (see Rancière: 1998) or Badiou's 'inexistent' (see Badiou: 2005). Is this testing of the nation with the internal other, present yet not fully belonging, not also what Rastafari has done and continues to do in Jamaica and elsewhere?

DIVISIVE UNIVERSALISM IN A GLOBALISED WORLD:

To conclude then, Rasta-influenced conscious roots reggae, as a logic of incompletion, utilises a different kind of universalism to the supposedly inclusive one of representational democracy which claims to count all parts equally and exhaustively. I call this 'divisive universalism' because it divides the symbolic unity of a national situation but exposes something universally true for that situation: it both foregrounds an excluded group and demonstrates the reliance of the entire situation on this very group. Broadly speaking, this same kind of universalism is already at work in Marx when, for example, in the *Critique of Hegel's Philosophy of Right* (Marx: 1970), he famously describes the proletariat as a class 'which has a universal character because its suffering is universal': it 'does not claim a particular redress because the wrong done to it is not a particular wrong but *wrong in general*'. So divisive universalism refuses juridical mechanisms of inclusion or representation but exposes the 'part of no part' that covertly founds those mechanisms. Where the Enlightenment universalism imported by European colonisers emphasised the administrative category of the unified nation, divisive universalism incompletes the nation to open its borders, be they political, racial, historical, or economic, to critical questioning.

In this sense, conscious roots reggae demonstrates the hypocrisy of claims to representational inclusivity, either that made at the level of Jamaica's 'Out of Many, One' slogan, or that of the globalized version of the same thing in the form of the putative 'global village'. It does so by rendering an account of the uncounted, a more radical category than the merely excluded. Today's refugees and slum dwellers, sweat-shop workers and displaced indigenous peoples all demonstrate that there are still wretched of the globalised earth. As it becomes globalised – and this should not be seen as a bad thing: both Rastafari and conscious reggae have always arguably been both symptoms of, and forms of resistance to, the forces of globalisation – roots reggae must hold on to its militant role as 'rebel music' for the world's disenfranchised if it is not to lose its capacity to function as a divisive universalism. Otherwise, the history of oppression it mobilises will become a series of empty signifiers that cannot support subjects living in conscious daily relation with that history; the critique of Babylon will become commodified as mere 'rebel chic', rather as elements of Rastafari have been mainstreamed in political and popular discourse in Jamaica and globally; and, finally, the core spiritual and political message of love, peace and unity will be replaced by a romanticized togetherness that conceals the world's growing schisms, and thereby becomes complicit with them.

As my example of Linton Kwesi Johnson suggests, however, this insistence on retaining its status as rebel music is not necessarily about imputing some kind of authentic and in the end exclusive 'Jamaican-ness' to the 'conscious' roots reggae. No doubt Jamaican musicians must lead the way, as they always have, but by emphasising divisive universalism, it is clear that it is a universalism that plays itself out differently in different contexts: suffering is everywhere, yet everywhere different. Reggae can continue to be the song of this common difference only if it recognises divisive universalism as, paradoxically, a universalism that must be manifested in locally differentiated ways.

With its slack lyrics and defiantly vernacular use of what Louise Bennett once called 'Jamaica labrish', current dancehall music is not making the international inroads that, *economically*, Jamaica really needs, leading many in Jamaica (perhaps of a certain generation) to call for a return to the roots tradition Bob Marley made so popular around the world in the 1970s. This was a call that was answered in the wake of the scandal surrounding Buju Banton's infamous 'Boom Bye Bye' record when 'conscious ragga' emerged in the early 1990s, as an albeit shortlived rootsical turn in dancehall. The more recent switch from dancehall to roots reggae in Buju Banton's own latest album, *Rasta Got Soul*, could be seen to respond to this call once again, but in truth these shifts emerge from, precisely, more *rooted* concerns which are part and parcel of the cyclical conversations between past and present internal to every musical tradition, especially one as rich as Jamaica's. However, the clarion call to 'return to roots' that comes not from musicians and fans, but from on high from government culture ministers, international promoters and entrepreneurs, is often phrased in terms of 'brand Jamaica'. Such branding necessarily involves the marketization of cultural integrity, and a competitive zeal to grab a greater slice of the international music market's considerable revenues. And yet it is this same 'brand Jamaica' that has succeeded so disappointingly in turning Rastafari into a quaintly exotic peace movement that literally adds 'colour' to the hippy movement, and Bob Marley into an unchallenging, establishment-friendly commodity mainly for consumption by tourists.

This sort of critique of dancehall, as failing to be as amenable to international marketing as roots music has been, too quickly assumes that this is what popular music should be doing; that it must be a business first, a living culture grounded in the everyday realities and struggles of a people very much second. Without taking a position on slackness and the controversial sex and gender politics of dancehall - which, it is true, doesn't sell well in Europe or the US - it is nonetheless possible to recognise that internationalisation as an exclusive measure of musical value is often both crudely economic and entangled with class-based distinctions of taste internal to Jamaican society (See Hope: 2011). Beyond branding national culture for non-Jamaican audiences in order to enhance national GDP, it is not clear how the chiasmus between global economics and local cultures, and local economics and cultures of globalisation, can ever support the oppositional militancy of Rastafari or the message music of reggae. Better to be Bunny Wailer's reviled 'black-heart man' than the inanely smiling pseudo-Rasta beloved of the Jamaican tourist board.

However, as I have tried to show, just as there is a divisive universalism that opposes Eurocentric nationalist universalism (not as oxymoronic as it sounds), so there is a kind of internationalisation that is neither narrowly economic, nor culturally impoverishing. The situation in Jamaica, with Rasta inspired conscious roots reggae increasingly subordinated to the logic of branding, poses the question of how divisive universalism can continue to be divisive after its rhetoric and its aesthetic have been included in what Rancière would call the 'police order': as he says, 'consensus consists [...] in the reduction of politics to the police' (Rancière: 2010, p.42). One answer to this comes in a form that Jamaican's understandably concerned with the economic plight of their country do not like: namely, in the on-going success of the roots reggae tradition *outside* Jamaica, in countries such as Italy, Germany, Japan, Hawaii and New Zealand as well as the Reggaeton coming out of Latin America. In all of these instances, the logic of incompletion that I have tried to describe operates to articulate the forms of oppression specific to those contexts, yet precisely in this way, they are arguably more faithful to the politics and ethics of Rasta roots reggae than those who would brand such music as 'essentially' Jamaican (and therefore 'stolen', invoking the language of property rights). This is the internationalisation not of a brand image, but of a spirit of resistance and solidarity that appeals to the most inclusive 'demographic': humanity itself.

REFERENCES

Amnesty International, *Killings and Violence by Police: How Many More Victims?*, AI Index, 2001.

Badiou, Alain, *De l'Amour*, Paris: Flammarion, 1999.

_____, *Logics of Worlds*, trans. Alberto Toscano, London: Continuum, 2009.

Bakan, Abigail, *Ideology and Class Conflict in Jamaica: The Politics of Rebellion*, Montreal: McGill-Queen's University Press, 1990.

Barrett, Leonard, *The Rastafarians: Sounds of Cultural Dissonance*, Boston: Beacon Press, 1988.

Bhabha, Homi K., *Locations of Culture*, London: Routledge, 1994.

Briener, Laurence, 'The English Bible in Jamaican Rastafari', *Journal of Religious Thought*, Vol. 42, No. 2, 1985, pp.30-43.

Campbell, Horace, *Rasta and Resistance: From Marcus Garvey to Walter Rodney*, Trenton New Jersey: Africa World Press Inc., 2001.

Cashmore, Ernest, *Rastaman: The Rastafarian Movement in England*, London: Unwin Paperbacks, 1983.

Chevannes, Barry, *Rastafari: Roots and Ideology*, Kingston: The Press, 1995.

Cooper, Carolyn, *Soundclash: Jamaican Dancehall Culture at Large*, New York: Palgrave Macmillan, 2004.

Craton, Michael, *Testing the Chains: Resistance to Slavery in the British West Indies*, London: Cornell University Press, 1982.

Dawes, Kwame, *Wheel and Come Again: An Anthology of Reggae Poetry*, Leeds: Peepal Tree, 1998.

Feltham, Oliver, *Alain Badiou: Live Theory*, London: Continuum, 2008.

Foehr, Stephen, *Jamaican Warriors: Reggae Roots & Culture*, London: Sanctuary Publishing Limited, 2000.

Hochschild, Adam, *Bury The Chains: The British Struggle to Abolish Slavery*, London: Macmillan, 2005.

Hope, Donna P., *Inna Di Dancehall: Popular Culture and the Politics of Identity in Jamaica*, Kingston: University of West Indies Press, 2006.

Hope, Donna P., *Man Vibes: Masculinities in Jamaican Dancehall*, Kingston: Ian Randall Publishers, 2010.

Johnson, Linton Kewsi, *Mi Revalueshanary Fren: Selected Poems*, London: Penguin Books, 2002.

Lee, Hélène, *The First Rasta: Leonard Howell and the Rise of Rastafarianism*, trans. Lily Davis, Chicago: Lawrence Hill Books, 1999.

Kostal, Rande W., *A Jurisprudence of Power: Victorian Empire and the Rule of Law*, Oxford: Oxford University Press, 2005.

Marx, *Contributions to the Critique of Hegel's Philosophy of Right*, trans. by Annette Jolin and Joseph O'Malley, Cambridge: Cambridge University Press, 1970.

Murrell, Nathaniel et al, *Chanting Down Babylon: The Rastafari Reader*, Philadelphia: Temple University Press, 1998.

Nojeim, Michael, *Gandhi and King: The Power of Nonviolent Resistance*, London: Praeger, 2004.

Rancière, Jacques, *Disagreement: Politics and Philosophy*, London: University of Minnesota Press, 1998.

Spivak, Gayatri, 'Can the Subaltern Speak?' in Nelson, C. and Grossberg, L. (eds.), *Marxism and the Interpretation of Culture*, Illinois: University of Illinois Press, 1988.

_____, *A Critique of Postcolonial Reason: Towards a History of the Vanishing Present*, London: Harvard University Press, 1999.

Thomson, Ian, *The Dead Yard: Tales of Modern Jamaica*, London: Faber and Faber, 2009.

Tomlinson, John, *Cultural Imperialism*, London: Printers Publishing Ltd, 1991

Turner, Mary, *Slaves and Missionaries: The Disintegration of Jamaican Slave Society, 1787-1843*, Kingston: The Press of the University of the West Indies, 1988.

10 DUBBING THE REGGAE NATION

TRANSNATIONALISM, GLOBALIZATION, AND INTERCULTURALISM

When I first heard the opening horn lines of 'Mandela' (1978)[1] by Jamaican tenor saxophonist Tommy McCook, I was convinced there was a mistake in the album's accompanying information. The introductory horn line and *riddim*[2] are nearly exact renderings of the earlier roots reggae classic 'Satta Massagana,' recorded by the Abyssinians in 1969.[3] After the first moment, however, a dramatic shift takes place immediately following the horn introduction; while the original version of 'Satta' immediately proceeds to the iconic harmony vocalizations of the Abyssinians, 'Mandela' instead offers a new instrumental melody played by the horns while the vocals remain absent for the remainder of the song. Emblematic of the dub remixing practices of the Jamaican popular music scene of the 1970s, this new *version*[4] of 'Satta' strategically reinvents the original song by disrupting our expectations. Using what Michael Veal describes as an '[a]esthetic of surprise and suspense, collapse and incompletion,'[5] the expectations of listeners familiar with the original song are subverted and refocused. Whereas the original lyrics of 'Satta' declare (rooted distinctly in Rastafarian and Ethiopianism) that 'there is a land, far, far away,' the new instrumental *version* replaces these lyrics with a different sense of *place* and arrival—the new song is a soundscape of strategically shifted signifiers ripe with symbolism.

In recent years, dub has increasingly become the subject of critical studies in Jamaican popular music.[6] Similarly, reggae performed by non-Jamaicans has become the subject of a growing body of literature that, generally speaking, examines the ways in which local musicians adapt varying forms of reggae to local social, cultural, and musical contexts.[7] Studies of reggae outside of Jamaica—in the Circum-Caribbean, the Americas, Africa, Europe, Asia, New Zealand, and elsewhere—have gradually moved into dialogue with more recent trends in the study of globalization and, by extension, transnationalism.[8]

In this essay, I develop a methodology drawn from dub to offer a reading of the term *reggae nation*,[9] a trope that appears in various ways in the global reggae community. A slogan used in multiple ways during musical performances, artist interviews, and product marketing, reggae nation invokes community within the scattered global networks of reggae performance and reception. Intrinsically transnational, it stands as a creatively articulated surrogate for an actually-existing nation state. While in dialogue with studies of reggae outside of Jamaica, my focus diverges from much of the discourse that looks at reggae practice in various local communities around the world. Instead, I am interested in the ways that *reggae nation* operates as a form of transnationalism generated through a shared, symbolic discourse of musical practices and specific face-to-face intercultural musical encounters. Such encounters are certainly ensconced in numerous trajectories of race, class, and gender; this preliminary study stops short of focusing on these important functions of different, but provides several important initial steps towards a more clear understanding of how transnational cultural flows are shaped by notions of race and class. By analyzing the music or lyrics of examples by McCook, Ivorian vocalist Alpha Blondy, and Panamanian-American vocalist Elijah Emanuel, I offer a reading of *reggae nation* that moves beyond immigration-based accounts of transnationalism; instead, I argue that *reggae nation* offers important insights into the ways that people articulate strategic social formations across national and cultural boundaries.

By drawing upon the soundscapes of dub mixing techniques, I hope to offer a 'reverberative' methodology to identify the meaning of 'nation' invoked by the recurring trope of *reggae nation* in the global reggae community. The *reggae nation* trope is both ubiquitous and elusive. Much like the echo created by radical uses of delay, reverb, and other effects in mixing techniques of Jamaican dub engineers, *reggae nation* is constantly transforming, evolving, echoing. Both dub echos and *reggae nation* might embody a kind of fractal geometry or series of constellatory relationships.[10]

In part, my reverberative methodology stems from Louis Chude-Sokei's metaphor of the 'echo chamber' and its relationship to shifting meanings of 'Africa' in reggae. Chude-Sokei argues that 'the cultural practices of memory assert [...] 'Africa' as both multivalent signifier and historical legacy still central to black modernity... However, it is true that the echoes of Africa that are new world black cultures have now bounced back, creating a complex scenario that can best be grasped by the metaphor of an 'echo chamber".[11] The echo or bounce back of African-diasporic cultures reformulates African cultural identity in ways intimately connected to processes of globalization and globalized cultural production. The myriad effects common in dub mixing techniques and *versioning*—most notably the echo—provide new ways to theorize globalization and transnationalism in reggae discourse.

My essay is divided into three dub sections, named in the manner that dub remixes of pre-existing songs have been titled since the 1970s.[12] In each of these sections, or dubs if you will, the central theoretical themes of my essay reappear in various ways, often bringing together specific musical examples with ideas from the evolving discourses centered on these themes. Each section focuses on a different series of musical examples. The first dub continues the analysis of 'Mandela' and 'Satta' that started the essay, identifying the *reggae nation* trope and giving way to my adoption of the term transnation.[13] Within this discussion, we discover ways in which Jamaican musicians have imagined their music within larger international—global and transnational—frameworks. The second dub explores Ivorian reggae icon Alpha Blondy's classic 1984 song 'Cocody Rock' and theorizes ways in which non-Jamaican musicians have drawn upon notions of *place* to articulate connections between their music and that of Jamaican musicians. That Blondy recorded the song in Kingston under the musical direction of bassist Aston 'Family Man' Barrett takes on special significance in my analysis and provides important insights on the intercultural nature of reggae transnationalism. The final dub focuses on ways that the music of Panamanian-American singer Elijah Emanuel forges a Pan-Latin American *reggae nation* by persistently articulating the relationship between the African diaspora and indigenous cultures in the Americas.

Ultimately, I argue that *reggae nation* offers a theory of transnationalism that moves beyond the dialectical relationship between nation and globalization often at play in prevailing understandings of transnationalism. *Reggae nation* references nation without the nation, a nation without geographic coordinates. If transnationalism highlights the global dispersal of people who share a common ethnic or national origin, an extension of *diaspora*, then where is *reggae nation*'s origin and where does it exist today? What is the role of *place* in such a 'virtual' nation? How might it be informed by ideas about *diaspora*, Pan-Africanism, or Pan-Latin Americanism? How might these discourses provide concepts of nation that diverge from current thinking about transnationalism? And how does music function as a technology of creating, maintaining, or challenging ideas about *reggae nation*? A dub-like, reverberative methodology may help to answer these questions.

Reggae nation dub: from 'Satta' to 'Mandela'

'There is a land, far far away'[14]

–The Abyssinians

McCook's 'Mandela' illustrates that 'Satta' became an alluring *riddim* among producers and performers in Jamaica's reggae scene of the 1970s. That 'Satta' became an important signifier of Rastafarianism, and remains so to this day is remarkable given the complicated history of the song and its relationship to the *versioning* culture of the time. Originally titled 'Land Far Away,' the Abyssinians—the vocal trio of Bernard Collins and the Manning brothers, Donald and Lynford— self-produced the recording and released the song on their own Clinch label in 1969.[15] Largely ignored by the established reggae industry, the release did little to garner the attention of the listening public. Within a few months of the release, however, producer Joe Gibbs recorded a new instrumental *version* of the song ('A So') featuring his Destroyers group, which included sax work by McCook. This re-recorded *version* received radio airplay and led to new interest in the Abyssinians' original, by this time renamed 'Satta Massagana,' a title drawing from the lyrics of the song. 'Satta' was released in 1971 as the result of this new attention.[16]

Almost immediately both versions of the song, by Gibbs and the Abyssinians, entered the rhizome-like laboratory of Jamaican *versioning* culture.[17] By 1978, several popular instrumental and talkover *versions* had been released, including I Roy's 'Satta,' Augustus Pablo's 'Pablo Satta,' Dillinger's 'I Saw E Saw,' and others.[18] Indeed, the Abyssinians themselves contributed to the proliferation of the 'Satta' riddim by almost immediately releasing talkover, dub, and instrumental versions, such as 'Mabrak' (featuring Bongo Jerry). Such a strategy served to catalyze the growing interest in the song and helped ensure its continued presence in the local scene.

Both the song and the *riddim* became almost foundational as the music scene witnessed a tremendous shift towards Rastafarianism. The prominence of the Abyssinians in Jeremy Marre's classic 1977 film *Roots Rock Reggae*[19] illuminates some of the ways that the group and their music served the formulation of a Rastafarian ethos in reggae. In a notable scene the Abyssinians perform an acoustic rendition of 'Satta Massagana' in a small one room shack below a sign celebrating the Ethiopian Emperor Haile Selassie I and containing the words 'cultural school.' The narrator then declares that 'the songs of the Abyssinians have become a spiritual thing; they're even sung as hymns in the Ethiopian churches.' As the performance scene fades, a new scene emerges as a crowd has gathered around and in a building labeled by the signage of the Ethiopian World Federation, an international organization designed to celebrate Ethiopia's relationship to African identity and the African diaspora.[20] Within the E.W.F. building, the film captures a group of people singing 'Satta Massagana' as a hymn followed by a woman reading aloud from a book describing Haile Selassie.[21]

This interest in Ethiopia was prominent in the Kingston community of musicians that included Collins and the Manning brothers. Indeed, an emergent Rastafarian presence in Kingston during the 1960s attracted many musician converts, most of whom were eager to explore the relationship between their beliefs and their music. When Collins moved to Jones Town (an area of Kingston near Trench Town) in 1965,[22] he was not a Rastafarian, although many of his ideas showed a propensity towards Rastafarian beliefs.[23] According to Collins, when he met Donald Manning (around the time he moved to Jones Town) Donald was already a lock-wearing Rastafarian, unlike his brother Lynford who was a 'church man from longer time.'[24] Even with these particular leanings, the Manning brothers frequently attended Ethiopian Orthodox Church services and were influenced by an older brother who was a well-known priest in the Church.[25] In part, this interest in the Ethiopian Orthodox Church evidences the fluidity between Rastafarianism and various forms of Christianity in Jamaica. That various parts of the lyrics of 'Satta Massagana,' including its title, are written in Amharic (the language of Ethiopia) is equally significant. According to Collins, he and Donald studied Amharic in community-based language classes, presumably related to the Ethiopian Orthodox Church and maybe the E.W.F.. From this perspective, the lyrics of 'Satta Massagana' betray the convergence of Ethiopianism, Rastafarianism, and the burgeoning early reggae scene.

Perhaps for these reasons, 'Satta Massagana' quickly took on special significance within the reggae scene, a significance that has persisted throughout many developments in Jamaican popular music. One of the prevailing tropes around the song suggests that it is 'reggae's national anthem.' Now inexorably linked with the song in virtually all contexts (press, radio, live performance), the title of 'anthem' proves very difficult to trace and its origins nearly impossible to find. For example, in his liner notes to the 1993 Heartbeat compilation *Satta Massagana* (which contains tracks from several different recording sessions), Chris Wilson writes that '[w]hen the Abyssinians [...] wrote 'Satta Massagana' little did they realize it would become reggae music's national anthem.' Indeed, this 'anthem' trope appears most frequently in promotional language surrounding the Heartbeat album, presumably written by a savvy publicist or marketing agent.

Even though the history of the term 'reggae's national anthem' is difficult to parse and may in fact be the product of clever marketing, I'm drawn to the ways it effortlessly invokes complex ideas about nationalism, belonging, and identity. As it echos throughout the global reggae community, it serves as an algorithm of unity, it argues for a sense of togetherness embodied in affinity intercultures centered on music.[26] That 'Satta' is deeply connected to Rastafarianism, Ethiopianism, and a patently African-diasporic cultural vision makes this implied 'reggae nation' a 'complex scenario,' to borrow again from Chude-Sokei. Like the echoes heard in dub mixing techniques, these 'new world black cultures'[27] reverberate a continually shifting, phasing, and flanging sense of identity and cultural continuity across time and space. Aspects of this process shape the ways that the 'Satta' *riddim* is reformulated in McCook's 'Mandela.'

'Mandela' contains many of the classic remixing techniques of dub practices pioneered by Jamaica's remarkably creative coterie of mixing engineers active in the 1970s. For example, an assortment of sounds from the original multitrack recording are brought in and out of the mix, often highlighting previously obscured details (like the tambourine), while strategic occasional elisions of the piano and guitar rhythms, the drums, or the bass guitar open new sonic spaces within the fabric of the recording. This 'combination of fragmentation and [...] manipulation of spatiality'[28] is blended with new horn lines and improvised horn solos. Unlike other trends in dub of this era that focus more on vocals, such as 'talkover' *versions* of the *riddim* made popular by Big Youth, Dennis Alcapone, and others, 'Mandela' belongs to a style of instrumental dub that prominently features horn sections and individual horn soloists. In part, this is a reflection of the large pool of professional horn players active in Jamaica in 1970s. Like the well-known horn players of the Skatalites in the 1960s (including McCook), and more broadly those players associated with the music program at Kingston's Alpha Boys School, many of these musicians were versed in jazz and rhythm and blues performance styles of the United States. As producers looked to capitalize on the popularity of certain songs in the 1970s by releasing subsequent dub versions, it became common for horn players to get in on the action.

McCook's performance on 'Mandela' strongly resembles dominant styles of American jazz saxophonists during the so-called 'post-bop' period of the 1950s and 1960s. This is heard most prominently during McCook's improvised solo that occurs roughly two thirds of the way through the recording. His deep, robust tone and angular melodic phrasing are markedly similar to those pioneered by African American jazz saxophonists such as John Coltrane, Sonny Rollins, Dexter Gordon, and others. This is no minor coincidence.

Born to Jamaican parents living in Cuba, McCook entered the famed Alpha Boys School in Kingston in 1933, when he was eleven years old.[29] Founded in 1890 by the Sisters of Mercy,[30] the school was dedicated to helping needy families with the education of their children, many of whom exhibited behavioral issues. Shortly after the founding of the school, an active music program developed, which under the direction of Sister Mary Ignitius Davies and bandmaster George Neilson produced a substantial number of top notch jazz musicians from the 1930s through the 1960s (and beyond). Jamaican bandleaders, like Eric Dean, regularly hired Alpha Boys School graduates into their jazz groups.[31] Many of the most influential jazz-educated horn players in Jamaica in the 1960s and 1970s also studied at the school, including Don Drummond, Cedric

'Im' Brooks, and a host of others. After recording several successful singles, in 1964 McCook became the first bandleader of the Skatalites, an all-star instrumental ska group that released recordings under its own name and as a session band for producers Coxsone Dodd and Duke Reid. Although they broke up in 1965 in the aftermath of trombonist Don Drummond's notorious mental breakdown, their short tenure as a group proved very influential in the history of Jamaican popular music.

Jazz was central to the music of the Skatalites. McCook recalled that '[o]ur music originally came from American big-band swing influences like Duke Ellington, Glenn Miller, Charlie Parker, Dizzy Gillespie and John Coltrane. We selected parts of these great artists' work and injected them into our own material.'[32] According to McCook, this jazz influence was directly related to the appeal their music had to Jamaican audiences of the period: 'I immediately became popular with the fans in Jamaica because of my jazz input into the ska. My solos were different from the other saxophonists.'[33] McCook's strongest connection with jazz began when he travelled to Miami in 1956, where he first encountered the music of John Coltrane. Coltrane's music had a tremendous impact on McCook's approach to the saxophone and improvisation.[34]

McCook's performance on 'Mandela' substantiates these strong historical connections to important developments in African American jazz. Furthermore, the articulation of new melodies and jazz-heavy solos within the framework of the 'Satta' *riddim* can be read as a transnationalizing move. 'Mandela' activates important links between Jamaican popular culture and African American music, illuminating the flow of sounds, ideas, and performance practices from various cultures within the African diaspora. Perhaps this is inevitable — as Stuart Hall argues, black popular culture is 'always conjunctural,'[35] it persistently upsets a politics of authenticity regulated by narrowly-conceived concepts of race, *place*, and national belonging. We might also read McCook's choice of naming the song after the then-imprisoned South African anti-apartheid activist Nelson Mandela as a transnationalizing move. Indeed, the 1970s witnessed the rise of a new anti-apartheid movement in South Africa, met by a reinvigorated white nationalism of the Botha regime in 1978. By naming the song 'Mandela,' McCook strategically created a new kind of 'black Atlantic'[36] framework that brought together the latest trends in Jamaican popular music, with African American jazz, and black South African resistance to apartheid. Loretta Collins claims that 'hegemonic discourses and sound fields are destabilized by the improvisational sound repertoires of emerging nations.'[37] Perhaps we could push this one step further. The kind of 'emerging nation' we may be witnessing in McCook's theoretically rich song may be a form of reggae transnationalism, an emerging transnation of sorts. This *reggae nation* is forged through new musical practices and embodied by the growing number of musicians and listeners around the world to whom reggae is a defining aspect in their lives.

Furthermore, this *reggae nation* challenges views of transnationalism tightly bound to processes of immigration. This standard view of trans-nationalism might be summarized as a field 'composed of a growing number of persons who live dual lives: speaking two languages, having homes in two countries, and making a living through continuous regular contact across national borders.'[38] Such an analysis assumes 'long-distance nationalism'[39] is in place that constitutes a dialectical[40] relationship between nation and globalization. On the other hand, the reggae transnation is grounded in a different rhetoric of nation-ness, a rhetoric less connected to specific political and geographic nation-alisms. It references nation without geographic coordinates. In other words, if standard conceptions of transnationalism highlight global dispersals of people who share common ethnic or national origins, in a sense a further extension of the concept of diaspora, where then is *reggae nation*'s origin and where does it exist today?

The term 'reggae nation' pervades reggae discourse but is rarely theorized. That 'Satta Massagana' is frequently cited as 'reggae's national anthem' is but one clue to its existence. It also appears in spiritualistic refer-ences steeped in Rastafarianism, as well as slick product marketing directed towards an international consumer base,[41] and in the language of Jamaican musicians seeking new ways of building community with their audiences. Many of these meanings are captured in a 2004 video

released by the web-based company called Reggae Nation whose eponymous *Reggae Nation: Island Movement, Volume 1*[42] combines recent reggae
recordings with footage of surfing, utopian images of island lifestyles,
live music performances, and interviews with various reggae artists
from around the world. The term is also used by a German recording
and concert production company. and a Guyanese reggae group, just to
cite a few examples.[43]

Trenchtown dub: from 'Trench Town Rock' to 'Cocody Rock'

> *'Groovin'… It's Kingston 12 now'*[44]
>
> –The Wailers

> *'We are the rockers from Zion Ivory Coast'*[45]
>
> –Alpha Blondy

New transnational conceptions of reggae began to emerge in the earliest years of the internationalization of reggae. Although record distribution networks and several entrepreneurial   British-based figures
helped West Indian immigrant communities keep in contact with nearly
simultaneous developments in Jamaican ska throughout the 1960s,[46]
the international success of Bob Marley after the release of *Catch A Fire*
on Island Records captured, on an entirely new level, the imagination
of people from all around the world. The successful tours carried out
by Marley and the Wailers in the mid-1970s allowed for other Jamaican
artists to begin to tour internationally. Combined with their recordings,
the live performances of these early touring pioneers of Jamaican roots
reggae inspired local musicians to adopt reggae as an important form
of musical expression.

The emergence of Ivorian vocalist Alpha Blondy is an excellent example
of the impact of this new touring circuit for Jamaican musicians. Born
Seydou Koné in Dimbrokro, Cote d'Ivoire—the Ivory Coast—Blondy
attended college in both Cote d'Ivoire and Liberia, and then lived briefly
in New York in the mid-1970s. During his stay in New York, Blondy

sang with various groups and attended a 1977 concert by legendary roots reggae singer Burning Spear. This reportedly had a dramatic impact on the young singer, who launched his music career shortly after this when he returned to Cote d'Ivoire to live in Abidjan.[47]

Because of his rising popularity in Francophone Europe, Blondy moved to Paris in 1984, where he signed with Pathé-Marconi, a subsidiary of EMI. In Paris and London, Blondy recorded his second full-length album, *Cocody Rock*.[48] For the title track of the album, however, he traveled to Kingston to record with the Wailers band, reorganized under bassist Aston 'Family Man' Barrett after Marley's death in 1981. This international, African-diasporic collaboration between Blondy and the Wailers band is extremely important.

We might draw from 'articulation theory'[49] and work on interculturalism to help parse the complicated cultural moves taking place in the seemingly innocent act of international travel and artistic collaboration. As we will see below, the conceptual differences between Marley's 'Trenchtown Rock' and Blondy's 'Cocody Rock' problematize the rather easily deduced similarities between the two songs. In his work on intercultural music making, Jason Stanyek suggests that 'today articulation theory is activated (although sometimes implicitly) in pretty much all music scholarship that concerns itself with issues of identity and power relations.'[50] On a fundamental level, these songs by Marley and Blondy are indeed about the complex intersection of national and African-diasporic identity, about the relationship between music making and specific places that anchor their identities.

Even if the relationship between *place* and identity tends to defy homologous, one-to-one matchings,

> 'space and place still matter; the global processes that shape us have very different inflections in different places. Cognitive mapping in the future will require both local and global knowl-

edge, demanding that we blend rootedness in specific cultures and traditions with competence at mobility and mixing.'[51]

As George Lipsitz argues, modern identities exist in a complex relationship between real, lived spaces, and a broader sense of belonging to larger global formations. In the literature on globalization, this tends to be mapped in the relationship between local and global, what some now call the 'glocal.'[52] We might push this further by examining the 'trajectory' of specific places in the songs by Marley and Blondy, the 'practice of a space' that emerges when they reference Trench Town and Cocody.[53] What we discover is precisely the 'cognitive mapping' that Lipsitz suggests is crucial to contemporary thought.

Although the symbol of Africa was central to Rastafarian-informed roots reggae, there appears to have been relatively little collaboration between Jamaican reggae artists and African artists during the prolific roots reggae years of the 1970s. At the same time, Marley's music had become the soundtrack for various liberation movements in post-colonizing Africa (evidenced in part by Marley's invitation to perform at Zimbabwe's 1980 independence celebration). For many young West Africans coming of age during the 1970s, such as Blondy, Rastafarian messages of Pan-Africanism, resistance, and liberation spoke directly to their hopes and aspirations. It was natural, then, that reggae would provide a kind of musical *lingua franca* amongst the decolonizing nations of Africa in the 1970s.[54] Intimately connected to these musical messages about Rastafarianism were ideas about *place*, images of both a *real* and an *imagined* Jamaica.

The Wailers first recorded 'Trench Town Rock' in 1970 while working with iconoclastic Jamaican producer Lee 'Scratch' Perry.[55] Certainly a product of Scratch's sometimes-eccentric tracking and mixing style, the recording features Peter Tosh playing keyboards, vocal harmonies by the Wailing Souls, and has the characteristic sound of other Scratch-produced Wailers songs of the era (like 'Duppy Conqueror' and 'Soul Rebel').[56] In the aftermath of the international success of *Catch A*

Fire (on Island Records), 'Trench Town Rock' (also spelled 'Trenchtown Rock') was included on the 1973 Trojan-released compilation *African Herbsman*.[57] Subsequent live recordings of the song have been released posthumously on reissued editions of earlier albums, such as *Rastaman Vibration*.[58]

As the epigraph to this section suggests, a strong sense of place pervades the song's lyrics:

> *One good thing about music, when it hits you, you feel no pain.*
>
> *Oh, oh, I say, one good thing about music, when it hits you, you feel no pain.*
>
> *Hit me with music, hit me with music now.*
>
> *This is Trench Town rock, don't watch that, Trench Town rock, big fish or sprat now,*
>
> *Trench Town rock, you reap what you sow, Trench Town rock, and only Jah Jah know,*
>
> *Trench Town rock, I'd never turn my back, Trench Town rock, I'd give the slum a try,*
>
> *Trench Town rock, I'd never let the children cry, Trench Town rock, 'cause you got to tell Jah, Jah why.*
>
> *Groovin', it's Kingston 12 [...]*[59]

The Kingston neighborhood of Trench Town, long associated with reggae history, draws its name from the Irish immigrant James Trench, who used the land that now comprises Trench Town for livestock in the nineteenth century.[60] Squatters began making the area their home throughout the 1900s and after the devastation caused by Hurricane Charlie in 1951, a government housing project was developed in the area that created the 'tenement yards' infamous in reggae history. The Wailers and many other important figures in Jamaican popular music made Trench Town their home at various points in the past and present.[61]

Marley invokes a strong sense of *place* in his lyrics to 'Trench Town Rock.' Using the old postal numbering system still in vogue today, 'Kingston 12' refers to the area of Kingston where Trench Town is located. In the 1960s and 1970s, as well as now, these numbers were used as a shorthand to refer to the various areas and neighborhoods of Kingston. Using 'Kingston 12' mythologizes Trench Town and reveals a nuanced transcript[62] within the music offering new fields of meaning to the inquisitive listener. The direct reference to Trench Town and the slightly more veiled reference through 'Kingston 12' idealizes the rough and tumble neighborhood, suggesting its potential opportunity for the poor and dispossessed in Jamaica—in Marley's words, he's tempted 'to give the slum a try.' At the same time, Trench Town is also marked by risk. While the music 'hits' with 'no pain,' the vicissitudes of life in Trench Town are accompanied by the threat of real violence. The 'rock' of Trench Town is less about the groove of the music; rather, 'rock' refers to the intensity of life in the neighborhood.[63] As an extension of the 'rude boy' phenomenon central to certain ska songs of the 1960s, 'Trench Town Rock' urges 'big fish or sprat' to not 'turn your back.'[64] We might read this as a cautionary warning for 'rude boys.'

Whereas 'Trench Town Rock' illustrates various notions of *place* at work in Marley's music, Blondy's 'Cocody Rock' similarly draws attention to a specific physical location, in this case a neighborhood in Cote d'Ivoire's port city of Abidjan.[65] Indeed, 'Cocody Rock' activates transdiasporic[66] linkages in multiple important ways. The face-to-face, inter-corpo-real music making embodied by the song evidences what Mark Slobin describes as a 'diasporic interculture'[67] and demonstrates the growing interconnection between Jamaica—reggae's birthplace—and other communities of musicians and listeners. That Cocody is on the African continent takes on special meaning in the song, providing a very real connection between Jamaican Rastafarian musicians and West African reggae musicians. When Blondy declares in the song that he is from 'Zion Ivory Coast,' he places himself within the Rastafarian discourses of repatriation and of Africa as the spiritual motherland.

Blondy's collaboration with the Wailers band on 'Cocody Rock' in Kingston in 1984 is particularly significant. While all of the other songs on *Cocody Rock* were recorded in Europe, Blondy travelled to Kingston to record the title track specifically under the direction of Aston 'Family Man' Barrett and with a group long-associated with Marley's music. By all accounts the collaboration was a success—'Cocody Rock' continues to sound musically fresh and articulate to this day. This initial song led to his next album, *Jerusalem*, being exclusively recorded in Kingston in 1986, also under Family Man's direction.

On a conceptual level, several elements of 'Cocody Rock' suggest that it is a direct counterpart to 'Trench Town Rock,' that it serves as a kind of West African reprise of the original. By interchanging 'Cocody' for 'Trenchtown,' Blondy achieves a kind of 'cognitive mapping' that conflates the two neighborhoods into a statement about diasporic belonging seen largely through the lenses of Rastafarianism and reggae. These elements come through in the first verse and chorus of the lyrics:

> *Rockin' rocker, rockin' rocker from Zion I.C.,*
>
> *we're ready ready ready, ready to rock.*
>
> *We are the rockers from Zion Ivory Coast,*
>
> *we're ready ready ready, ready to rock.*
>
> *We sayin' coco, coco, is Cocody rock,*
>
> *coco, coco, is Cocody Rasta.*
>
> *Coco, coco now, Cocody rock,*
>
> *coco, coco, is Cocody Rasta.*[68]

The use of 'rock' in Blondy's song acts as a fulcrum; on the one hand it signifies a connection to Marley's original, and the underlying argument that Cocody and Trench Town are symbolically the same. On the other hand, 'rock' may in fact problematize the similarities between the two songs. While 'rock' signifies the inner city reality of Trench Town for the Wailers, Blondy's 'rock' is more about celebration and music making.

This latter meaning is intimated by Blondy's reference to 'working out the soundsystem,' as he explains in the second verse of the song. Blondy's 'rock' also locates Rastafarianism within Abidjan—the chorus of the song strategically vacillates between 'Cocody rock' and 'Cocody Rasta.' Combined with later references to 'Jah,' Blondy's song is firmly ensconced in Rastafarian rubric. In 'Trench Town Rock,' however, 'rock' is less buoyed by Rastafarianism; the song stops short of clear references to Rastafarianism and draws instead from ideas about Kingston that come from a more broad Jamaican folk culture.

The symbolic connection between Trench Town and Cocody breaks down further through even a cursory comparison of the two neighborhoods. For example, accounts dating back to the early colonial period of Abidjan characterize Cocody as an affluent neighborhood within the city. In the 1970s and 1980s, during Blondy's formative musical years, Cocody continued to be known as an affluent part of the city, where many politicians lived and where much of the banking industry was based.[69] How, then, do we account for this seeming disjuncture? If the real similarities between Trench Town and Cocody, or more generally between Jamaica and West Africa, begin to break down, how might we theorize the kind of cultural moves taking place in transdiasporic collaboration? And how might these complicated aspects of cultural production help to decipher the symbol of *reggae nation*?

Rather than a literal remapping of an urban Jamaican landscape onto an urban West African landscape, I suggest that we view 'Cocody Rock' as a metaphoric dub version of 'Trench Town Rock.' 'Cocody Rock' creates the kind of 'sound bridge' that Chude-Sokei so eloquently illustrates about roots reggae. Like McCook's reworking of 'Satta,' Blondy's song demonstrates ways that globally dispersed musicians create strategic connections to other musicians and communities, ways that are sometimes lived and sometimes symbolic. The fact that it was recorded in Kingston with Jamaican musicians provides a theoretically rich counterbalance to the disjuncture we find in the differences between the neighborhoods of Cocody and Trench Town. In the midst of African independence and decolonization during the 1970s, however, the collaboration nevertheless activates important linkages between continental Africa and the burgeoning Pan Africanism of Jamaican roots reggae of the mid and late 1970s. The face-to-face collaboration engenders *reggae nation* through diasporic interculturalism, through a navigation of difference that may, as Stuart Hall suggests, be fundamental to African diasporic popular cultures around the world.[70] The fissures and disjunctures between Blondy's 'rock' and Marley's 'rock' provide important clues to the nature of global community formations around reggae. The actors in this *reggae nation* perform a fluid, flexible, and creative sense of identity and continuity. Common symbols, such as Trench Town, are creatively re-articulated with signal differences.[71]

Transnational dub: reggae and Pan-Latin American identity[72]

soy legal! ['I'm a legal citizen!']

— Elijah Emanuel[73]

Although my previous examples focus on a flow between Jamaican culture and African and African-diasporic communities, there are almost countless examples of articulations of global reggae culture with local cultures that demonstrate other kinds of transnational linkages. Notable examples include *Jawaiian* reggae, reggae that emerged in Hawaii after Marley's international success, or Maori reggae in New Zealand, or *reggaeton* in Latin America. These demonstrate James Clifford's observation that 'the articulation of reggae with indigenous projects in the Pacific and elsewhere is a resonant, if unorganized, form of 'globalization from below.'"[74]

Among many other possible examples, these issues are actively theorized in the work of vocalist and songwriter Elijah Emanuel. Born Elias Hernandez[75] in Colon, Panama, Emanuel grew up in two worlds, one in Panama and the other in San Diego, California, where he spent many of his formative teenage years. From 1997 to 2008 Emanuel collaborated with local roots reggae musicians in San Diego, where he first formed a group called the Revelations. Later the group would change its name to 'Elijah Emanuel and the Revelations' (under his sole leadership). In its final years, the group was known simply as 'Elijah Emanuel.' Over this period, Emanuel released three albums: *La Lucha Continua / The Struggle Continues...* (2001), *Vision Persistente / Persistence of Vision* (2004), and *Tres Sangres* (2008).[76] Often describing his music as 'reggae en Español,' Emanuel's performance style drew heavily from the practices of roots reggae of the 1970s and early 1980s.[77]

The press release for *Tres Sangres* draws attention to the bilingual nature of Emanuel's music.[78] On his recordings and in live performance Emanuel sings in English and Spanish, occasionally in both languages within the same song. Initially, this bilingualism was structured around specific songs. In his repertoire from *La Lucha Continua/The Struggle Continues...*, each song has a fixed language; for example, 'Revolución' was always performed in Spanish while 'Lazy Mind' was always performed in English. In live performances leading up to the recording sessions for *Vision Persistente/Persistence of Vision*, this gave way to more flexibility between the languages. It became increasingly common for him to switch the language of a song from one performance to the next (such as 'Two Roads' becoming 'Dos Caminos'[79]), sometimes even in the middle of an individual performance of a song. This trend culminated with several songs on *Vision Persistente /Persistence of Vision* having two versions, one in English and one in Spanish.

Bilingualism of this sort illustrates important aspects of Emanuel's work. Emanuel's music can be viewed as a form of cultural production that theorizes transnational identities in Latin America and beyond. In a certain sense, his music reaches towards a Pan-Latin American nationalism focused on ancient indigenous connections across nation state boundaries. As we see below, this is crucial in the lyrical construction of indigenous identity common in his songs. At the same time, however, we should also view Emanuel's message as one firmly ensconced in the politics of the transborder region of the United States and Mexico. The border, or *la frontera*, is a crucial point of reference in Emanuel's music. It is used as a symbol to generate modes of resistance and struggle within the complex border politics of the United States and Mexico, while also serving as a conceptual field of cultural creativity, exchange, and hope. As a physical reality, the border is also something that Emanuel crossed often in the late 1990s and throughout the first decade of the 2000s in order to perform semi-regular concerts in Tijuana, Playas de Tijuana, and Ensenada, Mexican cities just across the border from San Diego.

All of these issues come to the fore in the lyrics of Emanuel's anthemic song 'Yo No Soy Ilegal' used in the epigraph to this section of my essay. Written before the increased militarization of the U.S.-Mexico border now common in the post-911 political climate, Emanuel's song speaks remarkably well to current debates about immigration policy, the policing of national borders, and the isolationist stance of the G.W. Bush and Obama administrations that seem to contradict the transnational makeup of many American communities. On the contrary, much of Elijah's Spanish-language *oeuvre* offers a Pan-Latin American identity that resonates well with contemporary Chicano activism in the United States and related activist movements throughout Latin America.

In the introduction to 'Yo No Soy Ilegal,' Emanuel recites the names of several important historical figures in Latin American activism: Poncho Villa, Emiliano Zapata, and Che Guevara. Invoking these historical figures helps position his assertions that 'yo no soy illegal' ('I'm not an illegal alien' and 'sigo cruzando fronteras, sigo luchando'[80] ('I'll continue crossing borders, continue struggling') within much larger discourses about colonialism and national independence in Latin America. Horace Campbell argues 'the cultural resistance from the hills of Jamaica and the symbols of defiance become their form of resistance as they attempt to create their own cultural institutions.'[81] Drawing from the cultural politics of Rastafarian-inspired roots reggae, we see in Elijah's music an aggressive agenda of *de*nationalizing political nation states that serve to dissect and compartmentalize Latin American ethnicities, indigenous cultures—*indigenas*—and their connections to Caribbean culture and the African diaspora. Yet this agenda is also one of *re*nationalizing musical and cultural identities in new transnational ways, not as a kind of immigration-based 'long distance nationalism,'[82] through which global flows of people remain connected to their country of origin, but as a progressive transnation resembling the 'global citizenship' suggested by Darren O'Byrne and others.[83]

At the same time, however, 'Yo No Soy Ilegal' speaks to Emanuel's different audiences in divergent ways. When performed at San Diego venues, enthusiastic audiences frequently joined Emanuel in singing the response of the chorus, proclaiming 'soy legal!':

> *Yo no soy ilegal. Soy legal!*
> *Yo no soy ilegal. Soy legal!*[84]

For San Diego audiences, being 'legal' is intimately connected to highly politicized discourses about illegal immigration and cultural identity in the border region. Emanuel's references to Latin American activists in the introduction to the song might be read as a retort to the decidedly nationalist frames of reference often at play in American debates about illegal immigration. But how might these references be read by Mexican audiences just south of the border in Tijuana, where Emanuel performed regularly? Or in Panama, where Emanuel has periodically attempted to promote his music?

Emanuel builds a crafty ambivalence into the lyrics of 'Yo No Soy Ilegal.' While the chorus might signify debates about illegal immigration to American audiences, there is nevertheless a strong anti-colonial, anti-imperialism message in much of the lyrics that easily allow legal citizenship to be viewed from a Pan-Latin American perspective. In the second verse he sings

> *[p]or una falta de memoria, nos olvidamos de nuestra historia.*
> *Fuimos los primeros en esta tierra / California, Texas y todas*
> *las Americas. Y ahora andamos en el olvido, por tanto creer en*

los Estados Unidos. Aunque me pongan barreras sigo cruzando
fronteras, sigo luchando, sobreviviendo!

(Because of a lack of memory, we forget our history. We were the
first in this land / California, Texas and throughout the Ameri-
cas. And now we are being forgotten, for believing so much in the
United States. Even though they put up barriers, I continue crossing
borders, keep fighting, surviving!)[85]

By pluralizing 'Americas,' Emanuel frames the issue of legal citizenship in broader, regional terms. While speaking about the movement
of people across the border of the United States, he simultaneously
questions national borders 'throughout the Americas.' 'Our history' is
not limited to the relationship between the United States and Mexico;
instead, 'history' is conceived through indigeneity. This nuanced sense
of Latin American identity is frequently invoked in Emanuel's music
by reference to 'indigenas,' by which he means indigenous peoples of
the Americas.[86] As a result, the form of transnationalism that emerges
in Emanuel's music moves past immigration-based accounts of people
'having homes in two countries'[87] towards a form of transnationalism
that questions the nation state itself and challenges the basic dialectic
between nation and transnation.[88]

In June 2006, Emanuel and his group travelled from San Diego to Mexico
City to perform at a reggae festival celebrating Afro-Mexican culture,
what the organizers of the festival described as '[la] tercera raíz cultural'
('the third cultural root').[89] Held on the sixth anniversary of El Faro de
Oriente,[90] a large family-oriented community arts, crafts, and educational complex in the Fuentes de Zaragoza neighborhood of Mexico
City, the five day festival included various educational exhibitions, film
screenings, and musical performances all focused around the theme of
'rencuentro con nuestra negritud' ('re-encounter with our blackness'). A
major force behind the music presented at the festival was local reggae
musician and organizer Zopi (Gerardo Pimentel), known for his role as
bassist and vocalist in Rastrillos, a cornerstone group in Mexico City's

reggae scene, and for his Saturday radio program, Reggaevolución, on 105FM.[91] Zopi was key in bringing Emanuel and his group to the festival and was familiar with the ways that Emanuel's music formulates a Latin American reggae identity with clear linkages to the African diaspora.

Performing on a large festival stage with a massive canvas backdrop showing the African continent, Emanuel offered commentary on local issues in between songs such as 'La Consciencia Indigena,' 'Yo No Soy Ilegal,' and 'Todos Unidos.' Most of Emanuel's comments were aimed at issues revolving around the EZLN (Ejército Zapatista de Liberación Nacional) and indigenous land rights. Indeed, the Zapatista movement, named after the Mexican revolutionary-era figure Emiliano Zapata, has figured prominently in many Emanuel songs and serves as a crucial nexus of indigeneity, activism, and Pan-Latin American identity in his work.[92] In the days just prior to the festival appearance, Emanuel learned that Subcomandante Marcos, an educator turned Zapatista revolutionary leader, was in Mexico City to help advocate for local land rights. Emanuel visited an EZLN branch in hopes of meeting Marcos; although the meeting was unsuccessful, copies of Emanuel's music apparently reached the leader. These experiences with the local EZLN community inspired Emanuel's performance and commentary at the festival. While solidarity with the Zapatista movement was frequently expressed in Emanuel's performances in and around San Diego, his proximity to active EZLN contingencies energized the activist nature of his music that afternoon. Ironically, however, his comments in support of the EZLN and the Zapatistas fell on deaf ears at the concert, or so it seemed to this author.[93] To the organizers of the festival, Emanuel's music acted as a tool to help identify African-diasporic influences within Mexican culture. This comes in part from the association of reggae with modes of resistance within Afro-Jamaican culture. Zopi explains that '[l]as condiciones (de marginación) en las que surgió el reggae (en Jamaica) no han cambiado, hasta se han recrudecido a través del neoliberalismo. En Africa, Jamaica, Iztapalapa, son las mismas condiciones de marginación' ('the conditions (of exclusion) within which reggae emerged (in Jamaica) have not changed, they have worsened through neoliberalism. In Africa, Jamaica, Iztapalapa, are the same marginalizations').[94] Zopi's association of Africa, Jamaica, and Iztapalapa, the latter an area of Mexico City, speaks to the kinds of transnational connections often forged in global reggae communities. For Zopi, Emanuel's music embodies these transnational connections and provides a figurative roadmap for 'imagining community,' for parsing the ways that reggae might activate links between African diasporic cultures and both indigenous and modern forms of Latin American identity. This notion of the *reggae nation* is at once local and global; it recognizes specific locals—Jamaica, Itztapalapa—but does so in a patently global language. *Reggae nation* is potentially everywhere and offers strategies for connecting across national boundaries in ways that subvert the primacy of the nation state itself.

Emanuel's music articulates this through modes that are strategically transnational. For example, in his song 'Todos Unidos' ('We're All United'), Emanuel celebrates the mixture of various Latin American indigenous identities with African diasporic and European influences.

> *Somos aztecas, inca, maya, mestizos y negros / Somos todos unidos*
>
> *('We are Aztec, Inca, Maya, mestizo and black / we are all united')*[95]

By invoking ancient Latin American empires and putting them in dialogue with 'mestizos y negros' (Latin Americans with European and African mixed ancestry, respectively), Emanuel forwards a decidedly multiracial, Pan-Latin American notion of *reggae nation* that includes various articulations with the African diaspora. We can find this in his song 'Reggae en Español':

> *Traigo un sabor distinto, diferente / afro, latino, indio, fuerte.*
>
> *Traigo un amor multicolor / un amor sin fronteras, un amor sin barreras.*
>
> *('I bring a distinct, different flavor / African, Latino, indigenous, strong.*

> *I bring a love that is multicolored / a love without borders, a love without walls.')*[96]

By using the personal present indicative tense of the verb *traer* ('to bring'), Emanuel tells us that he embodies these different identities, that he is in fact part African, part Latino, and part *indigena* (he uses the term 'indio' to refer to indigenous peoples of the Americas). Emanuel's multiracialism is both literal and figurative. The son of a Puerto Rican father and a Panamanian mother, Emanuel traces his ancestry through these different racial identities. At the same time, however, he celebrates the inherent multiracial qualities of Pan-Latin American identity. In other words, our collective cultures are already racially mixed, already have global influences, are already conjunctural.[97] So why not acknowledge and celebrate this fact? This is the central point of the title track to Emanuel's latest album, *Tres Sangres*. In the song, Emanuel explains that his Panamanian heritage is a mixture of 'three bloods'—African, indigenous, and European:

> *Que viva la patria, raíces ancianas, que viva Panama, mi tierra natal.*
>
> *Sangre africana en mis venas, sangre indigena en mis venas, sangre europea en mis venas, tres sangres mezcladas.*
>
> *('Long live the motherland, ancient roots, long live Panama, my homeland.*
>
> *African blood in my veins, native blood in my veins, European blood in my veins, three mixed bloods.')*[98]

Emanuel's music creates a kind of Pan-Latin American transnationalism that moves beyond the nation by highlighting the multiracialism of his Panamanian ancestry. While celebrating Panama, Emanuel strategically calls to attention the presence of *la indigena*—the indigenous—in Latin American countries. As a result Panama is effectively *de*nationalized; the country becomes a vessel through which a new transnation emerges, one with roots in indigenous cultures of the

Americas, the African diaspora, and Europe. If Emanuel engages in 'polylateral exchanges,'[99] then the 'local' tradition represented through his music is a theoretically rich form of globalization, a transnationalism activated through reggae. This analysis is corroborated by the reception of Emanuel's music in the Latin American transborder region of the United States and Mexico. Yet audiences within Panama have not embraced Emanuel's music with similar enthusiasm.[100]

POSTLUDE

The creative articulations of *reggae nation* found in the music of Tommy McCook, Alpha Blondy, and Elijah Emanuel illustrate ways in which identities and social formations transcend nation state boundaries. By developing a 'reverberative' methodology that foregrounds the spatial sound dynamics of dub, I have argued that the *reggae nation* trope thrives in the 'echoes' of continuity, connection, and identity found in various musical practices of global reggae musicians. McCook's 'Mandela' brings into dialogue a rich, largely African-diasporic constellation of ideas and sounds; Blondy's 'Cocody Rock' challenges issues of place in the midst of intercultural collaboration; and Emanuel's music forges a remarkable Pan-Latin American identity that strategically intersects with the African diaspora. While embodying the reggae nation trope, these examples point to a remarkable fluid form of transnationalism.

Inextricably linked to the vibrant amalgam of Jamaican popular culture, this reggae transnationalism provides different ways of mapping Jamaican influence around the world. During her opening remarks at the 2010 International Reggae Conference, the Honorable Minister Olivia Grange made a passionate plea for increased ownership of Jamaican musical performance abroad. Central to her argument was a sense that Jamaican musicians were losing valuable performance opportunities at major reggae festivals in Europe and elsewhere—put simply, non-Jamaican reggae acts were receiving a majority of the performance opportunities while Jamaican musicians were losing opportunities. On the next day of the conference, during her plenary talk titled "Reggae

University:' Rototom Sunsplash and the Politics of Globalising Jamaican Popular Culture,' Professor Carolyn Cooper made a similar plea directed more at scholarship surrounding reggae—more Jamaican scholars are needed to foster an accurate critical discourse around the music. These economic and academic imperatives are partially the result of the increasing globalization of reggae and Jamaican cultural production. As we move into the future, the trope of *reggae nation* may help us reconcile a self-determined vision of Jamaican nationalism while recognizing the transnational flows of musical and cultural practices so common in our contemporary, globalize world.

REFERENCES

'The Abyssinians,' *Abyssinians Top Official Website Reggae Artists*. Accessed September 29, 2010. http://www.theabyssinians.com/bio.html.

'Alpha Boys School: A Mission of Mercy.' *Alpha Boys School*. Accessed September 29, 2010. http://alphahome0.tripod.com/abs/id1.html.

Ashcroft, Bill. 'Chicano Transnation.' In *Imagined Transnationalism: U.S. Latino/a Literature,*

Culture, and Identity. Eds. Kevin Concannon, Francisco A. Lomelí, and Marc Priewe. 13-28. New York: Palgrave Macmillan, 2009.

_____. 'Globalization, Transnation and Utopia.' In *Locating Trans-national Ideals*. Eds.

Walter Goebel and Saskia Schabio. 13-29. New York: Routledge, 2010.

Barrow, Steve and Peter Dalton. *The Rough Guide to Reggae: The Definitive Guide to Jamaican Music, From Ska Through Roots to Ragga*. 2nd edition. London: Penguin Books, 2001.

Bradley, Lloyd. *This is Reggae Music: The Story of Jamaica's Music*. New York: Grove Press, 2000.

Brecher, Jeremy, Tim Costello, and Brendan Smith. *Globalization from Below: The Power of Solidarity*. Boston: South End Press, 2002.

Campbell, Horace. *Rasta and Resistance: From Marcus Garvey to Walter Rodney*. Trenton: Africa World Press, 1987.

Chang, Kevin O'Brien and Wayne Chen. *Reggae Routes: The Story of Jamaican Music*. Kingston: Ian Randle Publishers, 1998.

Chude-Sokei, Louis. "Dr. Satan's Echo Chamber': Reggae, Technology, and the Diaspora Process.' In *Emergences* 9:1,1999, pp. 47-59.

Clifford, James. 'Indigenous Articulations.' In *The Contemporary Pacific* 13:2, Fall 2001, pp. 468-90.

Collins, Loretta. 'Rude Bwoys, Riddim, Rub-A-Dub, and Rastas: Systems of Political Dissonance in Caribbean Performative Sounds.' In *Sound States: Innovative Poetics and Acoustical Technologies*. Ed. Adalaide Morris. Chapel Hill: University of North Carolina Press, 1997, pp. 169-193.

Cooke, Mel. 'Trench Town Tour Visits Singers' Homes.' *Jamaica Daily Gleaner* (March 2, 2010). http://www.jamaica-gleaner.com/gleaner/20100302/ent/ent1.html.

de Certeau, Michel. *Culture in the Plural*. Trans. Tom Conley. Minneapolis: University of Minnesota Press, 1997.

Deleuze, Gilles and Félix Guattari, *A Thousand Plateaus: Capitalism and Schizophrenia*. Trans.

Brian Massumi. Minneapolis: University of Minneapolis Press, 1987.

Doyle, Laura. 'Toward a Philosophy of Transnationalism.' In *Locating Transnational Ideals*. Eds. by Walter Goebel and Saskia Schabio. New York: Routledge, 2010, pp. 63-88.

Eglash, Ron. *African Fractals: Modern Computing and Indigenous Design*. New Brunswick, NJ: Rutgers University Press, 1999.

Garnier, Christiane. 'Banana Boat to Abidjan.' In *Africa Today* 10:8 October 1963, pp. 4-8.

Gates, Henry Louis Jr. *The Signifying Monkey: A Theory of Afro-American Literary Criticism*. New York: Oxford University Press, 1988.

Gilroy, Paul. *The Black Atlantic: Modernity and Double Consciousness*. Cambridge, MA: Harvard University Press, 1993.

Guilbault, Jocelyne. 'On Redefining the 'Local' through World Music.' In *Ethnomusicology: A Contemporary Reader*. Ed. Jennifer Post. New York: Routledge, 2006, pp. 137-146.

Hall, Stuart. 'What is This 'Black' in Black Popular Culture?' In *Stuart Hall: Critical Dialogues in Cultural Studies*. Eds. David Morley and Kuan-Hsing Chen. New York: Routledge, 1996, pp. 465-475.

Henderson, Richard. 'Well-Rounded Labels: The Family Tree Of Genres Grows Far Beyond Its Roots.' In *Billboard* , February 10, 2001.

'History of the Ethiopian World Federation, Inc..' *E.W.F. Online*. Accessed September 29, 2010. http://www.ethiopianworldfederation.com/history.html.

Hitchcock, Peter. 'It Dread Inna Inglan': Linton Kwesi Johnson, Dread, and Dub Identity.' *Postmodern Culture* 4:1, 1993.

Katz, David. *Solid Foundation: An Oral History of Reggae*. London: Bloomsbury, 2003.

Lee, Hélène. *Voir Trenchtown et Mourir*. Flammarion, 2004.

Lipsitz, George. *Dangerous Crossroads: Popular Music, Postmodernism, and the Poetics of Place*. New York: Verso, 1994.

'Music is the Healing of the Nation' *Reggae Nation Germany Official Website*. Accessed September 29, 2010. http://www.reggae-nation.de.

O'Byrne, Darren J. *The Dimensions of Global Citizenship: Political Identity Beyond the Nation-State*. London: Frank Cass & Co. Ltd, 2003.

Partridge, Christopher. 'King Tubby Meets the Upsetters at the Grassroots of Dub: Some Thoughts on the Early History and Influence of Dub Reggae.' In *Popular Music History* 2:3, 2007, pp. 309-331.

Portes, Alejandro, Luis E. Guarnizo, and Patricia Landolt. 'The study of transnationalism: pitfalls and promise of an emergent research field.' *Ethnic and Racial Studies* 22:2, March, 1999, pp. 217-237.

'PRESS RELEASE: NEW ALBUM FROM ELIJAH EMANUEL - 'TRES SANGRES." Unknown origin. Dated September 29, 2009.

Ramirez, Tania Molina. 'El Faro de Oriente celebrará encuentro con nuestra negritud.' *La Jornada* (June 19, 2006. http://www.jornada.unam.mx/2006/06/19/index.php?section=espectaculos&article=a20n1esp.

'Reggae Nation Germany.' Accessed March 12, 2007.

www.myspace.com/reggaenationgermany.

'Reggae Nation Germany.' *Myspace.com.* Accessed September 29, 2010. http://www.myspace.com/reggaenationgermany.

'Reggaevolución on Myspace Music.' Myspace.com. Accessed on September 29, 2010. http://www.myspace.com/reggaevolucion.

'RFI Music – Alpha Blondy.' *RFI Musique.* Accessed September 29, 2010. http://www.rfimusique.com/siteen/biographie/biographie_6125.asp.

Robinson, Jason. 'Enacting Diaspora: Transdiasporic Collaboration and Musical Experimentalism.' Paper presented at Africa Meets North America: 3rd International Symposium and Festival, University of California, Los Angeles, Los Angeles, California,

Salewicz, Chris. *Bob Marley: The Untold Story*. London: HarperCollins, 2009.

Savishinsky, Neil J. 'Rastafari in the Promised Land: The Spread of a Jamaican Socioreligious Movement Among the Youth of West Africa.' In *African Studies Review* 37:3, December, 1994, pp. 19-50.

Scott, James C. *Domination and the Arts of Resistance: Hidden Transcripts.* New Haven: Yale University Press, 1990.

Skrbis, Zlatko. *Long-Distance Nationalism: Diasporas, Homelands and Identities*. Aldershot: Ashgate, 1999.

Slobin, Mark. *Subcultural Sounds: Micromusics of the West*. Hanover Wesleyan University Press, 1993.

Stanyek, Jason. 'Diasporic Improvisation and the Articulation of Intercultural Music.' PhD diss. University of California, San Diego, 2004.

'Sr. Ignatius—Alpha Boys' School.' Accessed March 12, 2007. http://www.alphaboysschool.com/iggy.htm.

Tracy, James F. 'Popular Communication and the Postcolonial Zeitgeist: On Reconsidering Roots Reggae and Dub.' In *Popular Communication* 3:1, February 2005, pp. 21-41.

Van Pelt, Carter. 'Bernard Collins: Keeping On . . .' *400 Years*. Accessed September 29, 2010. http://incolor.inebraska.com/cvanpelt/collins.html.

Veal, Michael E. *Dub: Soundscapes & Shattered Songs in Jamaican Reggae.* Middletown, CT: Wesleyan University Press, 2007.

'Welcome to the web portal of Reggae Nation Guyana.' Accessed September 29, 2010. http://www.reggaenationguyana.com.

www.reggae-riddims.com. Accessed September 29, 2010. http://www.jamrid.com/RiddimDBSearch.php?search=Satta%20massagana&type=Riddim.

Discography and Video Recordings

The Abyssinians. *Satta Massagana*. Heartbeat CD HB 120, 1993, compact disc. Title track originally released in 1969.

Blondy, Alpha. *Cocody Rock*. Shanachie 64011, 1988, compact disc. Originally released in 1984.

Bob Marley & The Wailers. *Rastaman Vibration*. Island B00005KBA0, 2001, compact disc. Originally released in 1976.

The Revelations. *La Lucha Continua /The Struggle Continues...,* self-released, 2001, compact disc.

Emanuel, Emanuel. *Visión Persistente / Persistence of Vision*, self-released EE1, 2004, compact disc.

_____. *Tres Sangres*, self-released, 2008, compact disc.

McCook, Tommy. 'Mandela.' On Abyssinians, *Satta Dub*, Taboo 1 TB1CD03, 1998, compact disc. Originally released in 1978.

McCook, Tommy. *Tommy McCook: The Best of Tommy McCook and the Skatalites, Tribute to Tommy*. Heartbeat CD 11661-7716-2, 1999, compact disc.

Reggae Nation: Island Movement, Volume 1. Resin Music, 2002. Video disc (DVD).

Roots, Rock, Reggae. Directed by Jeremy Marre. New York: Shenachie/Harcourt Films, 2000. Videocassette (VHS).

The Wailers. *African Herbsman*. Trojan, 1973, 331/3 rpm.

The Wailers. 'Simmer Down.' *Tougher Than Tough: The Story of Jamaican Music*, Mango B000003QLC, 1993, 4 compact discs. Originally released in 1964.

NOTES

1. Tommy McCook, "Mandela," on Abyssinians, *Satta Dub*, Taboo 1 TB1CD03, 1998.

2. In Jamaican musician-speak, *riddim* refers to reusable backing tracks from a recording.

3. The Abyssinians, "Satta Massagana," on *Satta Massagana*, Heartbeat CD HB 120, 1993.

4. In Jamaican musician-speak, *version* refers to a remake of an older song, often using the pre-existing *riddim*.

5. Michael Veal, *Dub: Soundscapes and Shattered Songs in Jamaican Reggae* (Middletown, CT: Wesleyan University Press, 2007), 77.

6. See, for example, Veal, *Dub*; Peter Hitchcock, "It Dread Inna Inglan": Linton Kwesi Johnson, Dread, and Dub Identity," *Postmodern Culture* 4:1 (1993), ; Christopher Partridge, "King Tubby Meets the Upsetters at the Grassroots of Dub: Some Thoughts on the Early History and Influence of Dub Reggae," *Popular Music History* 2:3 (2007), 309-331; James F. Tracy, "Popular Communication and the Postcolonial Zeitgeist: On Reconsidering Roots Reggae and Dub," *Popular Communication* 3:1 (February 2005), 21-41.

7. A brief list of citations would do little justice to the voluminous published work on local reggae scenes around the world.

8. This approach is beginning to find traction in the academy as well. For example, scholar Wayne Marshall offered a course titled "Global Reggae: Reggae as Transnational Culture" at MIT in the Fall semester 2010. Similarly, I began offering courses on the globalization of Jamaican popular music in 2002 at the University of California, San Diego, and later at the University of California, Irvine and

at Amherst College. Surely others have offered similar courses elsewhere.

9. As a way of drawing attention to its special meaning, I italicize *reggae nation* throughout the essay. I also omit the article "the," as in "the reggae nation," as an added way of focusing on the identity of this social formation. By omitting the article, we might view *reggae nation* as a place, even if it resists physical mapping.

10. As Horace Campbell suggested to me several years ago, one might draw connections between the recurrence of various tropes in Jamaican culture with fractal geometry present in African cultures. See, for example, Ron Eglash, *African Fractals: Modern Computing and Indigenous Design* (New Brunswick, NJ: Rutgers University Press, 1999).

11. Louis Chude-Sokei, "'Dr. Satan's Echo Chamber': Reggae, Technology, and the Diaspora Process," *Emergences* 9:1 (1999): 51.

12. Dub remixes are often renamed using part of the original name followed by "dub." For example, "The Same Song" by Israel Vibration might become "The Same Dub."

13. I borrow "transnation" from Bill Ashcroft, who describes it as "something more than 'the international' or 'the transnational,' terms that might be conceived as denoting a relation or crossing between states. Transnation is fluid, metaphorically, migrating *outside* of the state that begins *within* the nation" (14, original italics). In my usage of the term, I rely less on "migration"; instead, we might conceive the transnation as a flow of ideas rather than immigrants. Bill Ashcroft, "Chicano Transnation," in *Imagined Transnationalism: U.S. Latino/a Literature, Culture, and Identity*, ed. Kevin Concannon, Francisco A. Lomelí, and Marc Priewe (New York: Palgrave Macmillan, 2009), 13-28. See also Bill Ashcroft, "Globalization, Transnation and Utopia," in *Locating Transnational Ideals*, ed. Walter Goebel and Saskia Schabio (New York: Routledge, 2010), 13-29.

14. The Abyssinians, "Satta Massagana."

15. Although recorded at Studio One, apparently the song failed to capture the interest of impresario Coxsone Dodd. Although musically similar to other early reggae songs of the era, perhaps the strong Ethiopianism evidenced in the lyrics, including the use of Amharic, cast doubt on the song's marketability. Interestingly, it is precisely these elements that would later conjoin the song to Rastafarian symbolism. Steve Barrow and Peter Dalton, *The Rough Guide to Reggae: The Definitive Guide to Jamaican Music, Fro Ska Through Roots to Ragga.* 2nd edition (London: Penguin Books, 2001), 192.

16. Details about this history can be found in many places. See Kevin O'Brien Chang and Wayne Chen, *Reggae Routes: The Story of Jamaican Music* (Philadelphia: Temple University Press, 1998), 144; David Katz, *Solid Foundation: An Oral History of Reggae* (London: Bloomsbury, 2003), 149-150; "The Abyssinians," *Abyssinians Top Official Website Reggae Artists,* http://www.theabyssinians.com/bio.html; and the liner notes to The Abyssinians, *Satta Massagana.*

17. See "rhizome," see Gilles Deleuze and Félix Guattari, *A Thousand Plateaus: Capitalism and Schizophrenia,* trans. Brian Massumi (Minneapolis: University of Minneapolis Press, 1987).

18. For a list of songs that use the "Satta" *riddim,* see www.reggae-riddims.com, http://www.jamrid.com/RiddimDBSearch.php?search=Satta%20massagana&type=Riddim.

19. *Roots, Rock, Reggae,* videocassette, directed by Jeremy Marre (New York: Shenachie/Harcourt Films, 2000).

20. The E.W.F. was incorporated in the United States in 1937 after a delegation of African American community leaders from Harlem visited Selassie in England, while he was in exile during the Italian occupation of Ethiopia of 1935-1941. See "History of the Ethiopian World Federation, Inc.," *E.W.F. Online,* http://www.ethiopianworldfederation.com/history.html.

21. As the film suggests, Selassie's visit to Jamaica in 1966 undoubtedly had a tremendous impact on Rastafarianism, and Ethiopianism more generally, in Jamaica.

22. Donald Manning, quoted in the liner notes to *Satta Massagana*.

23. Bernard Collins, quoted in Carter Van Pelt, "Bernard Collins: Keeping On . . .," *400 Years*, http://incolor.inebraska.com/cvanpelt/collins.html.

24. Ibid.

25. Donald Manning, quoted in the liner notes to *Satta Massagana*.

26. "Affinity interculture" is a term first used by Mark Slobin. See Mark Slobin, *Subcultural Sounds: Micromusics of the West* (Hanover: Wesleyan University Press, 1993).

27. Although reggae communities around the world are comprised of many people who are not African or African diasporic, I nevertheless feel that "reggae" should always be understood by its connection to Afro-Jamaican cultural production. This is an historical frame of reference rather than an argument about authenticity. "New world black culture" is a term used by Chude-Sokei, "'Dr. Satan's Echo Chamber'," 51.

28. Veal, *Dub*, 77.

29. Brian Keyo, liner notes to *Tommy McCook: The Best of Tommy McCook and the Skatalites, Tribute to Tommy*, Heartbeat CD 11661-7716-2, 1999.

30. Opened as an orphanage sometime around 1883, the Jamaican government permitted and registered the school in 1890. "Alpha Boys School: A Mission of Mercy," *Alpha Boys School*, http://alpha-home0.tripod.com/abs/id1.html.

31. Keyo, liner notes to *Tommy McCook: The Best of Tommy McCook and the Skatalites*.

32. Quoted in ibid.

33. Quoted in ibid.

34. Ibid.

35. Stuart Hall, "What is This 'Black' in Black Popular Culture?," from *Stuart Hall: Critical Dialogues in Cultural Studies*, ed. by David Morley and Kuan-Hsing Chen (New York: Routledge, 1996), 465.

36. See Paul Gilroy, *The Black Atlantic: Modernity and Double Consciousness* (Cambridge, MA: Harvard University Press, 1993).

37. Loretta Collins, "Rude Bwoys, Riddim, Rub-A-Dub, and Rastas: Systems of Political Dissonance in Caribbean Performative Sounds," in *Sound States: Innovative Poetics and Acoustical Technologies,* ed. Adalaide Morris (Chapel Hill, NC: University of North Carolina Press, 1997), 171.

38. Alejandro Portes, Luis Guarnizo, and Patricia Landolt, "The study of transnationalism: pitfalls and promise of an emergent research field," *Ethnic and Racial Studies* 22:2 (March 1999): 217.

39. See Zlatko Skrbis, *Long-Distance Nationalism: Diasporas, Homelands and Identities* (Aldershot: Ashgate, 1999).

40. See Laura Doyle, "Toward a Philosophy of Transnationalism," in *Locating Transnational Ideals*, ed. by Walter Goebel and Saskia Schabio (New York: Routledge, 2010), 63-88.

41. The term "reggae nation" has been used by several companies (discussed below) and has been part of the catalogue-building strategy of Heartbeat Records. For the latter, see Richard Henderson, "Well-Rounded Labels: The Family Tree Of Genres Grows Far Beyond Its Roots," *Billboard*, February 10, 2001.

42. *Reggae Nation: Island Movement, Volume 1*, DVD (Resin Music, 2002).

43. See "Reggae Nation Germany," *Myspace.com*, http://www.myspace.com/reggaenationgermany; "Music is the Healing of the Nation," *Reggae Nation Germany | Official Website*, http://www.reggae-nation.de; and "Welcome to the web portal of Reggae Nation Guyana," http://www.reggaenationguyana.com.

44. See "Reggae Nation Germany," *Myspace.com*, http://www.myspace.com/reggaenationgermany; "Music is the Healing of the Nation,"

Reggae Nation Germany | *Official Website*, http://www.reggae-nation.de; and "Welcome to the web portal of Reggae Nation Guyana," http://www.reggaenationguyana.com.

45. Alpha Blondy, "Cocody Rock," from *Cocody Rock*, Shenachie 64011, 1988.

46. See Lloyd Bradley, *This is Reggae Music: The Story of Jamaica's Music* (New York: Grove Press, 2000), 133-153.

47. "RFI Music—Alpha Blondy," *RFI Musique*, http://www.rfimusique.com/siteen/biographie/biographie_6125.asp.

48. Alpha Blondy, *Cocody Rock*.

49. By "articulation theory," I'm referring to the work on "hybridity" forwarded by Stuart Hall, Lawrence Grossberg, John Fiske, James Clifford, Homi Bhahba, and others.

50. Jason Stanyek, "Diasporic Improvisation and the Articulation of Intercultural Music," (PhD diss., University of California, San Diego, 2004), 14.

51. George Lipsitz, *Dangerous Crossroads: Popular Music, Postmodernism, and the Poetics of Place* (New York: Verso, 1994), 180.

52. "Glocal" has emerged as a common term to reference the relationship between "local" and "global."

53. Both of these quotations are drawn from Michel de Certeau's *Culture in the Plural*: "[g]enerally speaking, the cultural operation might be represented as a trajectory relating to the places that determine its conditions of possibility. It is the practice of a space that is already constructed when it introduces an innovation or a displacement. By 'places' I mean the determined and differentiated places organized by the economic system, social hierarchies, the various types of syntax in language, traditions of custom and mentality, psychological structures." Michel de Certeau, *Culture in the Plural*, trans. by Tom Conley (Minneapolis: University of Minnesota Press, 1997), 145.

54. For an argument of the central role of reggae in spreading Rasta-farianism in West Africa, see Neil J. Savishinsky, "Rastafari in the Promised Land: The Spread of a Jamaican Socioreligious Movement Among the Youth of West Africa," *African Studies Review* 37:3 (December 1994), 19-50.

55. Chris Salewicz, *Bob Marley: The Untold Story* (London: HarperCollins, 2009), 175.

56. Ibid., 175-76

57. The Wailers, "Trench Town Rock."

58. Bob Marley & The Wailers, *Rastaman Vibration*, Island B00005KBA0, 2001 (originally released in 1976).

59. The Wailers, "Trench Town Rock."

60. For an account of the history of Trench Town, see Hélène Lee, *Voir Trenchtown et Mourir* (Flammarion, 2004).

61. Mel Cooke, "Trench Town Tour Visits Singers' Homes," *Jamaica Daily Gleaner*, March 2, 2010, http://www.jamaica-gleaner.com/gleaner/20100302/ent/ent1.html.

62. James C. Scott argues that "hidden transcripts" are crucial modes for resistance and solidarity. See James C. Scott, *Domination and the Arts of Resistance: Hidden Transcripts* (New Haven: Yale University Press, 1990).

63. Salewicz, *Bob Marley: The Untold Story*, 175.

64. The ambivalence between celebrating the life of the "rude boy" and warning those who adopt the aggressive social characteristics of the "rude boy" was certainly an aspect of ska in the 1960s. See, for example, "Simmer Down" by the Wailers. The Wailers, "Simmer Down," reissued on *Tougher Than Tough: The Story of Jamaican Music*, Mango B000003QLC, 1993.

65. Although still the economic capital of the West African nation, Abidjan was the political capital of Cote d'Ivoire from national independence in 1964 until 1983, when Yamoussoukro became the capital.

66. "Transdiasporic" is a term I use to help theorize collaborations between African and African-diasporic musicians. It brings to light modes of difference and diasporic belonging central to such collaborations. See Jason Robinson, "Enacting Diaspora: Transdiasporic Collaboration and Musical Experimentalism" (paper presented at Africa Meets North America: 3rd International Symposium and Festival, University of California, Los Angeles, Los Angeles, California, October 22-25, 2009).

67. Mark Slobin, *Subcultural Sounds*, 64.

68. Alpha Blondy, "Cocody Rock."

69. For an account of Abidjan and Cocody in the 1960s (even if rather colonialist), see Christiane Garnier, "Banana Boat to Abidjan," *Africa Today* 10:8 (October 1963), 4-8.

70. Hall, "What is this 'Black' in Black Popular Culture?"

71. I draw from Henry Louis Gates' notion of "signifyin(g)" to explain "repetition with a signal difference" (Gates, xxiv). See Henry Louis Gates, Jr., *The Signifying Monkey: A Theory of African American Literary Criticism* (New York: Oxford University Press, 1988).

72. This section of my essay draws extensively from ethnographic research developed over a period about eight years. During this time, I had close personal contact with Elijah Emanuel, the main subject of this section of my essay. This research occurred in formal and informal conversations with Emanuel while I was a performer in his group. Factual information without references draws from this "participant observation."

73. The Revelations, "Yo No Soy Ilegal," from *La Lucha Continua / The Struggle Continues...,* self-released, 2001.

74. James Clifford, "Indigenous Articulations," *The Contemporary Pacific* 13:2 (Fall 2001), 474. Clifford invokes Jeremy Brecher, Tim Costello, and Brendan Smith's book—*Globalization From Below*—on grass-roots organizations' roles in creating new alliances beyond national boundaries, certainly an apt metaphor for shedding light on the class politics often tightly woven within ideas about race, music, and nation. See Jeremy Brecher, Tim Costello, and Brendan Smith, *Globalization from Below: The Power of Solidarity* (Boston: South End Press, 2002).

75. The Judeo-Christian origins of "Elijah" and "Emanuel" are clearly invoked in Hernandez's adoption of his stage name. Very seldom does the fact that "Elijah Emanuel" is a created name enter into the discourse surrounding his music. Indeed, within the reggae scene in San Diego, even among musicians, he is known by his stage name only. In my close interactions with him, I have never heard him referred to by his given name.

76. The Revelations, *La Lucha Continua / The Struggle Continues...*; Elijah Emanuel, *Visión Persistente / Persistence of Vision*, self-released EE1, 2004; Elijah Emanuel, *Tres Sangres*, self-released, 2008.

77. He frequently adopts an oppositional stance against *reggaeton*, a kind of *sine qua non* today in discussion about reggae performed with lyrics in Spanish. Although this analysis is problematic—there are indeed many examples of Spanish-language roots reggae—it nevertheless acts as a very tangible force in the way that Emanuel understands the reception of his music among potential audiences. Although *reggaeton* has become a sine qua non of Spanish-language reggae, there is a rich tradition of Spanish language roots reggae throughout Latin America. Several more recent examples of well-known groups include Gondwana, Los Cafres, Pericos, Cultura Profetica, Gomba Jahbari, and others. We might even add to this list Brazilian groups such as Tribo de Jah, Cidade Negra, Edson Gomez, and others.

78. The release may even go too far. With implications that "reggae" means "roots reggae" (a limitation excluding dancehall and *reggae-*

ton), the release states that Emanuel is "arguably the first artist to write and sing reggae songs in Spanish and English." Despite this claim, that bilingualism is conceptually crucial to Emanuel's music is beyond a doubt. See "PRESS RELEASE: NEW ALBUM FROM ELIJAH EMANUEL - 'TRES SANGRES,'" unknown origin, dated September 29, 2009.

79. See Elijah Emanuel, *Visión Persistente / Persistence of Vision*.

80. Both quotations are from the lyrics of "Yo No Soy Ilegal."

81. Horace Campbell, *Rasta and Resistance: From Marcus Garvey to Walter Rodney* (Trenton: Africa World Press, 1987), 150.

82. Skrbis, *Long-Distance Nationalism*.

83. See Darren J. O'Byrne, *The Dimensions of Global Citizenship: Political Identity Beyond the Nation-State* (London: Frank Cass & Co. Ltd, 2003).

84. The Revelations, "Yo No Soy Ilegal."

85. Ibid.

86. See, for example, see his song "La Consciencia Indigena" from Elijah Emanuel, *Tres Sangres*.

87. Portes, Guarnizo, and Landolt, "The study of transnationalism," 217.

88. For the "dialectic" of nation and globalization, see Doyle, "Toward a Philosophy of Transnationalism."

89. Tania Molina Ramirez, "El Faro de Oriente celebrará encuentro con nuestra negritud," *La Jornada* (June 19, 2006). http://www.jornada. unam.mx/2006/06/19/index.php?section=espectaculos&article=a20n1esp.

90. Officially known as La Fábrica de Artes y Oficios de Oriente.

91. Reggaevolución has been on the air for more than ten years. See "Reggaevolución on Myspace Music," Myspace.com, http://www.myspace.com/reggaevolucion.

92. See, for example, his song "Revolución," in which he expresses solidarity with "hermanos y hermanas en Chiapas," the southern Mexican state stronghold of the Zapatistas.

93. The audience, some four or five thousand strong, reciprocated Emanuel's comments about the Zapatistas with little applause. In part, this could be due to the demographic of the audience; most appeared to be teenagers with little to indicate their political or activist affiliations. Similar comments made at concerts in California and northern Mexico almost unerringly produced huge applause and signs of agreement.

94. Quoted in Ramirez, "El Faro de Oriente celebrará encuentro con nuestra negritud."

95. Elijah Emanuel, "Todos Unidos," from *Visión Persistente / Persistence of Vision*.

96. Elijah Emanuel, "Reggae en Español," from *Tres Sangres*.

97. Hall, "What is This 'Black' in Black Popular Culture?," 465.

98. Elijah Emanuel, "Tres Sangres," from *Tres Sangres*.

99. Jocelyne Guilbault uses this term to recognize ways in which world musicians represent local traditions within larger global markets. Jocelyne Guilbault, "On Redefining the 'Local' through World Music." In *Ethnomusicology: A Contemporary Reader*. Ed. by Jennifer Post (New York: Routledge, 2006), 141.

100. Even after radio interviews in Colón, Panama, Emanuel failed to build a local audience in his birth country. His group has yet to perform in Panama. There is little evidence to indicate that his music has garnered attention in other Spanish-speaking countries of Latin America and the Caribbean.

11 MEXICA BINGHI I

CHICANO REGGAE IN SAN DIEGO

INTRODUCING SAN DIEGO

San Diego, California is arguably the reggae music capital of the U.S. and North America. It has produced some of the U.S.' top grossing reggae music acts; is a major destination for reggae music tours and festivals; home to the annual Bob Marley Day Festival and 'Tribute to the Legends' concert, as well as home to many independent reggae music labels and recording studios, and to many reggae oriented local businesses such as Makeda Dread's World Beat Center. San Diego's neighborhoods and schools, moreover, are rife with youth and young adults sporting dreadlocked hairstyles, speaking in Jamaican patois, and devoting themselves to the religious faith of Rastafarianism.

Jamaican culture is thus heavily imprinted across the cultural landscape of San Diego. There are, however, very few Jamaicans living there. In fact, San Diego has the smallest Jamaican and general Caribbean immigrant populations of the ten largest cities in the U.S. San

Diego's demographics make it an odd location for Jamaican culture in other ways. Reggae and Rastafarianism are also commonly understood as essentially Afro-centric, as expressive cultures produced within the dynamics and a subsequence that Paul Gilroy (1993) captured with his theorization of the 'Black Atlantic.' San Diego, however, is not easily connected to the histories or dynamics associated with the Black Atlantic. Its history has generally been shaped by a different set of circumstances, ones more tied to histories of U.S. imperialism in the U.S.-Mexico border region and to the Pacific Rim. San Diego, moreover, has the smallest Black Diasporic population of the ten largest U.S. cities (US Census, 2006). To be sure, it would be wrong to presuppose that Black expressive cultures are embraced across the African Diaspora without impediment or conflict. It is rather well known, for example, that Jamaican roots reggae artists strived for more support amongst African Americans, a phenomenon that was most recently chronicled in the biopic film, *Marley*, on the life and works of Jamaica's most famous reggae icon. Nonetheless, the vivid appropriation of Marley and of Jamaica's reggae music tradition and Rastafarian aesthetics amongst San Diego's generally non-Black population is a curious phenomenon deserving of a critical scrutiny.

It is, in sum, the product of a unique conjuncture of historical and contemporary circumstances. On the one hand, it seems clear that reggae and Rastafarianism have been uncritically appropriated in San Diego similar to how Black Diasporic cultures have been routinely appropriated by non-Black populations in the U.S. and the world over. The capacity to appropriate and perform subaltern cultures has been a trademark characteristic of colonial authority from the outset (Said, 1999). This condition is well evidenced in the literature regarding minstrelsy in U.S. Jazz culture (Lott, 1995) and, more recently, in analyses of the appeal of African American gangsta rap music and culture amongst middle class white Americans (Kitwana, 2005). White performances of black subjectivity are, in short, a symbol of white supremacy.

The appropriation of reggae and Rastafarian aesthetics beyond Jamaica and beyond the African diaspora, as Marvin Sterling (2008) has demonstrated, is also commonly associated with beach tourism the world over, an industry reflective of the global wealth disparities exacerbated by late global capitalism. The privileged travel to exotic destinations whereas the underprivileged remain a figment of exotic landscapes, to be exploited, thus exacerbating the effects of colonialism albeit under the veneer of post-colonial discourses. San Diego is like many southern California locales in that it is one of the prime beach tourist destinations within the continental U.S., thus making it a prime location for the proliferation of stereotypical Jamaican images such as the ganja smoking Rastaman, or the hula aesthetic appropriated from Polynesia.

There is more, however, to this story. Similar to the effect of the tourist industry of the Caribbean or Polynesia, San Diego's image as a beach tourist destination glosses over the region's racial formation and, namely, the legacy of conquest and settler colonialism towards indigenous populations (namely, Native American and Chicano) there (Trask, 1999). This history and its effects thus provide for a unique 'contact zone' (Pratt, 1991), for the interaction, if not amalgamation, of Jamaican, Native American and Chicano subjectivities. Beyond the uncritical appropriations of Jamaican culture that are associated with San Diego's beach tourism, there is also evidence of the native Chicano populations appropriating roots reggae and its Rastafarian ethos as a method to engage in similar forms of counter-hegemony, that is, as a method to critique displacement, exploitation, and expendability in the same ways that Jamaican reggae artists like Peter Tosh and Bob Marley were critiquing the effects of slavery and colonialism in the mid to late 20th century.

This essay highlights this unique imaginative link between Jamaica and San Diego via the evolution of the San Diego based band *Big Mountain*, one of the most commercially successful reggae acts to have emerged from the U.S., and a band that has been historically comprised of Jamaican and Chicano members. Big Mountain's history is intriguing. The band has benefitted in large part, from the beach tourism industries of the U.S. west coast, Polynesia, and parts of Latin America. They have recorded some of the most popular beach reggae tunes of the late 20th century.

The band's artistry, however, also reflects the dynamics of what political theorists like Gilroy, Stuart Hall (1992, 1996), and Walter Mignolo (2000) have described as a cultural hybridity, fusions between local histories of displacement that are enabled by many of the time/space compressions or vivid transnationalism associated with neoliberalism and/or globalization. Such fusions map out a significance of the Black Atlantic and its critique of European modernity, beyond the Black Atlantic. This hybridity is most evident with recent works by Big Mountain, tunes that do not attempt to precisely mimic the sounds and styles of Jamaican artists, but that blend those elements within cultural traits that are indigenous to southern California. The title of this essay is appropriated from one such example, to be explained in full detail within the ensuing pages. The history of Big Mountain offers a template for understanding the advent of other hybrid reggae musical forms such as the Jawaii tradition of Polynesia and Latin America's reggaeton.

(E)Race-ing San Diego History

Tourism is San Diego's third largest industry due, largely, to its temperate climate, picturesque beaches, golf courses, and bevy of amusement parks. San Diego has the third largest hotel occupancy rate of any city in the U.S., a compelling statistic considering how it is only the 8th largest U.S. city. San Diego is much like much of southern California. It is a place where social imaginations soar, that many Americans imagine as a blank slate, a place of refuge and of new beginnings, and a place that is not troubled by the conflicted histories of regions like the Upper East Coast, the South, and the Midwest. Southern California is the location for 'California Dreaming,' an ethos that is further evident in the mystique of Hollywood and theme parks such as Disneyland and Sea World. Much of this theme park motif is buttressed by a strong tinge of U.S. nationalism and a generally conservative political climate when compared to most major cities on the west coast and a reflection of the incredible wealth of many San Diego communities (Clemence,

2005). The nationalism of San Diego is, in part, the result of its proximity to the Mexican border. It is, in larger part, the result of a heavy U.S. military presence in San Diego as the city was originally strategized as an important location for the U.S. military presence across the Pacific Rim. The city was long established as a major naval base, is home to a large Marine training facility, and is nearby one of the largest U.S. Marine bases in the U.S.

Southern California, however, was never a blank slate or paradise waiting to be discovered. The military and beach tourism industry of places like San Diego and Hawaii are also products of genocide and settler colonialism. Prior to European arrival, the area was inhabited by the indigenous, Kumeyaay. Joao Rodrigues Carbrilho, a Portuguese born Spanish explorer, encountered what is now known as San Diego Bay in the fall of 1542. San Diego Bay and the region at large were given its current name in 1602 by Sebastián Vizcaíno as he mapped out the coastline of Alta California on behalf of the Viceroy of New Spain (San Diego Historical Society)

The presidio and mission provided the structural foundations for European settlement in San Diego. Much of this depended upon the conquest or colonization of the Kumeyaay people. They were not, however, passive victims to this encroachment. In 1775, the Kumeyaay revolted by burning down the mission and killing the Franciscan friars who built and maintained it. This action elicited a more forceful response by Spanish colonizers as they concentrated more military forces in the region, rebuilt the mission, and embarked upon the project of forced colonization of the Kumeyaay and other smaller indigenous groups of the region. These realities led to the steady erasure of the Kumeyaay presence in early San Diego (Shipek, 1976, 1986).

Mexico achieved its independence from Spain in 1821 and San Diego became part of the Mexican state of Alta California. It became part of the U.S. following the U.S.-Mexico War of 1846-1848, an imperialist war motivated by the discourse of manifest destiny and that allowed for the

U.S. to triple its geographic size. Westward expansion in the U.S. was always already tied to the racial demonization of indigenous peoples there, a pervasive legacy that is evident today. Native Americans and Mexicans were thus produced as part of the wilderness to be quarantined or obliterated in the U.S.'s quest to spread its dominion and 'civilizing' mission. The effects of this demonization have been quite evident over time.

The Mexican folk hero, Joaquin Murrieta, is widely recognized for his vigilante exploits against white oppressors and on behalf of indigenous peoples throughout the San Diego region during the 19th century. During the civil unrest of the 1960s and 1970s San Diego was a hotbed of activism related to the Chicano movement, one amongst an assortment of 'racial power' movements in the 1960s and 1970s, within which non-white populations rebelled against the pervasive legacy and effects of conquest and settler colonialism. The Chicano movement in particular, was one informed by mythologies that linked Latinos, and more specifically Mexicanos, to ancestral ties to the lands of southern California and the southwest (Mariscal, 2005). Much of this was inspired by anti-colonial movements across Latin America, Africa, and the Caribbean, thus creating a pretext or the kinds of cultural hybridity evident within the work of Chicano reggae acts such as Big Mountain.

One of the more notable events in San Diego's Chicano movement history was the establishment of what is now known as Chicano Park in the neighborhood of Barrio Logan in the late 1960s. Mexican immigrants and Mexican Americans began to settle in a neighborhood called Logan Heights in the late 19th century and 'Barrio Logan' grew into the second largest Mexicano population on the west coast outside of East Los Angeles. The residents of Barrio Logan began to experience a series of displacements starting in the early 20th century when the U.S. Navy and defense related industries series moved into that area. The militarization of Logan Heights and the south bay section of San Diego displaced many Mexicano families from waterfront homes and communities. Decades later, the city of San Diego re-wrote zoning laws regarding Logan Heights, allowing for environmentally hazardous industries to locate there and severely curtailing the quality of life for Barrio Logan residents (Chicano Park Association, Steering Committee, 2000).

In 1963, the State of California constructed a highway through the middle of Barrio Logan. This caused many families to flee the neighborhood. Six years later, in 1969, the State of California announced that it would build a California Highway Patrol Station on land that Logan residents had identified as a preferred site of a community park. Already squeezed by a growing industrialization of San Diego Bay and the expanding Naval base, and incensed by the enduring history of displacement, residents of Barrio Logan began to rebel.

They organized as a series of coordinated sit-ins and other acts of civil disobedience to obstruct further displacement by government agencies. Their activism was a success. In 1970, CHP authorities abandoned the plans for the station and Barrio Logan residents launched a grass roots initiative to build a community park to commemorate their history and their small victory. Part of that construction included the painting of large murals depicting the plight of indigenous peoples and leftist heroes in the Americas. Renowned mural artists from across the Southwest contributed to the project. The victory at Chicano Park is commemorated each year via a celebration known as Chicano Park Day, one of the U.S.'s largest Latino cultural and most politically charged festivals.

NATIVE SON

One of the most common features of Chicano Park Day celebrations of the past decade, have been performances by the reggae singer, Quino, a native of San Diego and a self described Chicano. Quino's full name is Joaquin McWhinney, named in honor of the aforementioned Mexican populist hero, Joaquin Murrieta. Quino is also the founder and lead singer of the band Big Mountain. Quino chose that name for his band as an emblem to his dedication to indigenous histories in the Americas. The name Big Mountain derives from the Dineh (also known as

Navajo) people of northern Arizona. The Navajo Indian reservation is the largest in the U.S. and the Navajo nation represents the largest American Indian community in the U.S. Quino visited there in the early 1990s along with a team of human rights activists while the Navajo were involved in a struggle with the Peabody Coal Mining Company over mining rights on a mountain that they considered sacred. Quino named his group in honor of that mountain and the pervasive struggle for indigenous rights across the U.S.-Mexico border region.

Big Mountain's first album, titled *Wake Up,* was released in 1992 on a record label named Quality. The highlights of that album are the roots 'one drop' tunes 'Back in the Hills' and 'Rastaman,' both tunes that advocate an anti-capitalist and anti-Eurocentric view of the world and a dedication to the anti-modern and rustic 'Nayabinghi' lifestyle of Rastafarianism that Chicanos like Quino were exposed to via the global spread and popularity of reggae music. Those tunes, however, were not the most commercially successful for Big Mountain. The single 'Touch My Light' from that album reached number 51 on the U.S. pop charts and was also included on the soundtrack for the hit television show titled, 'Beverly Hills 90210.' The success of that song attracted the attention of the global reggae music audience and industry (VH1.com)

Big Mountain's rise to prominence led to changes in the band's lineup. They added legendary Jamaican artists such as guitarist, Tony Chin and drummer, Santa Davis. Chin and Davis were rather well recognized roots artists in Jamaica's reggae music industry. Both were native Jamaicans and were part of the original Soul Syndicate band that backed artists like Peter Tosh in the 1970s. Kevin Batchelor and Jerry Johnson, the former horn section of Steel Pulse, joined the band in the late 1990s as well, further boosting Big Mountain's reggae credentials. Jamaican artists remain prominent in the band's current lineup with Paul Kastick (Maxi Priest, Kymani Marley, and Beres Hammond) on drums, Taddy P (Maxi Priest) on bass, and Richard 'Goofy' Campbell (Maxi Priest) on keyboards.

The addition of Davis (currently backing Ziggy Marley) is particularly telling of how Big Mountain was viewed, by some, as a refreshing and exciting new addition to the reggae music world in the 1990s. Davis is widely recognized as one of the originators of the one-drop reggae music rhythm and the roots reggae sound that Bob Marley and the Wailers made popular the world over. Davis became a professional drummer in the 1960s and his skill landed him spots with legendary roots reggae acts such as the Wailing Souls, Soul Syndicate, Bob Marley, Jimmy Cliff, Andrew Tosh, and Peter Tosh. Upon joining a group of young and Chicano reggae artists from southern California, Davis explained to one music journalist, 'This is the best thing that's happened to me in a while. They're young and open to new ideas it's like working on a whole new level' (Reggae Report, 1994).

With Chin and Davis on board, Big Mountain began recording their first album for the Giant Label of Warner Brothers in the mid 1990s. While doing so, they were approached by pop music producer Ron Fair about recording a reggae style cover song of Peter Frampton's 'Baby I Love Your Way' for a soundtrack he was working on for the film, 'Reality Bites.' The band accepted the challenge and, as a result, that song was included on their 1994 album titled Unity. Big Mountain's version of 'Baby I Love Your Way' reached number six on the U.S. pop chart, number one the UK pop chart, and was a smash hit worldwide. The band followed that success with other tunes such as 'Sweet Sensual Love' (number 51 on UK Charts), and 'Caribbean Blue,' a tune produced by the renown Jamaican drum and bass duo, Sly and Robbie. Unity sold over 1 million copies worldwide, a major accomplishment for a reggae music artist of the 1990s. The success of the Unity album allowed for Big Mountain to headline Reggae Sunsplash USA in 1994 and 1995, a tour that included stops across Europe, South America, and Asia. According to journalist George Vargas, Big Mountain was the first U.S. band and the only act from California to ever headline the Reggae Sunsplash world tour (Varga, 2012). The band followed up with two other albums for Warner Brothers with Resistance in 1995 and Free Up in 1997.

QUINO PERFORMING AT REGGAE SUNSPLASH, 1994 WITH GUITARIST AND BANDMATE TONY CHIN. (PHOTO COURTESY OF BIG MOUNTAIN).

Quino reportedly never sought fame or notoriety as a pop artist. He became famous for singing pop reggae tunes about love and romance and yet, he was far more motivated as a political artist/activist. Much of this is evident within Quino's unique biography, much of which I have been exposed to over the past few decades as his friend and political activist ally. Quino spent the first eight years of his life living on a banana plantation in Honduras. His father worked for the United Fruit Company and was sent to Honduras from the U.S. to work as a foreman. Quino lost his father to a tragedy in Honduras and returned to the U.S. with his mother and infant brother. They relocated to the Coachella Valley in California where his mother's family ran a small farm. While there, Quino was inspired by the Mexican folk music that his grandfather and uncles performed and soon began to accompany them as a vocalist. His talent and charisma were quite evident at an early age. His mother remarried soon thereafter, to an African American, and they relocated to the city of San Diego. From an early age, his subjectivity was linked to the histories of Central America, the Caribbean, the U.S.-Mexico border region, and to African Americans.

In 1979, he was exposed to a method and language that help him to bring all of those elements together. Quino and his stepfather were watching the news program *60 Minutes* when it aired a brief documentary titled *Reggae Rebels,* an exposé about Jamaican history as well as the social and political relevance of reggae music and Rastafarianism to impoverished residents of cities like Kingston in Jamaica. According to Quino, that documentary changed his life in that it instilled in him an awareness of the political and spiritual power of music, and also a method of expressive rebellion that he found applicable to the struggles of the disadvantaged Native American and Latino population of San Diego. Bob Marley's appearance in that *60 Minutes* segment was especially inspiring to him as he reported to have found a new role model. This became evident not only in his embracement of Rastafarianism as a religious creed and lifestyle, but also in his transition into a roots reggae performer, and eventually global star. Quino's transition to Rastafarianism was also encouraged by an aunt of his who had married a Rastafarian. His primary interest in the faith was its universality, or emphasis on Africa as a homeland for all of humanity or a unifying force. In one of his first interviews regarding his sentiments towards reggae, Quino commented, 'Reggae people are conscious people. I see reggae as being a rallying cry for this new time' (*Reggae Report*, 1994). In a more recent retrospective interview he commented on his appreciation of Marley in particular and of reggae's political significance, 'To me reggae music still has this mystic, revolutionary part to it. I got into reggae music because I wanted to change the world. To me Bob Marley was Che Guevara with a guitar' (Leighton, 2009).

And yet, despite his dedication to being what the music media was describing as 'a driving force behind reggae music in America,' Big Mountain's success was largely fueled by its ability to cross over into the world of pop music and by Quino's unique charisma and vocal skills. Big Mountain's success made them an easy target for criticism from reggae music purists, and especially those dedicated to the roots tradition. Upon their headlining the Reggae Sunsplash USA festival in 1993 in Los Angeles, the tensions were evident within the press. When asked how he felt about headlining a reggae bill full of legendary reggae artists from Jamaica and being the only artist who was phenotypically not Black, Quino commented:

> They're musicians who follow the Rastafarian religion and have that Rasta spirit. We're an American band, and many of the

reggae musicians look at American reggae bands as intruders. They think we're bastardizing their music and capitalizing on it. They may be cold toward us backstage at the show--and I can't say I blame them.

A noted reggae and music journalist also commented on the tensions surrounding Big Mountain's success. He commented:

The success of an American reggae band like Big Mountain can be disturbing to Jamaican musicians...Lots of Jamaican artists have worked for a long time to crack the American market. It could be upsetting to them to see an American band accomplish in a few years what they have not been able to accomplish in many, many years of trying...Many of these bands co-opt the music and distort it away from what it's supposed to be. There are so many examples of American bands going wrong and totally missing the point of reggae's message--which is basically a spiritual and social message about making the world a better place (Hunt, 1993).

The fact that this journalist was making such statements with a direct reference to Big Mountain, implies that Quino's group became the poster child for reggae's political essence having 'gone wrong.' These critiques were exacerbated by Quino's open advocacy of Rastafarianism, a trait that conflicted with his non-Black phenotype. To be sure, such phenotype is not a prerequisite for the faith as indicated by the global appeal of Rastafarianism. Quino, however, was one of the first major public figures to be non-Black and yet to also embrace Rastafarianism. His appearance as a dreadlocked rasta on stage thus conflicted with the image of Black Rastafarian artists that the reggae audience had become so accustomed to. As a trailblazer in this regard, Quino and his band was thus the target for much unfair criticism. These tensions seemed to elicit two responses.First, Big Mountain soldiered on and remained dedicated to roots music and to Rastafarianism's stress on universality. The second response was an increasingly critical attention paid to topics and histories that were less familiar to reggae purists. The band thus did not distort or miss the point of reggae's 'spiritual and social message,' they merely applied those messages to the oppressed populations of their home region.

MEXICA BINGHI I: A CONCLUSION

This was evident in early Big Mountain tunes such as 'Border Town.' The regional and ethnic ties, however, have become more pronounced over time. The best example of this is a recent tune titled Mexica Binghi I. Mexica is coterminous with the Aztecs, and their capital city of Tenochtitlan. The fall of Tenochtitlan to the Spanish conquistador, Hernan Cortes has been marked as the foundational moment for European modernity. While Columbus' supposed 'discovery' of the Americas in 1492 is highlighted for its importance, Todorov (1997) argues that it was the discovery of the great and lavish Mexica empire and city two decades later that was more important. Cortes' ability to conquer the most exquisite and powerful example of indigenous history in the Americas has been described as the definitive moment where Europeans 'discovered themselves.'

The fall of Technotitlan is a central theme within Chicano history and culture. A central tenet of the Chicano movement was that Mexican Americans were direct descendants of the Mexica, and that the U.S. southwest was Aztlán, the original homeland of the Mexica prior to their migration to the central valley of Mexico and their construction of Tenochtitlan. As a result, the conquest of the Mexica by the Spanish in 1519 represented the originating moment in a long history of suffering by native peoples across the Americas. The term, Chicano, is popularly perceived to have originated from the term Mexicano which is also viewed as coterminous with 'being Aztec. (Mariscal, 2005).

The term 'Binghi I' emerged from a different geographic space, yet from similar conditions. It is derivative of the broader term, nayabinghi, which is the name of one of the four houses or 'mansions' of Rastafarianism. The term Niyabinghi literally translates to 'black victory.' The term originated from anthropologists to describe clans in Uganda/ Rwanda whose culture was based on the veneration of the goddess spirit, Niyabinghi. Although, Niyabinghi has no tangible connections to Ethiopia or to its Emperor Halie Selassie or Ras Tafari, Nayabinghi are considered to be the most orthodox of the Rastafarian branches in that they dedicate themselves to the idea of a global theocracy headed by Emperor and messiah Haile Selassie. From this context, the term Binghi man or Binghi-I signifies someone who envisions Ethiopia as humanity's zion or sacred homeland.

By amalgamating the history, espistemology, and meaning of terms such as Mexica and Binghi I, into the slogan Mexica Binghi, Quino offers an emblematic example of hybridity that carries with it an important political commentary of unity and solidarity across national, ethnic, and racial borders. It is a term that derives from the wounds wrought by white supremacy and as inflicted in variant regions of the world, that is, in Africa, the Caribbean, and Aztlán. It is also, however, a term that has been produced by the migration of ideas, symbols, and sounds via media technologies. The fact that the song is played over a classic one-drop style roots reggae beat, whose tempo and rusticity is reminiscent of songs produced by Jamaican artists in the late 1970s, is yet another example of how Jamaica's unique influence on Black music and politics has been outsourced to shape the oppositional conscious-ness of artists and activists far from the Caribbean. One of the most telling verses of that song borrows from a classic line of Bob Marley about the spirit of Rastafarianism as a force that heals colonial wounds. As Quino sings, 'Nacimos inocentes. Sin identidad. Y quien lo siente lo sabe. Y pide nada mas.' Translated this means 'We are born innocent, without identity. But who feels it knows it, and can ask for no more.'

Quino's lament on the limits of ascribed identities, of the categories and systems of categorization that are inherent to settler colonial projects, is reminiscent of Stuart Hall's rumination on the tenuous nature of identity politics in the late 20th century. Nothing remains pure or uniform. Jamaica appropriates Africa and Chicanos appropriate

Jamaica. All are linked within a narrative of modernity and its discontents. Hall, for example, explains that relations of power and legacies of colonialism often manifest within expressive cultures, modalities that contribute to the advent of new forms of collective consciousness that unsettle the hegemonic discourses of nations and nationalism. He argues that the abilities of subaltern groups to draw from and blend together a diverse array of knowledge, experiences, and epistemologies when forging of subjectivities, moreover, make them less manageable by colonial powers and, thus, create new visions for social change. Hall (1996, p.4) has described such blends as 'new ethnicities' that have emerged from variant time-space compressions associated with neoliberalism. As he explains:

'Identities are never unified and, in late modern times, increasingly fragmented and fractured; never singular but multiply constructed across different, often intersecting and antagonistic, discourses, practices and positions'.

The evolution of Big Mountain can thus be linked to what Hall would describe as a unique conjuncture of histories, geographies, and expressive cultures.

Ultimately, the success of Big Mountain can be assessed via the opportunities it has created for newer artists. U.S. Rastafarian acts such as Soldiers of Jah Army (SOJA), Groundation, and Rebelution have all followed in Big Mountain's footsteps. Quino has also blazed a path for Chicano Reggae and as evident in groups like Elijah Emmanuel and the Revelations, The Devastators, Roots Covenant, Tribal Seeds, Quinto Sol, and Maiz have been a major force in the U.S. roots reggae scene for some time now. The recent success of Tribal Seeds is most notable. With a sound modeled very much after the famed roots reggae group, Israel Vibration, Tribal Seeds' self titled debut and sophomore album titled, *The Harvest*, has been in the top 50 reggae albums sold on Itunes. The former is currently in the top 20 reggae albums sold worldwide.

REFERENCES

Bakari Kitwana. *Why White Kids Love Hip-Hop: Wankstas, Wiggers, Wannabes and the New Reality of Race in America*. New York: Basic, 2006.

Canclini, Nestor Garcia et al. <u>*Hybrid Cultures: Strategies for Entering and Leaving Modernity*</u>. Minneapolis: University of Minnesota Press, 1990.

'City of San Diego website: Economic Development'. Sandiego.gov. http://www.sandiego.gov/economic-development/glance/economy. shtml. Retrieved 2010-07-01.

Clemence, Sara (October 28, 2005). 'Richest Cities In The U.S.'. Forbes. http://www.forbes.com/2005/10/27/richest-cities-US-cx_ sc_1028home_ls.html. Retrieved April 22, 2009.

Entertainment Weekly, July 29, 1994

Gilroy, Paul. *The Black Atlantic: Modernity and Double Consciousness*. Cambridge: Harvard University Press, 1993.

_____. 'British cultural studies and the pitfalls of identity', In J. Curran, D. Morley, & V. Walkerdine (Eds.). *Cultural studies and communication* (pp. 34-49). London: Arnold, 1996.

Hall, Stuart. 'New Ethnicities' in *'Race', Culture and Difference*, ed. by, James Donald, James, and Ali Rattansi. London: Sage, 1992, pp. 252-259.

_____. Who needs 'identity'? In S. Hall & P. du Gay, (Eds.). *Questions of Cultural Identity*. London: Sage, 1996, pp. 1-17.

Hunt, Dennis. 'Big Mountain Scales the Heights' *Los Angeles Times*, June 10, 1993.

Lott, Eric. *Love and Theft: Blackface Minstrelsy and the American Working Class*. New York: Oxford University Press, 1995.

Mignolo, Walter. *Local Histories/Global Designs.* Princeton: Princeton University Press, 2000.

Money Magazine, 'Best Places to Live 2006'. MONEY Magazine. 2006. http://money.cnn.com/magazines/moneymag/bplive/2006/snapshots/PL0666000.html. Retrieved November 29, 2009.

Pratt, Mary L. 'Arts of the Contact Zone.' In *Profession,* No. 91 (1991), pp. 33-40.

Reggae Report, Volume 14, Number 5, 1994. 'Big Mountain, New Album, New Lineup, New Tour.'

Shipek, Florence C. 'History of Southern California Mission Indians. *Handbook of North American Indians.* Volume ed, Heizer, Robert F. Washington, DC: Smithsonian Institution, 1978, pp. 610-618.

_____. 'The Impact of Europeans upon Kumeyaay Culture.' *The Impact of European Exploration and Settlement on Location Native Americans.* Ed. Raymond Starr. San Diego: Cabrillo Historical Association, 1986: 13-25.

Sterling, Marvin. *Babylon East: Performing Dancehall, Roots Reggae and Rastafari in Japan.* Durham: Duke University Press, 2010.

U.S. Census, 'Table 1: Annual Estimates of the Population for Incorporated Places Over 100,000, Ranked by July 1, 2008 Population: April 1, 2000 to July 1, 2008' (CSV). *2008 Population Estimates.* United States Census Bureau, Population Division. 2009-07-01. http://www.census.gov/popest/cities/tables/SUB-EST2008-01.csv. Retrieved 2009-07-01.

U.S. Census, ^ 'Find a County'. National Association of Counties. http://www.naco.org/Template.cfm?Section=Find_a_County&Template=/cffiles/counties/usamap.cfm. Retrieved 2008-01-31.

Varga, George. 'Big Mountain Turns Twenty at 'Reggae Legends' Fest. *San Diego*

Union Tribune. February 16, 2012.

I-I, Artists Biography, Big Mountain, http://www.vh1.com/artists/az/big_mountain/bio.jhtml

BIG MOUNTAIN ALBUMS

Free Up, Warner Bros. Records, 1997.

Resistance, Warner Bros. Records, 1996.
Unity, Warner Bros. Records, 1994.

Wake Up, Quality Records, 1992. (Contributor) *Reality Bites* (soundtrack), BMG/RCA, 1994.

CONTRIBUTORS

NICKESHA T. DAWKINS is a PhD candidate in linguistics, and part-time lecturer in the Department of Language, Linguistics and Philosophy at the University of the West Indies, Mona. Her areas of interest include phonology, sociolinguistics and dancehall music. She is also an aspiring dancehall recording artist going by the performing name 'Gemstone'. with a debut album titled 'Diamond In Da Ruff' and collaborations with both local and international artists from Jamaica, Spain, Peru and Italy. She has performed live at Sting and Reggae Sumfest, among many other reggae/dancehall events.

CHUCK FOSTER has written about Jamaican music for over twenty-five years. He wrote the 'Reggae Update' column for *Beat Magazine* for two decades, and currently pens the 'Reading and Reasonings' column for the annual *Reggae Festival Guide*. He is the author of *Roots, Rock, Reggae: An Oral History of Reggae Music From Ska to Dancehall* (1999) and *The Small Axe Guide to Rock Steady* (2009). Chuck has been actively involved in Los Angeles public radio for nearly 20 years and plays ska, rocksteady, reggae, dub, roots and dancehall, drawn from one of the largest collections in the U.S., from vintage 7' singles to the latest Jamaican chart hits, on his radio program, Reggae Central on KPFK in LA.

DONNA P. HOPE is Cultural Analyst, and Senior Lecturer and Director in the Institute of Caribbean Studies & the Reggae Studies, at the University of the West Indies, Mona. She has conducted extensive research and published widely on Jamaican popular culture and music. Dr. Hope's books include *Inna di Dancehall: Popular Culture and the Politics of Identity in Jamaica* (2006), *Man Vibes: Masculinities in the Jamaican Dancehall* (2010) and *Drum and Bass* (Forthcoming 2013). Her articles have appeared in multiple journals including *Small Axe, International Journal of Cultural*

Studies, *Journal of Pan African Studies*, *Discourses in Dance*, *Interventions: International Journal of Postcolonial Studies*, *JENda*, *Revista Brasileira Do Caribe*, *Social and Economic Studies* and *Journal of West Indian Literature*.

DAVID KATZ is author of *People Funny Boy: The Genius of Lee 'Scratch' Perry*; *Solid Foundation: An Oral History of Reggae*, and *Caribbean Lives: Jimmy Cliff*. He also contributed to *The Rough Guide to Reggae*, *A Tapestry of Jamaica*, and *Keep On Running: The Story of Island Records*. Katz's writing and photographs have appeared in many periodicals and books, and he has annotated over 100 retrospectives of Jamaican music. Katz has also co-hosted radio programmes, released original records, and contributed to documentaries and feature films, while his Dub Me Always DJ nights are regular features of London's nightlife.

ELLEN KÖHLINGS made her first 'record deal' at the tender age of four when she agreed to swap her pacifier for a turntable. During her punk-fuelled teenage years she made frequent trips to the UK, during which time reggae entered the equation. While finishing her university course in English and Communication Art (1995) at Heinrich-Heine University in Düsseldorf, she was given special dispensation to write her Master's thesis on hip-hop and then worked as a freelance music journalist for daily papers, magazines and various radio stations. Her first trip to Jamaica in 1996 resulted in reggae becoming her sole musical diet, whether of a roots or dancehall flavor, and her being appointed as the editor-in-chief of RIDDIM on its launch in 2001.

PETE LILLY, journalist, photographer, editor and reggae aficionado, was born and raised in a small village in Germany. His first trip to Jamaica in 1996 at the age of 30 changed his life and reduced his journalistic work more and more to one topic: Reggae. He became the chief editor of *RIDDIM* Magazine at its launch in Cologne in 2001 and, as a result, work on Reggae music began to loom even larger in his life. Today, twelve years and sixty-five *RIDDIM* issues later (plus one special issue on Bob Marley and seven English issues), together with 18 trips to Jamaica under his belt, Pete remains wholly absorbed by Jamaica's musical culture and its creativity, which he continues to explore in-depth in his writing.

JOHN D. MÁRQUEZ is Assistant Professor in the Department of African American Studies and Latina and Latino Studies Program at Northwestern University. A Chicano and native of the Gulf South, Dr. Márquez has worked with numerous grassroots organizations to address border militarization, police brutality, and gang violence. His work has been widely featured in the media and has been published in academic journals including *Subjectivity, American Quarterly*, and *Latino Studies*. His book, *Black-Brown Solidarity: Racial Politics in the New Gulf South* is forthcoming from the University of Texas Press (2013). Dr. Márquez's research interests include Critical Ethnic Studies Critical Race Theory, Conquests and Settler Colonialism, Borders, Biopolitics, and Sovereignty, Ghetto Violence and Latino/a Studies.

ANNA KASAFI PERKINS is a former Dean of Studies at St Michael's Theological College. Her research interests include quality assurance and enhancement, faith and political life, sex and sexuality, religion and popular culture, gender and the scriptures, business and professional ethics. Her first book, *Justice as Equality: Michael Manley's Caribbean Vision of Justice* (2010), joins several articles and chapters she has written. A second co-edited volume entitled, *Justice and Peace in a Renewed Caribbean Contemporary Catholic Reflections* (2012) is now available. Dr. Perkins is currently Senior Programme Officer, Quality Assurance, University of the West Indies, Regional Headquarters, and Adjunct faculty, St. Michael's Theological College.

LISA TOMLINSON is a scholar of Jamaican origin residing in Toronto, Canada. She holds a Masters degree in Education and has recently completed her Doctoral studies in Humanities at York University. Her research and teaching focus is in the area of literary and cultural studies of the Caribbean and African diaspora. She is currently Adjunct faculty in communication courses at University of Ontario Institute of Technology.

MAUREEN WEBSTER-PRINCE holds Diplomas in Education and Library Science, a BA in History and Social Sciences and a Masters in Library Studies (UWI) and also studied media management at the Aberystwyth University (Wales). She has worked at the National Library of Jamaica as Consultant, Deputy Director, Head of the Audio Visual Department, Coordinator of the Audio Visual Information Network and Advisory Committee Member for the National Information System. Ms. Webster-Prince was the first appointed Reference Librarian at Radio Jamaica, and Chief Archivist on the team that facilitated the development of the Caribbean Advanced Proficiency Examinations. She is currently the Manager of the Information Resources Department at the Government Information Services Limited, Trinidad and Tobago.

COLIN WRIGHT is Co-Director of the Centre for Critical Theory, University of Nottingham, UK, and was born in Montego Bay and raised in Kingston, Jamaica. Dr. Wright's research interests include contemporary French theory, particularly psychoanalysis, poststructuralism, postcolonialism and continental philosophy. He is the author of *Philosophy, Rhetoric, Ideology: Towards a Sophistic Democracy* (2006), *Psychoanalysis: Orientations* (2008), and *Badiou in Jamaica: The Politics of Conflict* (forthcoming, 2013), as well as co-editor of the special issue of *Paragraph: A Journal of Modern Critical Theory* devoted to 'Psychoanalysis and the Posthuman' (November 2010). He is also a trainee Lacanian analyst with the *Centre for Freudian Analysis and Research* in London.

TERNATIONAL
REGGAE

TERNATIONAL
REGGAE

EDITED BY:
DONNA P. HOPE

PELICAN PUBLISHERS LIMITED
Kingston, Jamaica W.I.

First Published in Jamaica, 2013 by Pelican Publishers Limited

44 Lady Musgrave Road
Kingston 10, Jamaica, W.I
Tel: (876) 978-8377 Fax: (876) 978-0048
Email: pelicanpublisers@gmail.com
Website: www.pelicanpublishers.com.jm

© 2013, Institute of Caribbean Studies, University of the West Indies
Mona, Jamaica

ISBN 978-976-8240-12-5

Cover design by Pelican Publishers Limited

TABLE OF CONTENTS

PART 3 - MUSICAL CONVERSATIONS

ACKNOWLEDGEMENTS

The second staging of the International Reggae Conference in 2010, which generated the articles in this volume, owes a great deal to the contribution of the staff and student assistants of the Institute of Caribbean Studies/Reggae Studies Unit at the UWI, Mona Campus – in particular Nicole Edwards, Georgette McGlashen, and Latoya Tulloch. In her capacity as Director of the ICS/RSU in 2010, Professor Claudette Williams provided the necessary foundation, backed by financial support and professional guidance for the staging of the IRC2010. The UWI Open Campus office, then headed by Dr. Luz Longsworth, gave sterling contribution to the overall planning and execution of the IRC2010, with staff members Jennifer White-Clark, Delroy Banks, Delroy Waugh and Stacey Meggo working above and beyond the call of duty to ensure that every single aspect of the conference was efficiently and effectively executed. The overall IRC2010 Conference Committee who gave unstintingly of their time and effort throughout the entire process deserve high commendation, including Dr. Anna Perkins, Dr. Livingston White, Dr. Michael Barnett, Dr. Lloyd Waller, Charles Campbell, Patricia Valentine, Ava-Loi Forbes, Lenford Salmon, and Dennis Howard.

Many thanks to Professor Gordon Shirley, Principal and Pro-Vice Chancellor at the UWI, Mona, for his continued support for the International Conference, and the work of the ICS/Reggae Studies Unit.

Where this publication is concerned, Tanya Francis-Thomas' sterling support in the final editing and indexing of this work is commendable. I owe her a debt of gratitude. Latoya West-Blackwood and the team at Pelican Publishers worked assiduously to meet the demands of a rigorous publication schedule. And to all the reviewers of the chapters published herein, your contribution to this work is highly appreciated.

If I have inadvertently omitted anyone by name or designation, Nuff Respect to you for your contribution to the continued dissemination of knowledge on Jamaican culture and music.

INTRODUCTION

Jamaican popular music has enjoyed a rich history since the first strains of drums resonated from the slave plantations during plantation slavery. The cementing of its music industry in the 1950s and the seminal contribution of songwriters, singers, players of instruments and their financial backers over several decades, has contributed to the development and spread of several Jamaican music genres, including mento, ska, rocksteady, reggae and dancehall, that have become internationally renowned, loved and replicated. The dissemination of thought on these genres and the exploration of socio-cultural, political, gendered and other interconnections, plus the exploration of regional and international movements across multiple borders, has been an integral part of the development of these genres.

The essays that make up this collection all originated from presentations made at the 2010 International Reggae Conference. As a component of the move to enable multiple conversations across genres, the International Reggae Conference provides a platform for academics, researchers, artistes, musicians, scholars, journalists, cultural practitioners, entrepreneurs and music lovers from around the world to share their experiences with and perspectives on Jamaican culture and popular music as well as on popular music internationally. These essays represent the research, reflection and interrogation of Jamaican popular music from varying intellectual perspectives, methodologies, spaces and geographical locations in what is a truly internationalized frame of thought and idea on music and cultures that began in the physically small location of an island in the Caribbean Sea - Jamaica.

This volume has four sections. In Part one, Cultural Interpretations, focus is placed on Jamaican popular music, reggae and dancehall, in relation to contemporary debates on violence, homophobia and youth identity negotiation in Europe, Jamaica and Canada. In Part two, Gendered Ruminations, debates on gender and sexuality in the dancehall are interrogated through Christian theology and linguistic methodology. Part three, Musical Conversations, presents important conversations with Jamaican popular music, particularly reggae, in varied formats, including an interview, journalistic discussion and an analysis of a seminal component of Jamaican culture – radio serials. In the final Part four, Reggae/Rasta International, the emphasis shifts to the internationalization of Jamaican music and culture with focus on manifestations of Reggae and Rastafari in diverse spaces, and the raising of an international reggae nation which all re-turn to the nexus of Jamaican music and culture for their birth and sustenance.